The Story of
Churchdown

For the People of Churchdown

Past and Present

The Story of

Churchdown

Gloucestershire

A Village History

Gwen Waters

GLOUCESTER REPRINTS

Published 1999 by Gloucester Reprints, 3 Campden Terrace, Linden Gardens, London, W4 2EP.

ISBN 0 904586 04 9

Produced by Past Historic, Kings Stanley, Gloucestershire, GL10 3HW
Printed and bound in Great Britain by MPG Books Ltd, Bodmin, Cornwall

Contents

List of Illustrations

Plans and Maps

Illustration credits

Photographs and illustrations were supplied by, or are reproduced by kind permission of the following:

Peter Copeland Collection pp. 24, 61 (Cheltenham Chronicle), 41, 161 (Gloucestershire Newspapers Ltd.), 60, 123 (G. Garness), 84, 117, 122; Dr. H. G. Dowler p. 184 (upper); Garness Collection pp. 87, 108, 110, 184 (lower); Peter Garness p. 185; David Goodman pp. 79, 111, 149; Mrs. J. Johnson Collection pp 49, 86, 101; Miss D. M. Jones pp. 127, 150; Brian Waters p. 13 (by courtesy of Mrs. Sheppard), p. 15 (by courtesy of Gloucester City Museum), p. 17 (by courtesy of Doreen Cratchley), pp. 20, 35, 38, 39, 40, 52, 69 (by courtesy of the Vicar and Churchwardens), pp viii, 6, 9, 11, 23, 50, 59, 68, 75, 95, 97, 118, 119, 134, 142, 176, 177, 182, 190, 194; Henry Western pp. 170, 179.

Maps:

Ordnance Survey Map p. xii: Reproduced from the O.S. Map Scale: 6″ to the Mile Gloucestershire Sheet No. XXVI.S.W. (Provisional Edition Revision of 1921 with additions in 1938).

Maps pp. 2, 4, 47: Brian Waters .

View of Churchdown from Chosen Hill today.

Preface and Acknowledgements

I have had two aims in writing this account of the village in which I now live; the first has been, obviously, to find out as much as I could about its past, tracing its development from a small rural parish to a popular, and populous, residential area; the second has been to consider how much - or how little - such a community as this has been affected by events taking place in the wider, national sphere.

Churchdown is perhaps particularly suitable as a subject of study in this latter respect because it is provincial being distant from London and other major cities, and it is not a place of great renown - neither a well-known beauty spot, nor the scene of some important event in history or the birthplace of a celebrity. In fact, like thousands of others, it ranks as 'an ordinary place' - but, of course, no place *is* 'ordinary'! W. G. Hoskins, the well-known authority on local history, makes this point when he writes:: 'There is no part of England, however unpromising it may appear at first sight, that is not full of of questions for those who have a sense of the past.' (Editor's Introduction, *The Gloucestershire Landscape,* H. P. R. Finberg, p.19.)

Churchdown is a very pleasant village, held in much affection by those of us who live here, so it is not 'unpromising' in that sense, but it is a rather scattered community, without any anciently-defined centre, and it is not as well-endowed with archive material as some fortunate places (no really significant charter, for instance, has been found so far); certainly, though, it can provide its full share of the 'questions' of which Hoskins writes. Persistent 'delving' over many years with the following up of reference-leads from a wide range of sources, has revealed more about Churchdown's past than at first seemed possible and some surprising facts have come to light - but several mysteries remain to puzzle us.

The histories of the village that already exist - and I hasten to acknowledge the debt I owe to their compilers - have proved a valuable starting point for this study, but time and events have moved on since they were written and there is much that can now be added. I have had the privilege of talking with older residents and their reminiscences have provided a rich fund of first-hand, and often very amusing, anecdotes which make the village's recent past really come to life. For Churchdown's more ancient history I have relied on documents found for me at the Gloucestershire Records Office, at the Shire Hall Archives Department and Library Headquarters, at the Gloucestershire Collection Department at Central Library, Gloucester, and at our local Branch Library, and without the patient and specialist help I have received from their staff this book could never have been attempted. The third source of factual discovery has been provided by Churchdown itself - its buildings (and I have much appreciated the kindness of householders who have allowed me to see over their homes), its farms, roads and fields and, above all, of course, by exploration of the hill which has always dominated this village, almost certainly being the determining factor in original settlement and important as a place of religious significance from the very earliest times.

The late Hermione Oram and the late Sid Richings had a fund of interesting memories and amusing anecdotes to relate and it has been a great pleasure to include many of these in this study of Churchdown. I am very grateful to the Rev. Martin Oram for kindly giving me access to his mother's pictures and papers. The diaries of William Swift, first headmaster of the village school, have been both a source of great enjoyment and of valuable insight into village life in the late nineteenth and early twentieth centuries. The summary of these entries compiled by the late Dr. H. G. Dowler has proved very useful. Winifred Mills' account of 'Churchdown before the Change' has also been a source of enjoyable information.

I am indebted to David Smith, County Archivist, for giving me valuable advice regarding the use of archive material in his departments, and I also wish to thank Peter Lowe, present headmaster of Churchdown Village Primary School for so helpfully allowing me to use and quote from the school logbooks.

I am grateful to the Rev. Edward Mason and the Rev. Malcolm Northall for allowing me access to the parish records, and to John Rhodes and Malcom Watkins for showing me artefacts in the Gloucester City Museum which were found in Churchdown. My husband and I were privileged to visit the home of Mr. and Mrs. Sheppard where we shown, and had the opportunity of photographing, the stone hand-god image which they had found in their garden.

While conducting an investigation of the mound on which St. Bartholomew's Church stands, Sean Cooke, the archaeologist, kept me fully informed of his findings and permitted me to view the excavations and this I much appreciated.

I wish to thank Peter (L. E.) Copeland for so generously allowing me to benefit from his considerable knowledge and photographic record of Churchdown's more immediate past.

Carolyn Heighway, archaeologist and local historian, replied most helpfully to my enquiries and very kindly allowed me to see Michael Hare's paper on the Early History of St. Oswald's Priory which was a great privilege. I also wish to thank Professor Barry Cunliffe and Dr. Nicholas Herbert for the trouble they have taken in answering my letters of enquiry.

Joyce Johnson, a previous owner of the Manor House, has told me many interesting facts about the ancient house and I am very grateful for the loan of her personal collection of local material. Kathleen and Henry Western have provided me with accounts of wartime Churchdown which are both most amusing and informative and I am most grateful for their help and the interest they have shown; Roger Western has kindly answered all my questions about local government. Owen Hyett, too, has given me the benefit of his memories of the village in the past and I wish to thank Victor and Mary Colville, son and daughter of William Colville, a past owner of the village shop and bakery, for telling me much about Churchdown in those earlier days. Cora Gough and Susan Stone have taken considerable trouble to find me details about the local library service and I thank them for their help. My husband and I wish to thank Anthony Garness, owner of the Old House at Home in Brookfield Road, for all the interest he has shown and for giving us permission to use photographs in his family's possession. I am also indebted to David Goodman for permission to reproduce his photographs.

It has been a great privilege to be shown over three of the very old houses in the village, Draggett's Court, Ye Olde House and Chosen Hay, and I wish Angela and Stewart Fincham, June and Robert Smith and Anne and Anthony Boden to know how much I have appreciated this opportunity.

Peter Ford very kindly gave me information about Pirton Court of which he is the present owner and also gave me a copy of the house's history written by Ian Lord, grandson of a previous owner.

The late Charles Rouse answered my questions about the bells of St. Bartholomew's and I thank him for allowing me to benefit from his great knowledge of the subject.

Gillian Clegg took great care in editing my script and has given me valuable guidance from her own considerable experience in local history work and I very gratefully acknowledge this, as I do the friendly help given to me by Richard Bryant of Past Historic regarding the layout and typesetting of this book.

I wish to thank my son, Richard, for being my fellow investigator and very particularly for the work he did for me on the field systems of the parish.

My publishers and friends, Peter and Carolyn Hammond, have encouraged, supported and advised me from the outset and I am most deeply indebted to them for the production of this book.

My husband, Brian, has been my photographer, co-researcher, adviser and helpmate in every possible way; in fact, the input to this account by local people, past and present, by my publishers and my family has been so great that I am very happy to acknowledge that this story of Churchdown may be considered a communal effort.

G. M. W.

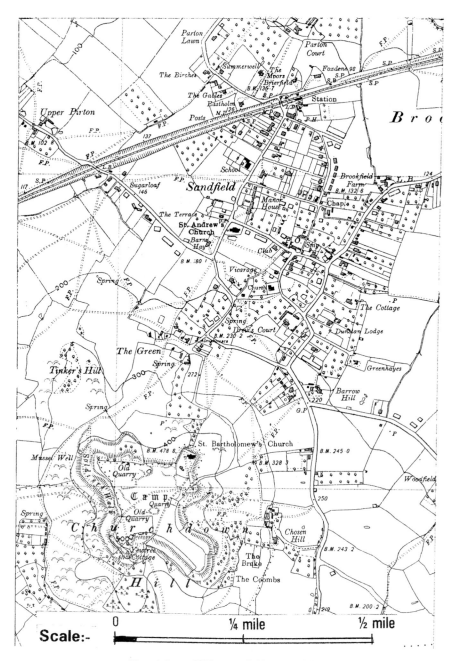

Churchdown Village and Chosen Hill.
Reproduced from the Ordnance Survey Map - Scale: 6″ to the Mile -
Gloucestershire Sheet No. XXVI.S.W. (Provisional Edition Revision of 1921 with
additions in 1938).

Chapter 1

The Hill and the Vale

At what point in time does the story of a place begin? We may say with the coming of the first people, but then we have to ask: 'Why did they come here?' The nature of the terrain has obviously great influence on where settlement takes place and, undoubtedly, in the case of Churchdown the hill was the attracting factor for it provided on its summit both a defensible area and a dry, flat expanse which could provide living space.

So, perhaps, the formation of the landscape, 140-170 million years ago in the geological era known as the Jurassic, should be the starting point for it was then that the lias clay which is the base rock of the whole locality was laid down, and this clay is soon apparent whenever a trench is dug, or a new road cut, in this part of the Severn valley. The lias was a sedimentary deposit on the floor of the deep, muddy inland sea which covered this region and in its murky depths swam creatures whose fossilised remains survive to surprise us when we find them today. The fortunate local fossil-hunter may discover a specimen of a beautifully coiled and whorled ammonite, but by far more common, in fact abundant, are the belemnites, the bullet-like cases of primeval relatives of the cuttlefish or squid.

In some parts of the village the top soil is still heavy clay and this has been dug for brick-making in the recent past. (The grassed-over remains of a brickworks can be seen in the field below Barrow Hill at the top end of the road to Brockworth). A sandy loam, however, predominates in much of the parish and, if a pit is dug, pure sand can often be excavated; this is the case in Chapel Hay where a quarry for sand existed not long ago. Farther back in time, when farming in Churchdown was organised under the open field system, one of the great fields was called 'Sandfield' and this name has been given to two residential developments today - Sandfield Road and Far Sandfield.

The sand may have been spread across the clay stratum during a hot dry spell occurring in more recent geological time - a mere 200,000 years or so ago[1] - creating a landscape, flat for the most part, with a soil that is quick-draining and easy to cultivate. When early settlers had learned to make tools with which to clear the dense forests then covering the

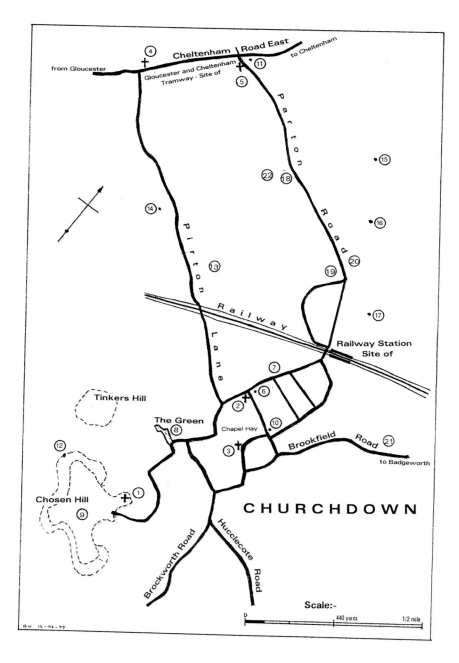

Map of Churchdown showing location of sites mentioned in text

lowland, and had developed some form of plough with which to till the soil, they moved down from the uplands, spreading in time across the valley and forming small farming communities. Apart from the urban stretches, the valley is still mainly pasture land today.

The Cotswold range, which borders the valley to the east, is, too, formed of a sedimentary rock, limestone, laid down like the clay, under water but in a warmer, shallower sea. A variety of life forms flourished in this kindly environment and so the stone can be rich in fossils, many minute, but others quite large like the splendid scallop shell which is embedded in the stone wall of the churchyard cottage on the hill.

Silent and peaceful as this long process of calcite precipitation and slow reef-forming was, there was nothing gentle about the tremendous forces which tilted the strata and then eroded them, producing eventually the high, cliff-edged plateau of the Cotswold ridge. This originally encroached much farther into the Severn valley but the relentless action of weather and water swept much of the more porous and softer rock away, leaving just two outliers, Churchdown (Chosen) Hill and its neighbour, Robinswood, rising like islands from the plain.

Why were these two hills spared the great denudation? The answer may lie in the fact that they are capped by a layer of hard, marly rock composed of limestone, ironstone, sand and clay. The ancient retaining wall below the east end of the church is constructed of hill stone and blocks of this material are also incorporated in the fabric of St. Bartholomew's Church. In the nineteenth century the stone from Churchdown Hill was used extensively for road-making and the Rev. Frederick Smithe, first resident vicar of the parish, tells us: 'The two principal excavations on the hill are kept open for the purpose of supplying the surveyor of roads with materials. Churchdown stone is sometimes used in the parish roads to form a foundation.'[2] It was apparently valued for its special hardness but it was difficult to quarry

---

Key to plan on p. 2 :

1	St. Bartholomew's Church	12	Muzzle Well
2	St. Andrew's Church	13	Churchdown School
3	Methodist Church	14	Pirton Court
4	Church of Our Lady and School	15	Parton Farm
5	St. John's Church	16	Parton Manor
6	The Manor or Great House	17	Parton Court
7	Village School	18	Library
8	Old School House	19	Community Centre
9	Iron Age Fort	20	Parish Council Office
10	Bat and Ball Inn and site of the Old Elm Inn	21	Chosen Hill School
11	Hare and Hounds Inn	22	Parton Manor School

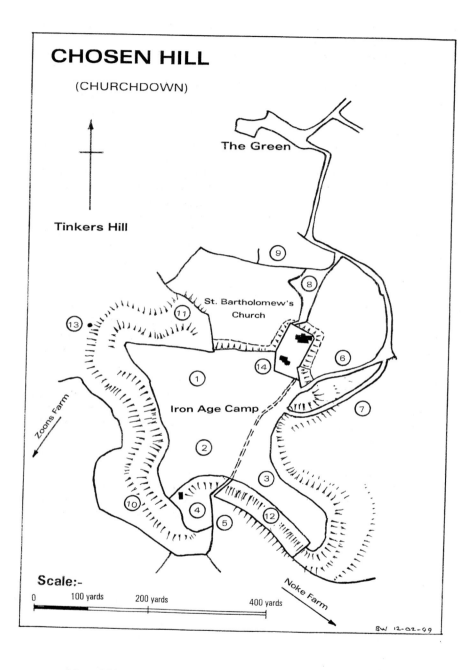

Map of Chosen Hill showing location of sites mentioned in the text

and therefore expensive and when cheaper materials could be obtained these were preferred and the hill stone was used to a much lesser extent. During the First World War, however, there was a demand for it again and German prisoners, interned in the locality, were employed to extract the stone, using explosives - which must have sounded very alarming to the people living in the village below! The mounds and hollows of past diggings can still be seen on the hill beneath the thick mantle of scrub and bramble.

The hill, besides having been subjected to much excavation, is also very unstable and liable to slippage. This is because the hill base is clay of the lower lias and when water percolating through the upper, more porous, rock reaches this impermeable stratum it becomes trapped, thus forming a very slippery layer. In past ages portions of the hillside evidently slid down to form the 'tumps' which are such a feature of the hill landscape. Land movements on such a massive scale seem, fortunately, not to occur now but observation of tree growth will often show a tendency to contortion as if the roots have scrabbled frantically to maintain a secure hold. Gorse grows in profusion and this is indicative of disturbed ground as the plant quickly colonises such an area. Whether the lower hill, called Tinker's (or Rabbits') Hill, is a 'tump', or merely a lesser part of the main formation which has become more reduced by denudation, is a matter of opinion.[3] Writing in 1939, J. Cooke lists the hills and tumps, but it is quite difficult to work out which is which, perhaps because there is more growth all over the hill area now than there was then.[4] Starting on the south side of Chosen he begins with the intriguingly-named 'Devils's Oak Tump' where, he says, there once stood a 'solitary, famous oak' , the site of which is now covered with fir and larch. Below this, on the Hucclecote road, are Noke Court and Noke Farm - 'Noke' being a corruption of the mediaeval 'atten oak' ('at the Oak'). Was there some deep significance, a pagan connection perhaps, about this tree that it was commemorated in these names?

Continuing around the hill he names 'Low Knoll' and, above it, 'High Knoll', and then, going westwards, the 'Kissing Tump', (also less romantically known as 'Zoon's Tump', Zoons Farm being below),

---

Key to plan on p. 4

1	Reservoir 1	8	Jubilee Plantation
2	Reservoir 2	9	Dunns Elm
3	Reservoir 3	10	Beacon and Soldiers Walk
4	Site of Fishlock's Tea Gardens	11	Soldiers Walk
5	Hucclecote Path	12	Soldiers Walk
6	Hollow Way	13	Muzzle (Mussel) Well
7	Present Day Road	14	Church (Sexton's) Cottage

'Green Hill', 'Rabbits' Hill', 'Saddle Hill', 'Tinker's Hill' and, finally, Howcroft, the tump below the church. Few residents of Churchdown will know these names now and there are diverse opinions as to which is Rabbits' Hill and which Tinker's.

Another feature resulting from the trapping of water between the permeable and non-permeable strata is the existence of a spring line. Small ponds ring the hill at this level and a number of springs emerge along the line; the one at the top of Duns Elm above The Green was an important water source for the village until water was piped, but it is the Muzzle Well, on the west flank of the hill, that is the most noteworthy.

It is the generally held belief that this well is ancient; in fact, its alternative name is the 'Roman Well' but it may actually long pre-date the Roman occupation and be associated with a prehistoric settlement. The origin of the name has given rise to much conjecture including the suggestion that it is derived from the same root as the German 'Musenquelle' which means 'Well of the Muses' (prophetic nymphs of wells and springs).[5] An element of mystery does seem to have long been associated with it (as is the case with most ancient wells) and the tradition is recorded that local maidens would consult its tree-shadowed water and whisper their romantic hopes to it.

The Muzzle Well, also called The Roman Well, an ancient spring on the north-west slope of Chosen Hill.

In the past a hollow way led from The Green to the well and this may still be traced beneath the ferns and tree roots; there is evidence, too, of a trackway in the field above Green Farm for the well was once a much-used water source for the villagers who lived around the hill, and must have been, in fact, the only supply of fresh water for those who actually lived at the top.

It is with the early settlers of these locations that the story of Churchdown begins.

Chapter 2

The Early Years from Pre-History to the Norman Conquest

Early Settlement

When in its long history the name 'Chosen' first became attached to Churchdown Hill we do not know. Versions of 'Churchdown', via (among many other variations) the form 'Churson', arrive at 'Chosen' in the eighteenth century,[1] but Canon Bazeley, writing early this century, says 'Churchdown has always been called Chosen by its older inhabitants,' so it could be that this colloquial form is of some antiquity.[2]

However, whether the name is ancient or not, it may be assumed that the hill, rising as it does above the surrounding lowland and having, as has already been seen, a conveniently flat and inhabitable summit, would have been a chosen spot from the earliest times. Unfortunately all traces of any Neolithic or early Bronze Age settlements which may have existed on the hill have been completely lost through centuries of digging, quarrying and excavating, but neighbouring sites such as Crickley, Leckhampton and Barnwood have yielded plenty of evidence of habitation from these times and there is no reason to think Churchdown would have been neglected by early settlers. Excavations of the Roman Villa site below the hill on the Noke side have, in fact, revealed evidence of Late Bronze Age and Early Iron Age dwellings existing there before it became a Roman homestead. There is, also, some indication from recent archaeological investigation that the mound on which St. Bartholomew's Church stands may be, partially at least, man-made and date from as early as the Bronze Age.[3]

It has even been suggested, by those who are attuned to such mysteries, that Chosen Hill was a focal point on a ley line - one of those prehistoric trackways believed to be associated with earth magnetism - but, here, we are deeply into the realms of conjecture. Two large, roughly-shaped stones, one lying in the hedge by the road up the hill and the other in use as part of a stile in a field on the Hucclecote side, may be very ancient marking or guiding stones of some significance.

The only certainty we have about Churchdown's prehistoric past is that we now know that an Iron Age hillfort was established on Chosen Hill.

The existence of the camp seems to have been first acknowledged in writing by Thomas Lloyd Baker early in the nineteenth century when he prepared a list of fortifications along the Cotswold ridge.[4] He is dismissive about Churchdown's: 'It is on a small steep hill in the vale. Its shape is very irregular conforming entirely to that of the ground. It is rendered very imperfect by stone digging and little or nothing satisfactory can be said for it.'

We have, today, the advantage over Lloyd Baker; in 1972, when excavation for a new pipeline cut through the bank on the western approach to the summit, the opportunity to carry out a detailed survey was taken and the conclusion reached was that: 'Churchdown Hill must now be treated as an Iron Age fortified site.'[5] In the course of the construction of the third reservoir actual evidence of habitation was revealed and this will be described later in this chapter.

A rampart and ditch were observed on the west with earthworks following the contours, the whole area enclosed being just under 18 acres. What is known as 'glacis construction' is indicated, as, on the western to south-eastern side, there is evidence of a steep-sided ditch above which there would have been defensive structures of stone and/or wood with earth piled on the inner face, but the long passage of time has

Ancient Hollow Way leading to the top of Chosen Hill

reduced what were probably once quite formidable earthworks to gentle banks much overgrown with a tangle of gorse, scrub and bramble. On the north the naturally precipitous nature of the scarp precluded the need for a ditch.

A hill fort usually had a heavily-protected entrance in the form of a corridor between raised banks and here the defenders were well placed to repel an enemy attempting to break through - where would this have been on Chosen Hill? There is some slight indication of such an opening on the north side more or less in line with the ascent path known as the 'Roman Steps' - one of several paths leading up to the fort which are probably ancient; Churchdown Lane on the Hucclecote side, for instance, is called 'an ancient trackway' in an account of the Roman villa nearby,[6] and the deeply-sunken lane, now a bridle path, which leads up from the metalled road, has all the signs of being undoubtedly very long-established. This path would have led directly to the enclosure; it now emerges by the churchyard gate.

The Churchdown site is one among many local hillforts; there are at least seventy-eight in the county and a dozen are within 25 km., so it is generally held that some form of signalling could have been operated from one to another, possibly by beacon fires.

Large or small, hillforts usually follow a general pattern, with convenience seemingly almost invariably sacrificed to the exigencies of defence, and nearly all having one great deficiency - no natural on-camp water source. The nearest spring for the Chosen fort is the Muzzle Well, so it is thought unlikely that a prolonged siege could have been withstood.

Why then, and when, were these forts built? They were to repel invaders, the string of Cotswold Edge forts presenting a formidable front, and to provide refuge for the people and their livestock when danger threatened; but they were also 'power-houses', the seat of the chieftain and other elite, from which the surrounding territory, and the inhabitants of the small farming communities within it, could be controlled. The great building time for the forts was from 550-400 B.C., although a date as early as 800 B.C. is possible, and their use continued into the first century A.D. The Churchdown fort was occupied probably more in the later than the earlier years but it is not known whether or not evidence of previous habitation has been destroyed The Hurst report suggests that there may have been two phases of construction, the second being necessary because renewed danger threatened. During quieter, more trouble-free periods, the fort may have fallen out of use, or have been garrisoned only by a small force - it was, after all, an inconvenient place in which to live permanently having no water supply and being on a site unsuitable for extensive farming.[7]

The hillfort builders were Celtic Britons who had been settled in the area from about the 7th century B.C. onwards, and their enemies were fellow Celts who were neighbouring tribes or fresh invaders. Friend or foe, they

St. Bartholomew's Church viewed from the north-east.

were equally fearsome warriors, positively delighting in war and having little regard for the sanctity of human life. Their belief in reincarnation, with the soul passing into another body at death, made the ending of one life of little account and it was especially glorious to die in battle.

There was a general period of frenetic strengthening of forts in the 1st century B.C., and this may well have been when the apparent second construction of the Churchdown fort took place. The reason was the inexorable advance of a new wave of invaders from the Continent - the Belgae, named from their place of origin which was in the region of present Belgium.

It is probable that the Chosen defenders soon fell before their superior adversaries as did those of the Bredon fort, fourteen or so miles away. Here excavations have revealed the mutilated skeletons of about fifty men, in early manhood, apparently cut down in hand-to- hand fighting by the inner entrance where it seems they had been making a last stand.[8]

The Dobunni, the tribe who had settled in the Cotswold area and established their headquarters at Bagendon, were strongly penetrated both by Belgic might and Belgic culture, but this was not so with the Silures who inhabited the west bank of the Severn and so, consequently, *they* became the enemy. The Chosen camp was on the fringe of Dobunni territory and was, perhaps, retained as a military outpost, even, possibly, into the time of the Roman invasions.

Despite short periods of stability, life in Iron Age Britain was mostly turbulent and survival always precarious, but settlement in and around Chosen Hill may never have been entirely abandoned; almost certainly, though, the local inhabitants would have been caught up in the battles and skirmishes which were so much the pattern of life in Celtic Britain.

Direct evidence of such battles having taken place on the Churchdown site has not been revealed, but burnt material, clay daub and charcoal, has been found in excavated material (this, however, could be just domestic debris). It is alleged that a former sexton, while digging graves in the churchyard, disinterred, 'from time to time' remains of human charred bones.[9] These, it was then suggested then, could be relics of human sacrifices offered to the god, Thor, during the Saxon era, but this idea was probably more fancy than fact. Human burnt sacrifice *is* popularly believed to have been one of the gruesome customs practised by the ruling Druid priesthood of the Celtic religion, but it is also possible that these remains were of bodies slain in battle and, very possibly, burnt by the victors. However, some support for the idea that these remains were those of sacrificial victims is the statement that the sexton found them *while digging in the churchyard*, that is, on or around the mound on which the church stands - and this, as has already been stated, seems to be partially, or entirely, man-made and, therefore, may be assumed to have been an especially significant place..

The report of the geological survey made in May, 1992, states: 'The plateau top of the hill is the site of late Iron Age earthworks with ramparts formed around the entire plateau edge. The mound on which the church stands may well have been part of this system, as the site of a fort or lookout tower, or could conceivably have been a purpose-made mound either for St. Bartholomew's Church or, much more likely, for some pre-Christian place of worship or ritual.'[10] So we are back to the premise that here we have a pagan temple site where, possibly, human sacrifice was offered. (The excavations in 1992 revealed courses of very large blocks of stone below the surface on the south side of the church; without more extensive investigation it was not possible at the time to make any definite statement as to what these were - whether they were the foundations of a very sizeable building or just extensive reinforcement of the mound).

An alternative theory with regard to the mound is that it was a sacred burial place - a barrow in fact? The mystery may never be solved, but the long-held belief that Churchdown Hill was a *chosen* spot for religious observance long before Christianity reached this island can, at least, be given some credence.

One of the most fascinating finds connected with Churchdown's heathen past was discovered, not on the hill, but in the valley below, in a garden in Pirton Lane.[11] It is the likeness of a human head, blunt-featured and austere, carved from Forest of Dean red sandstone, and, being only

Small image of a god probably intended to be carried in the hand.
Found in Pirton Lane, Churchdown.

about four inches long, may have been intended to be carried in the hand. It is thought to be the image of a Celtic god as it is similar, but in minuscule, with two large carvings from a water shrine in the Forest of Dean. (The latter are now exhibited in Gloucester City Museum).

This hand god, if that is what it is, was found by a garden well and, as the well was a purely domestic one and not, as far as is known, ancient, there can be no significance in this; but water sources were revered in pagan times and human heads and skulls, actual or in image form, were very often cast into them.[12] Why this little relic was found where it was is just another mystery, but it is undoubtedly a link with Churchdown's pagan past and probably with the Druid religion, the worship rituals of which often took place near water or in sacred groves.

The oak was venerated above all other trees and any plant, mistletoe for instance, which grew upon it was thought to absorb some of its sacred essence and magical properties. The oak is a tree that grows well on

Chosen, with mistletoe, too, being abundant in the area, and, as has been seen in the previous chapter, at least one oak seems to have been accorded special notice.

Generally though, much of the dense woodland in the lower reaches and the valley was cleared by the settlers, and the land then cultivated with the new, improved heavy ploughs pulled by draught oxen. The hill site has produced evidence that domestic animals were bred, deposits of sheep and ox bones having been found; storage pits have also been unearthed, providing proof that grain was grown and harvested. It is thought that the layers of charcoal found in such pits indicate deliberately burning of the stored corn when it became rotten. Fragments of pottery, mostly pieces from storage jars, have been discovered in some quantity; these are of varying colour and texture but those stamped with the duck motif have been identified as from ware typical of that produced in the Cotswold/Herefordshire region over a long period of time from the 1st century A.D. to well into the Roman era.[13] It is known that the rotary quern, a handmill by which the grain was crushed between a stationary and a revolving stone, was in use, for the Belgae had introduced this as their culture spread; there were also by this time wheeled vehicles for transporting produce, and an advanced form of coinage for the conducting of marketing transactions.

The Churchdown people may have dwelt on the hill, within the camp, or, except when danger threatened, lower down in fenced compounds. They lived in well-constructed round huts, made of wood and wattle, with thatched roofs and stone floors, and wore clothing of leather or dyed woven cloth, fastened or decorated with metal clasps and brooches fashioned with great skill.

The Chosen site has not yet yielded any especially noteworthy artefact but the 'best' find to date is a cast copper alloy strap junction which was discovered in the debris of a collapsed bank on the summit path known as the 'Soldiers' Walk.' Although simple in design, it is very well fashioned and in excellent condition and was probably made for use on the person rather than as part of horse harness. It is similar in design to examples found in the prehistoric villages at Meare and Glastonbury in Somerset and this suggests that there was some trading contact between these communities and the settlement at Churchdown. Chronologically it may be placed as having been made between 100 B.C. and the 1st century A.D.[14] In the realm of craftsmanship, and probably in husbandry, the Chosen folk of the Iron Age cannot be classed as really primitive people, and their Druid priesthood had a sophisticated knowledge of natural lore, including astronomy.

It was during the early years of the 1st century and while the Later Iron Age people of Churchdown were acclimatising themselves to Roman rule, that there occurred the event which was to have a most profound effect on Western civilisation - in an eastern outpost of the engulfing

Iron Age Strap Junction of cast copper alloy. Found on Chosen Hill.

Roman Empire Christ was born. When knowledge of the Christian message first reached Britain is unknown but the legend that Joseph of Arimathea brought the Gospel early to the West Country is a persistent tradition. There can be a ground of truth in such ancient beliefs, often distorted by the sentimental imaginings of later centuries, but what *is* sure is that the ancient gods were not easily vanquished, and even when it seemed they had been, they kept a toehold through the power of superstition. We shall see this struggle against paganism surfacing again in Churchdown's religious history.

The Roman Occupation.

The Roman occupation of Britain began in A.D. 43 and extended over a period of 400-500 years and during this time the people of Churchdown lived in close association with a civilisation far in advance of their own. The Chosen Hill settlement existed in an area rich in Roman influence. At a distance of about fifteen miles eastward was Corinium Dobunnorum (now Cirencester), a town which, by the 4th century A.D. had become the third most important in Britain, and to the south-west, and only 4-5 miles away was Glevum (Gloucester) and the suburban military base of Kingsholm. Joining these two important military and commercial centres, passing close to the large native settlement at Barnwood and skirting the Churchdown area, was the great arterial road, Ermine Street. It is possible that local inhabitants were persuaded, conscripted or press-ganged into the workforce labouring on the construction of this highway.[1]

It is likely that the native people bought and sold in the Glevum markets and that some were employed in the city, as a number of service personnel would be needed to maintain the highly organised and sophisticated lifestyle of Roman urban society. In time, some particularly able members of the local tribes may have risen to occupy administrative posts, it being Roman policy to create links with the native population, but, for the most part the Iron Age people kept to their own culture.

Roman infiltration into the rural life of the area which included Churchdown was however extensive; the Cotswold plateau and the surrounding foothills are dotted with Roman villas, and there are, undoubtedly, many more which have not yet come to light; these homesteads are so numerous that the region has been described as a 'paradise for the well-to-do.'[2] Such wealthy suburban dwellers were often retired members of the Roman army many of whom may not have been Roman-born but had acquired Roman citizenship, while others may have been local Britons of status or descendants of mixed marriages.

Villas were often the centres of estates sometimes exceeding 1,000 acres in territory and consisting of a complex of buildings and out-buildings; in the former lived the owner with his family and domestic staff, while in the latter the farmworkers were housed. The main living quarters were decorated and furnished to a high degree of luxury with baths, underfloor heating and mosaic flooring, the walls colour-plastered and often mural-painted.[3]

The villa builders favoured 'a valley slope, facing south or east, not too high up, with shelter from the wind, exposure to the sun, and water close at hand,'[4] and the villa discovered at the Noke (on the Hucclecote side of Chosen) occupied just such a position. This site, which is on the land surrounding what is now the Hucclecote Centre, was excavated in 1910-11 and again in 1933.[5] The villa seems to have been a dwelling site with a long history of, initially, pre-Roman habitation, and then continuous occupation from the 1st to the 5th centuries A.D. (that is until after the Roman withdrawal.) The majority of coins and pottery which were found date from the early 4th century.[6]

Building had obviously taken place in stages but the final dwelling seems to have been about 60ft. by 110ft. and to have comprised quite a complex of room divisions, two forming bath compartments. A wealth of artefacts was retrieved from the site including pottery, knives, keys, rings, pins and buckles, spindle whorls, and discs for the game of fivestones, but among the most interesting finds was a small piece of plaster on which a sketch of a gabled building had been roughly scratched, representing, perhaps, a drawing of the villa itself. Other fragments of plaster were probably from internal walls and were in a range of colours, red, pink, yellow, blue, brown and white, some being patterned. There was a great deal of broken glass and pieces of roof tiling with some evidence that the house had been mosaic-floored, the workmanship dating from the end of the 4th century or later.

Trenches dug in the area brought to light some human remains including a skull, the jaw of a child and fragmentary remains of two adult skeletons; there was also a quantity of animal and poultry bones and among the former was the canine tooth of a bear. A bear in Gloucestershire? A captive animal perhaps.

Around this villa/farmstead stretched an expanse of open fields, extending up to and including the southern slopes of the hill, and this area would have been part of the estate, and probably terraced for fruit-growing. There is evidence of vine-growing in Churchdown at least by mediaeval times; it may well have been practised earlier.

The Noke villa was not the only Roman habitation in the environs of Chosen Hill as pieces of Roman brick and pottery have been found near Chapel Hay and Parton Court. A Roman lamp was discovered in a garden near the junction of Brookfield Road with Oldbury Orchard and, interestingly, this has the cross symbol in relief.[7]

There is also the question as to whether or not there was a military

Roman Lamp found in Churchdown.

station on Chosen Hill for this was a site within the defensive lines extending from the River Humber and including the Severn valley. There has long been a popular belief in Churchdown that there was such a Roman occupation of the hill - hence the name 'Roman Well' for the Muzzle Well and 'Roman Steps' for the, now almost non-existent, stone-set ascent path on the northern flank. The title deeds of land on the southern side of the summit are reported to refer to 'part of the Roman camp'[8] and the row of dwellings above Zoons Farm are known locally as the 'Oystershell Cottages', reputedly because so many shells of oysters, a delicacy much favoured by the Romans, were unearthed there.

Chosen Hill has also been suggested as a Roman temple site (and it will be recalled from the previous section that a course of large stone blocks was unearthed during the excavations in 1992); Jupiter is the deity most favoured as the object of local worship, this god being the patron of the Roman colony in Glevum, but Juno, Mercury and Minerva are also known to have been reverenced in Gloucestershire.[9] A coin, stamped with the likeness of Minerva, with her shield and javelin, (and minted in the reign of the Emperor Claudius, A.D. 41-54), was actually dug up in Pirton Lane, Churchdown, but this does not, of course, necessarily reflect local religious adherence; coinage circulated widely through trading usage. It is thought that, by the 5th-6th centuries, hillforts, such as that on Chosen, were used more as religious sites, whether pagan or, later, Christian, than as military outposts.[10]

The Celtic gods and goddesses and the spirits of the natural world may have been loosely accepted as local representatives of these Roman deities and worshipped at the same temple sites.[11] The villa dwellers at the Noke, following the custom existing in many Roman homesteads, almost certainly venerated the household gods, the spirits of home and hearth, and honoured them at a domestic shrine. The reverence of the Emperor, who, as head of state, represented the greater family of the empire and embodied its ethos, was an extension of this cult. Mithraism, a sacramental religion in which certain rituals foreshadowed those of Christianity, flourished among the military personnel and so may have been established in and around Gloucester.[12]

It is also possible that Christianity had its early adherents in the locality for it is thought that the new faith was spread by the movement of troops from the Eastern Mediterranean to Western Europe, thus reaching places like Churchdown where there was a military establishment. In the small collection of coins found in the area is one of the Emperor Magnentius (A.D. 350-353) which would have been minted at the time when the Empire was officially Christian.[13] This coin, found in Chapel Hay in the village centre, is inscribed with the Christian symbol the Chi Rho, the monogram of the first letters of the name of Christ in Greek. It has been suggested that Gloucestershire was already more Christian than pagan by the time of the Saxon takeover, the faith never having been entirely extinguished in these more western parts of Britain.[14]

The end of the 4th century saw the power of Rome declining and her armies withdrawn for defensive duty nearer home; by A.D. 410 all the Roman soldiery had left this island. The amenities of Gloucester no doubt deteriorated rapidly and the great highways fell into disuse, but, topographically, the effects of the occupation were more long-lasting and may even remain today for it is now thought that the pattern of the Roman estates survived to form the basis of parish divisions previously believed to be no earlier than Saxon.[15]

During the disturbed years that followed the Roman withdrawal the people of Chosen were subjected to the constant threat of harassment from the marauding bands of Irish raiders who swept up the Severn; when these piratical attacks occurred the local people may have, once again, taken to the relative safety of their ancient hillfort.

In A.D. 577 the invading Saxon warlords captured Gloucester[16]. It was during the ensuing years of Saxon domination and gradual integration that the Churchdown community began to take on its own identity and become a place with a recorded name, *Circesdune*. The first syllable of this name, being Celtic/British, suggests some retention of the usages of the past, while the Saxon second part unites the incoming culture with the old.[17]

The Saxon Period.

In the half-millennium between the withdrawal of the Romans and the coming of the Normans, during the time of invasion by the Saxons and their eventual settlement of the area, the people of Churchdown, like all their fellow countrymen, ceased to be 'Celtic' and became 'English,' and the village, although proof of this is hard to find, became the centre of a barony and so attained some importance.

During the years of infiltration it is likely that the indigenous population 'stayed put.' It is not now generally believed as it once was that the local people fled before the invaders and took refuge in the far west, for only the wealthy and most mobile could have done this; the peasant farmers who lived around Chosen would have carried on their usual pattern of existence as well as they could.

The Battle of Dyrham, (A.D. 577) regarded as a 'turning-point in English history,'[1] had brought the lower Severn Valley, probably including Churchdown, under West Saxon control, but by A.D. 628 the territory had been surrendered to Penda, who became king of the Mercians in 632. The sub-kingdom of the Hwicce, of which Churchdown must have been part, was formed about this time and the inhabitants of the region, with whom the settlers were beginning to intermingle, have been described as being both 'British' and 'Christian.'[2]

Stone insets, possibly
from an earlier Saxon
building, in the north
chancel wall of St.
Bartholomew's Church

Too much credence should not be given to the popular local belief that
a temple to the Norse god Thor was established on Chosen Hill. This idea
seems to have been started by Canon Lysons in 1865 when he claimed to
have in his possession a document which named the hill as 'Thorsdown,'
but later writers have considered this something of a myth.[3] By A.D. 660
the leaders of the Hwicci were probably Christian, and, in 675, Osric,
one of the sub-kings of the Hwicci, created the Bishopric of Worcester,
in which diocese Gloucestershire remained until Henry VIII made it a
separate diocese in 1541.

The years from the early 7th century onwards must have been a very
formative period for Churchdown but there is little archaeological
evidence to illuminate this long, important but obscure era. There are two
or three shaped stones in the north chancel wall of St. Bartholomew's
Church which are possibly pre-Norman, and the human remains and
carved stones, of uncertain date, found in Chapel Hay may be earlier than
mediaeval; as previously noted, the second syllable of the name

Circesdune is Saxon, and hidden Saxon word roots survive in local terms like 'Hay' (enclosure) and in many field names. Evidence of the Saxon influence though, is, in fact, all around us, for it was in those centuries that Churchdown took on the 'shape' that it still retains, despite the sprawl of modern development and the severing motorways. It was in Saxon times that the boundaries of the parish (which, as has been said, may have originated in the Romano/British estates) were definitely established, and it was then that the roadways were trodden out, the woodlands tamed and field patterns laid down.[4]

Boundaries often followed the course of a stream (as does part of the boundary along Norman's Brook); some were marked by the remaining stretches of wildwood, while others were artificially created by the planting of shrubs and trees on a raised bank with a ditch below. The Churchdown/Badgeworth boundary provides an example of this which can be seen in the hedgerow at the bottom of the fields below Badgeworth Church. Old hedgerows consist of varied tree and bush growth and usually meander pleasantly as they follow the natural features of the land.

The old roads remaining in the parish are the successors of the Saxon tracks which wandered from farmstead to farmstead, hamlet to hamlet, parish to parish, skirting obstacles such as marsh, pond or tree as they wound their haphazard way from one place to another. Modern traffic conditions have necessitated the straightening of many of their eccentric twists, but where they remain it is interesting to guess how and why they came to be there.

When we try to locate the site of the Saxon village of Churchdown we are unable to come to any definite conclusion. For one thing the dwellings were made of wood, as were, too, many of the objects the people used, and so no trace is left of them; for another, later development has often overlaid any evidence of an earlier community; thirdly, we cannot be sure that there was what is called a 'nucleated' village at all. The settlement of *Circesdune*, recorded in Domesday, may have consisted of a number of homesteads scattered over the area which comprises the present village centre, The Green, Pirton and Parton, and possibly extending farther afield to include The Noke, Elmbridge, Hucclecote, and even Brickhampton. It is perhaps more accurate, therefore, to designate the settlement as a 'township' or 'vill,' but it seems reasonable to place its heart (or 'nucleus') on The Green, for here was access to a good water supply and the present arrangement of dwellings around a central open space follows the pattern of many an anciently-established village.

By Saxon times the once all-enveloping forest had been greatly reduced, but the wooded stretches that remained were carefully managed, preserved and enclosed, and that such an area existed in Churchdown was later recorded in the Domesday survey. Wood was the building material most favoured by the Saxons and it also provided the main fuel for heating and cooking. Oak was favoured for load-bearing beams in house construction and elm was prized for its long, thick timbers.[5]

There was very little land left uncultivated around the village except, perhaps, for the top of the hill which was designated as common grazing. During the second half of the post-Roman/pre-Norman period a renewed attack was made upon the 'waste' and on the encroaching woodland, for, during the 5th and 6th centuries, when there was a fall in population, this had crept forward again.[6] As the number of inhabitants grew, more land was needed for crop-growing and so the process known as 'assarting' became a feature of land development. (This term meant, literally, 'to grub up trees').[7] Vegetation and undergrowth were cleared by axe or fire and then the land was either taken into cultivation, or used for rough pasture if unsuitable for ploughing; it is likely that the latter was the case on the slopes of Chosen which, still today, are used mostly for pasture.

Above all, it was ploughland that was needed and every yard of land that could be tilled was put under cultivation. In the earlier Saxon period the small, enclosed fields favoured by the Celtic Britons had been opened up into two or more large areas of tillage, probably in order to facilitate working with the new heavy ploughs, pulled by ox teams, which, by this time, had superseded the lighter hand ploughs of previous years.

The fields were divided into strips arranged together in furlongs (a term not necessarily related to the unit of measurement of the same name) and ploughed in ridges to facilitate drainage. The corrugated appearance of these ridges and furrows still shows in many fields, once ploughed but now long given over to permanent pasture, and from Churchdown Hill these 'fossilized' ploughing patterns can be seen in much of the surrounding countryside, especially when there is a light dusting of snow. It is also obvious that many present day roads and hedges cut through the old plough lines which can then be seen continuing in the next field; it is apparent, too, that the ridge patterns change direction, lying, for instance, east-west in one furlong and north-south in an adjoining one. The plough-patterning was obviously determined to some extent by the nature of the terrain, but also by the fact that it was the practice to plough across the length of the headlands, rather than up and down, as this gave a long 'drive' for the team. Evidence of this can be seen around Churchdown, but it must be remembered that open field farming continued for a very long time and actually how far it had advanced by Saxon times is a matter of some uncertainty.[8] The huge fields had their distinguishing names and four of these - Sandfield, Brookfield, Woodfield and Hillfield - are recorded in Churchdown documents in the 19th century, but we do not know if these are the ancient names. The main pattern of farming seems, however, to have been established in this pre-Norman era.

Ridge and Furrow Patterning showing in local fields.

All the familiar cereal crops were grown where conditions were suitable, but barley predominated, (the Anglo-Saxons consumed ale 'on an oceanic scale!'[9], and the term 'Barton', common in the Gloucester area, refers to the growing and storing of this grain. Beans were almost a staple food for the peasant classes and were grown so extensively in the fields and cottage plots that it has been said that our ancestors were, literally, 'full of beans!' (Bamfurlong Lane, which is in the locality, means 'Bean Furlong.') Grass and hay were of the utmost importance for the feeding of livestock and the main hay meadows of Churchdown were along the low-lying borders of Norman's Brook, an area very subject to flooding.

Apart from their cattle, sheep and pigs, the villagers kept geese, ducks and poultry which were allowed to forage on common ground. The straying of beast and bird provided a constant source of local litigation and most communities maintained a pound in which these wanderers were penned until claimed by their owners. A pound is recorded as having been sited on Chapel Hay, near the present St. Andrew's Church, but how ancient this was is not known. (Later, the village pound was moved to The Green but all trace of this, too, has now disappeared).

The Chapel Hay area seems to have been important right from ancient times and has produced very interesting archaeological finds which are undoubtedly of considerable antiquity. The footings of a length of ancient wall were discovered in the ground between the church and the church hall and are preserved under a flagged pathway; but the most spectacular find to date was that, already briefly referred to, which took place in 1924 when the bowling green and tennis courts behind the Churchdown Club in Chapel Hay were extended.[10]

These excavations revealed a number of skeletons, fragments of tile and pottery, the remains of a kiln, a quantity of ironstone dross and a collection of building stones. The latter were piled irregularly and consisted of larger and smaller blocks of local stone, roughly-shaped and, in some cases, with mortar still adhering. A piece of worked stone was found separated from the two main heaps and the carving was assessed as being 'Gothic', probably 14th-century. In all, it was calculated there was sufficient stone to form the base of a chapel, perhaps the chapel of 'Chapel Hay.'

The skeletons were evidence of burials having taken place over a period of time as some were deeply interred, a number were arranged in layered tiers, and others lay more superficially. Almost all were orientated east/west, suggestive of Christian, as opposed to pagan, burial, but one was facing north and buried in a sitting position with knees extended.[11] Most of the remains were those of adult men and

Human skeletons, of date unknown, found in Chapel Hay, Churchdown, during excavations in 1924.

women. There were no traces of coffin burial but this was not surprising as the bodies of humble folk were usually just shrouded and laid directly in the earth. The fact that these were multiple burials has led people to believe that they were of plague victims, but when mass epidemics occurred burial was usually in a communal pit, well apart from habitation.

The skeletons show that these people were quite tall, 5'4" to 5'10" in height; they had excellent teeth, although the adult molars were worn flat, and the teeth of the upper and lower jaws met instead of being aligned to overlap as do ours. The report then goes on to state that several of the skulls were sent to the Royal College of Surgeons in London for examination, and the statement consequently issued by the Royal College said that they were 'typical Saxon skulls', but, rather confusingly, added: 'I would rather say British, for they are probably nearer the 14th than the 11th century'.[12] Presumably, all the human remains were re-interred, although the report does not mention this, and so these early Churchdown people still lie buried beneath the present Recreation Ground - together, most possibly, with many others whose rest has not been disturbed.

The name 'Hay,' being Saxon and meaning an enclosed area, suggests that the site was in use before the Conquest and for some special purpose, but if it was designated, even then, as a burial place this does not, necessarily, mean that the central village was in the very immediate vicinity, Saxon cemeteries seldom being close to habitation.

The alleged remains of a chapel opens the question of the possibility of there having been a Christian place of worship in Saxon Churchdown, despite the stones, found in 1924, seeming to be evidence of a later, probably mediaeval, church. In 679, Osric, lord of the Hwicci, established a house of religion in Gloucester (a forerunner of St. Peter's Abbey which, after the Dissolution in the reign of Henry VIII, became the present cathedral), and it was very possibly from this 'minster' - the name given to a main monastic church - that the monks came into the surrounding countryside preaching the Gospel, and so, in all likelihood, to Churchdown.[13] A cross may well have been set up (perhaps on the mound where St. Bartholomew's now stands), for it is recorded from Anglo-Saxon times that: 'on the estates of the noble and good men of the Saxon race it is a custom to have a cross which is dedicated to Our Lord and held in great reverence, erected on some prominent spot for the convenience of those who wish to pray daily before it.' What more prominent spot than Chosen Hill?[14]

Later some form of shelter may have been put up, followed, perhaps, by a simple chapel, which, being built mainly of wood, would leave no trace of its existence, but one thing would have been necessary, however basic the nature of the place used for worship, and that was water suitable for use in the rite of baptism. It is possible that converts were led down to the Muzzle Well, but it is perhaps more likely that water was carried up to fill a simple font. There are, inserted in the north chancel wall of the hill church, some shaped stones one of which is crudely basin-like in outline, but if inverted this could be a window or door lintel from an earlier chapel in Churchdown.

But was such a chapel, if it existed, built on the hill or down below on Chapel Hay?

No church is mentioned in the Domesday entry for Churchdown, either on the hill or down below on Chapel Hay, but this omission does not necessarily mean that none existed - a matter to be considered a little later.

As we move forward in time to the last two centuries of the period, we come to the association, real or imaginary, between Churchdown and that pious, but martial, lady, Aetheflaed (or Ethelfleda). Local historians have liked to believe that she was Lady of the Barony of Churchdown and, as such, may have built a church, perhaps on Chapel Hay. In accordance with this belief she has pride of place in the stained glass of the window in the south chancel window of St. Andrew's Church - although, so far, no direct evidence of her having a personal involvement with Churchdown has come to light.

Aethelflaed enters the national stage at the time of Viking invasion and how much Churchdown was affected by the terrifying inroads of these fierce Norsemen we cannot say. One of the towns she fortified and made a 'burg' was Gloucester, and there is every reason to believe that she and her husband, Ethelred of Mercia, visited Gloucester and probably stayed at the palace at Kingsholm. It is an established fact that she and Ethelred endowed a new minster just outside Gloucester and, in A.D. 914, enshrined there, certain relics of St. Oswald of Northumbria. This monastery, (later to become the Priory of St. Oswald), and Churchdown co-existed in close relationship for about six-hundred years, that is until the Dissolution severed the connection. It is thought probable that the Barony lands were part of the endowment of the minster but it seems that the properties passed quite soon into the hands of the Bishops of Worcester - in whose diocese both the minster and the Barony then were.[15]

This transference of ownership to the Bishops of Worcester marks the beginning of the relationship between estates in Gloucestershire (which included the Churchdown Barony) and the Archbishopric of York; this strange and complex situation has been researched in considerable depth by A. Hamilton Thompson and published in a paper printed in the Transactions of the Bristol and Gloucestershire Archaeological Society in 1921.[16] Thompson sees the origin of the connection stemming, from A.D. 972 onwards, when there occurred the successive elevation of three Bishops of Worcester to the Primacy of York, with, in each case, their being allowed to retain the Worcester Bishopric.[17]

In A.D. 1061, Ealdred of Worcester, too, became Archbishop of York; he, also, held the two sees together but was obliged to submit to the Papal wish that a suffragan be appointed to oversee the spiritual care of the Worcester diocese. By way of compensation, Ealdred was allowed to retain twelve 'vills' that had been in the ownership of the Worcester church, and these may have included Churchdown and the member manors of the Barony.[18]

These properties, or at least some of them, were not held by York without interruption, for, in 1033, King Cnut granted to Duduc, a royal clerk who later became Bishop of Wells, the 'new minster' at Gloucester - but whether the endowment lands were included is not recorded[19] After Duduc's death in 1061, ownership of the Gloucester minster probably reverted to the king and was, later, possibly in the reign of Edward the Confessor, obtained by Stigand, Archbishop of Canterbury - apparently 'with unjust ambition'[20] - and thus, at the Conquest, we find Stigand holding the estates of St. Oswald. What may be particularly relevant to Churchdown is the statement that the Archbishop 'may have consecrated churches on some of the estates belonging to the new minster.'[21] Was one of these at Churchdown?

While all these political and ecclesiastical manoeuvres were going on how were the ordinary people of Churchdown faring? Perhaps they were little affected by the changes of ownership for these great overlords must have seemed very remote from the hard but simple lives of the peasantry who toiled on their estates.

By the close of the Saxon era manorial life had taken on much of the social pattern that was to last throughout the mediaeval years; it was a structured society, as later evidenced by Domesday Book, with the peasantry graded in degrees of servitude to the lord, and having very little, if any, personal freedom. Nearly all worked the land, that is their own strips and the lord's demesne to which they had to give hours of service each week, but some did specified tasks such as swine-herding, beekeeping or managing the woodland and hay meadows. The blacksmith held a slightly 'upper class' position, as did the miller if there was a local mill, while the beadle was responsible for maintaining law and order.

There was very little the Saxon peasant could really call his own (although even the poorest people were allowed to sell surplus produce if they had any); his land, cottage and livestock were really the property of his lord to whom, on the peasant's death, they could revert, but there was, nevertheless, a certain security provided by the system and, on a well-run manor, no doubt there existed a great sense of community. Living conditions were squalid by our standards, hygiene was primitive or non-existent, sickness or injury, when it struck, was a disaster and life-expectancy was short. Nevertheless, all was not doom and gloom, for the very most was made of every chance for merrymaking, and the stories, drawings and carvings that the people of this time have left us show they enjoyed a crude, but robust, sense of fun; loneliness was not the curse of society that it can be today, and, once outside their, no doubt, stinking hovels, there was the fresh, unpolluted air and the abundance of an unspoilt countryside.

The coming of the Normans would not alter these basic things.

Chapter 3

From the Conquest to the Eve of the Reformation

The Norman invasion has been described as the 'most decisive event in English history' which, sooner or later, changed 'every aspect of English life'[1] and certainly 1066 is the date which, above all others, has imprinted itself on the national mind; but how much did it alter life in a small, established settlement such as Churchdown? The answer may be not very much, although we cannot, from the safe detachment of 900 years, really know how traumatic the takeover was at the time.

King William favoured Gloucester by visiting the town annually and, following the custom of his Saxon predecessors, by holding council there and 'wearing his crown' on these occasions.[2] Norman control was firmly established in the area by strengthening the fortifications of the town, by the building of a castle and by appointing as its constable the sheriff; this officer was responsible for the collection of taxation revenue from the county as well as the town.[3] Churchdown, however, being an ecclesiastical estate, owned successively by the highest churchmen in the land, was not materially affected by change of monarch. At the time of the invasion Stigand, Archbishop of Canterbury, was the holder of the barony, but, after his deposition in 1070, the estates were ceded to Thomas of Bayeux, the Norman Archbishop of York.[4]

The minster of St.Oswald's remained a free chapel royal and continued to hold the churches of Churchdown, Norton, Sandhurst and Compton Abdale in appropriation, that is, it exercised spiritual control, provided a priest to say Mass, and received the tithes and dues by way of income. It maintained this rectorial position throughout the Middle Ages, but the minster, with its dependent churches and chapels, passed under the jurisdiction of York at the end of the 11th Century and became designated a 'peculiar' of the northern see. This was confirmed to Gerard, Thomas's successor at York in 1103, and, again, in 1177, to Archbishop Roger du Pont L'Evêque, but although the grant was thus officially confirmed it remained a contentious issue.[5]

The minster became a priory of Augustinian canons in 1153. These canons, although observing the monastic ideals of poverty, chastity and obedience, were freer than members of the more enclosed orders to go about the locality preaching, teaching the young and caring for the sick; this meant that they could visit a parish such as Churchdown to perform the priestly offices, undertake care of the religious, and some of the more secular, needs of the people, practise a healing ministry and, possibly, even run a school for the more promising boys.

We know something of the pattern of life in Churchdown because from this time onwards there is gradual increase in documentation, and this begins with Domesday Book.

Domesday Book

It was at Gloucester in 1085 that the king had 'important deliberations and exhaustive discussions ('deep speech') 'about this land, how it was peopled and with what sort of men' and within a year the survey had been made and the particulars entered in what we now call Domesday Book. The reason for its compilation, as given in a document of 1179, was to 'place the government of the conquered on a written basis and subject them to the rule of law.[6] Exactly how this massive survey was undertaken we do not know - and, certainly, we do not know how willingly the information was supplied, or how accurate it really was; nevertheless, our knowledge of this country at that time would be infinitely the poorer without it.

The Churchdown entry appears under the heading *In Dudstone Hundred* and is shown as being 'Land of Archbishop Thomas' and this establishes the pattern of lordship which was to prevail in Churchdown over the next four centuries. The component manors of the barony changed over the years but Churchdown was always central and Norton and Hucclecote were 'constants.' It then states that Archbishop Stigand (of Canterbury) had previously held *Circesdune*. The first syllable is considered by a recognised authority on etymology to have been formed from the Celtic hill-name *crouco* and it is thought, also, that later it may have been influenced by (but not derived from) the Old English *cirice* (church).[7] Another expert in place names suggests *crug* as its source, and as this had the meaning not just of 'hill' but also of 'tumulus', it could be significant as we now know that the church stands on a man-made mound. It is also stated that *cirice* (church) may be the source of the first element in cases where a church and a barrow exist together. The Saxon *dun* may have the additional sense of a place of defence sited on a hill, and this would certainly 'fit' in Churchdown's case.

The names of the two sub-manors, Pirton and Parton, both stem from 'pear' - 'pear orchard' or 'pear-tree farm' - and the outliers, Elmbridge and Brickhampton, from 'bridge by the elm tree' and 'Brihthelm's farmstead' respectively.[8]

But to return to the main substance of the Survey; it is stated that in '*Circesdune*'' there were 15½ hides, whereas in Hucclecote and Bishop's Norton, neighbouring parts of the same barony, there were only 4 and 5½ hides. It is not certain whether the extent for Churchdown includes the four sub-manors as well, minor settlements are not usually named in Domesday, but, presumably, it does as the number of hides seems so much larger by comparison with those of Hucclecote and Bishop's Norton.[9] The hide as a unit of measurement varied greatly from region to region, ranging from 48 acres to 120, but one authority thinks the Gloucester hide was at the larger end of the scale.[10]

An area of woodland, half a league long and three furlongs wide, is recorded and included in the total extent of the Churchdown manor. A league is commonly taken to have been about three miles.

We are told that 'in lordship' there were '2 ploughs' and this refers to the lord's personal demesne land and the plough teams working it; land service on the lord's demesne was undertaken by the villagers in return for the tenancy of their own strips and was obligatory. They themselves had 30 ploughs which suggests they worked quite a large area as Hucclecote had only 11 and Bishop's Norton 15, with 2 in lordship in both cases.

The tenants are listed as '18 villagers' ('villani or villeins'), '5 small-holders' ('bordarii' or 'borderers') and '7 ridingmen' ('radchenistri'). Hucclecote had 11 villagers and 5 smallholders and Norton had 15 villagers and 4 'slaves.' A steward was overseer of these workers and he would make periodic visits to inspect the accounts and officiate at the manorial courts, a bailiff was responsible for the actual organising of the workforce, and a reeve organised the daily work programme.

The villeins appear as the dominating social category in Domesday but the term is rather elastic and the distinctions between them and their fellow workers are often blurred, but, generally, they held anything from 10-60 acres, whereas the borderers had only 1-5 acres. The land and the tools necessary to cultivate it were loaned to them by the lord and, in return, they worked his land on a stated number of days and gave service at special times such as harvest and sheep-shearing. In some cases they were also liable to pay rent and, in later years, it became possible for service on the lord's land to be commuted to a money payment.[11] The smallholders occasionally worked for their better-off villein neighbours and so their subsistence level benefited a little.

There were in Churchdown a rather surprisingly large number, seven in all, of the upper group known as 'riding-men' ('Radchenistri' or 'Radknights') whereas there were none at all at Hucclecote or Norton. They ranked as freemen but they, too, had their specified duties which included a certain amount of demesne work. They paid rent and certain communal dues but, more importantly, they rendered personal service to the lord in the form of escort and guard duties, message carrying, boundary supervision and the undertaking of special assignments, the latter often incurring a certain amount of free riding.[12] Stenton describes them as a 'link between the lord's household and the peasantry' and, as such, not fitting 'neatly into any clear-cut scheme of social classification.'[13] Does such a large representation of men in this category in Churchdown reflect the high-standing of the lord of the barony, who was, of course, the Archbishop of York?[14]

The serfs (or 'slaves') who formed the lowest social order are unrepresented in the Churchdown Domesday entry but, as has been seen, there were four in this category at Bishop's Norton. Little is known about these humblest members of society who were 'chattels' of the lord and worked mostly on his land; occasionally, however, it seems they were allowed to earn a little money by working for the more affluent members of the community.

To this community all manor-dwellers, whatever their degree, were intrinsically bound. An entry in the Manorial Courts Rolls later in the Mediaeval period[15] gives instance of this, for it was ordered that two villeins, John Bonde, Senior, and John Bonde, Junior, (the names suggest family serfdom) who had absconded into Herefordshire, should be 'take(n) and seize(d) by their bodies' as quickly as they could be apprehended. Sometimes, however, freedom was granted; in 1462 Richard Willys, 'native of Chirchedon, co. Glouc.,' and all his household received freedom from bondage from the Archbishop of York,[16] and, very interestingly, John Ive of Hucclecote was granted his freedom in 1457 so that he could go to university to train for the priesthood.[17].

The lord controlled the working lives and movements of his people and this was the accepted norm for most inhabitants of manors throughout England (and, therefore, for most of our own ancestors). All the villein laboured to earn or produce, was, nominally at least, owned by the lord. He paid 'tallage' (a tax imposed as his master decreed), 'merchet' on his daughter's marriage, and 'heriot' at his death, his best beast then being forfeit to his lord - a seemingly hard custom to impose on a bereaved family.

The Domesday record gives us no further information about the manor of Churchdown - but there are two notable omissions. It was the general rule that all corn should be ground at the lord's mill and there is no mill recorded for Churchdown or Norton; there is, however, one for Hucclecote, presumably that known as the Pitt Mill, or an earlier one on the same site. (This mill existed until recently and is remembered in the name 'Pitt Mill Gardens' which are near the Horsbere Brook). If this was really the nearest mill for the inhabitants of Churchdown then this made life very hard indeed for them, for the journey, carrying a load of corn, would have meant a climb all the way up and over the hill, or the long detour round its base - a distance of two to three miles. (It seems strange that there should be no mill in the main village for an ideal site would seem to have existed at the confluence of Norman's Brook and the Brookfield stream in the fields near the cottages called 'The Folly'; one of these fields is called 'Mill Meadow'). Later in the period, however, there are references which suggest other mills may have existed in the locality, although not actually in Churchdown. There was one, known as 'Wythegenemull', or 'Withygun', at Elmbridge[18] and there was another at the Noke where the miller is named in the Subsidy Rolls of 1320 as 'Gafro le Mulleward'.[19] Either of these two mills would have been easier for the people of Churchdown to reach than the Pitt Mill, but it appears that the Noke mill belonged to St. Margaret's Hospital, Wotton, Gloucester, and this ownership may have precluded it use by the Churchdown villagers - unless, perhaps, they were able to pay for the privilege.[20]

The second striking omission is that of any church or chapel in Churchdown, Norton or Hucclecote, but this does not, necessarily, mean that none existed. Many churches, some very notable and definitely known to have existed before 1086, are excluded from the survey, and there is, also, considerable inconsistency, from one county to another, in the recording of churches with most of them being included in one area, while few are entered in another.[21] The Survey for Gloucestershire is singularly deficient in record of churches in the county. Seemingly, if a church was of little financial interest to the commissioners, it may have not been recorded and the point has been made that Domesday was 'neither a gazetteer nor a compilation of things ecclesiastic'.[22]. We can, though, assume with reasonable certainty that there was a place of worship somewhere on the manor, either on the hill or in the valley.

The Building of St. Bartholomew's

No documentary evidence earlier than the 13th century has so far come to light to give a definite date for the existence of a church in Churchdown, but the emergence in 1175 and 1176 of the 'Churche' or 'Cherche' element in the name has been thought to indicate that there was a church (possibly a very conspicuously sited one) at least by these dates. It has been pointed out that the carved stones which are dispersed over much of the fabric (excluding the tower) are similar to ones at Berkeley Castle which can be dated to about 1180.[23]

The earliest reference discovered so far to there being any places of worship in the barony area is one to 'chapels and churchyards' at 'Nortuna' (Norton), 'Periton' (Pirton or Parton) and 'Streta' (perhaps Hucclecote which is on Ermine Street), all of which were 'built since the death of Archbishop Turston' in 1140.[24] It will be noticed that Churchdown itself does not figure in this list, perhaps because its church already existed and these others were new buildings established to meet a specific need.

In 1252 the right to hold a fair in Churchdown on the 'eve, feast and morrow of St. Bartholomew' was granted, the choice of this saint's tide suggesting that St. Bartholomew was the patron of the parish church, which by then was in existence and dedicated to him.[25] (Dedications to this particular saint were very popular in the 12th and 13th centuries).

The first actual reference to the (presumed) existence of a church comes in 1289 when Archbishop Romeyn prohibited the parishioners of Churchdown from interfering in any way with the 'trees and herbage of the churchyard' as these were the responsibility of the Prior of St. Oswald's who, in turn, was forbidden to remove growing trees (although he was allowed to deal as he would with barren trees or fallen timber).[26]

The question of the date of the building of the church on the hill therefore remains open, but as the oldest parts of the building are undeniably Norman in architectural style, it is generally assumed to date from that period, probably from the second half of the 12th century. The carved blocks with typical Norman chevron patterning (voussoirs) which, as mentioned above, are incorporated in the stonework in many places, give evidence that much rebuilding and re-use of material has taken place at St. Bartholomew's over the centuries.

The most striking survival from the Norman church is the carved arch now over the inner side of the south door. This arch, which has a pattern of stylised plant forms interspersed with rather charming little heads wearing conical caps, is believed to have been originally over the north entrance which is now enclosed by the Early English north porch. The bases of the piers in the latter are formed from reversed Norman capitals probably part of the arcading of the entrance, and the stones at the base of the font may, too, be part of the Norman building, possibly from the original tower.

The walls of the nave are thought to be those of the early church, though the north wall is now pierced through with larger windows and the south wall by an arcade The piers of the latter have the sturdy, plain character of the Norman period but, as they probably date from the 13th century, they can be termed 'Transitional.'

Much of the stone would have been quarried on site and then shaped and cut to the orders of the masons. These craftsmen were itinerant, going from location to location and overseeing the construction of buildings so, while working in a locality they, and a small selected workforce, usually lived in temporary wooden shelters called 'lodges'. When St. Bartholomew's was being built, therefore, it is likely that the construction team had their quarters on the hill site. Each master mason signed the work for which he was responsible with his own 'trade-mark' and such 'logos', as they might be called today, can be traced throughout

Carved Norman
head, part of the
decorated interior
arch over the
south doorway of
St. Bartholomew's
Church.

the area in which he operated, some incised examples being discernible
in the stonework of the North Porch at St. Bartholomew's.

As far as is known it was usual practice to first mark out on the ground
the basic plan of the building. The site on Chosen imposed limitations
and it is likely that the original Norman church was a simple, single-cell
structure with either an apse or a small rectangular sanctuary at the
eastern end. The original windows would have been small and unglazed
and deeply-splayed to reflect as much light as possible. It is likely that
the roof was stone tiled as it is today. It is thought a tower was built at the
west end, probably a little later in the Norman period, but that this fell
down, or was taken down, at some time; the present tower was built in
the late-Elizabethan/early-Stuart period.

As the date of the building of the church is undocumented so, also, is
the name of its founder but a strong case can be made that Archbishop
Roger Du Pont L'Evêque, noted as being a munificent builder, can be
regarded as such.

Archbishop Roger, who had been appointed to the primacy of York in
1154, (and so, of course, became lord of the Barony of Churchdown) was
present at the coronation of Henry II whom he later supported in his
quarrels with Thomas Becket, Archbishop of Canterbury, - to the extent
that Archbishop Roger was even suspected of complicity in Becket's

murder.[27] The antagonism between the two archbishops was fuelled by Roger's insistence on his right to have the cross carried before him when he visited his Churchdown lands, which were, geographically, in the Southern Province of Canterbury's jurisdiction. Some have thought he built a church high on Chosen as an aggressive gesture emphasising his rights over the surrounding territory - and if this was so, he effectively made his point!

That Archbishop Roger *was* actively engaged in the affairs of his southern manors is instanced by the report of an alleged miraculous incident which occurred at Churchdown, the account of which is recorded in the archives of Canterbury and also commemorated in the 12th-Century 'Miracle Window' in the cathedral.[28] The story is as follows:-

'Roger, Bishop (sic) of York....a man very learned in secular and spiritual matters.....whose brotherly love kept peace in the church, led water in his vill of Cherchesdone from the top of a hill about 500 paces away. It was driven also into the midst of the hill, surrounded by level fields, looking down from its lofty crown to a depth of about 24 feet; which work, in order that it might be rapid, was dug through so that the water being thus led, conveyed by a wide pipe, should be taken in a straight line. There was standing in the work a certain William who had contracted for his work from the neighbourhood of Gloucester, upon whom, when he was placing the lead pipe in the bottom of the ditch in the hill, fell a ruinous mass of earth.'

The entombed William called on Almighty God and the Virgin Mary for help but, this not being immediately forthcoming, he addressed his cries to the blessed martyr, St. Thomas; the saint instantly intervened by appearing in a dream to a local woman, who, being thus told of William's dire predicament, but also being assured that he was not dead, informed the bailiff of the accident as soon as she awoke. A search party was organised and William was rescued from the trench - still alive.

There is some evidence of such a pipe if credence can be given to the recollections of 'aged people of the village' when in conversation with the Rev. Dr. Frederick Smithe who was vicar at the end of the last century.[29] He records that 'when their minds turned to the past' they told of a supply of water which had been brought down from a source on the hill in leaden pipes to 'the meadow known as Chapel Haye.' There is also a persistent local rumour that the remains of very thick pipes were discovered when digging took place on this site.

Another rather strange story provides a tenuous link between Archbishop Roger, King Henry II and Churchdown. In 1176, so we are told, the king sent his son, Prince Henry, to France and requested that he should be accompanied by one, Adam of Churchdown, who was a deacon in the retinue of the archbishop. Adam, like his master, was a very loyal supporter of the king, and when he saw the prince consorting with unsuitable company, sent word of this back to court 'in paragraphs most foul and horrible to hear.' The prince, perhaps understandably angry, sought to punish Adam with death, but the Bishop of Poitou, who did not approve of the death penalty, refused to sanction execution and so the prince had to content himself with subjecting Adam to public humiliation, scourging and imprisonment. When the king heard of this he sent four knights to bring the man home to England, and the last we hear of this is that he was given into the custody of the Abbot of Winchester.[30]

These two incidents do not *prove* that Archbishop Roger took a personal interest in his Churchdown manor, but they do suggest that he may have done so, and this strengthens the belief that he instigated the building of St. Bartholomew's; but many and varied are the suggestions put forward for his choosing to site it on the top of Chosen.

There is the possibility that Roger wished to make a show of penance for any part he may have played in the tragedy of Becket's murder in 1070, or at least for his lack of Christian brotherliness towards his fellow archbishop; the great difficulties which would have to be faced in building a house of God in such a situation would add lustre to his contrition.

A popular idea is the one already suggested - that he built in a spirit of 'one-upmanship,' or, more worthily, from the urgings of genuine piety; some have thought that the site was chosen because it was a conspicuous central point for much of the barony, (but Chosen Hill is certainly not visible from outlying manors such as Oddington and Compton Abdale). An attractive theory is that it was built as a pilgrim station but, if so, en route to where - St. Oswald's shrine in Gloucester? Or was it a 'staging post' on the pilgrim route to Compostella in Spain, as was the little chapel at Stoke Orchard (built c.1170) which is 7-8 miles eastwards from Churchdown?

An explanation often offered is that it was built half-way between Churchdown and Hucclecote in order to be 'fair' to the worshippers of both communities, but, apart from the fact that it would seem that a less inconvenient spot could have been found to meet this requirement, it is likely that Hucclecote, at least in the early years, had its own chapel at 'Streta'.

Local legend has it that the *Devil* insisted it should be there. The story goes that a church was begun in the valley, but every night, under cover of darkness, the Devil carried the building blocks to the top of the hill, and this happened so many times that the 'down below' project was abandoned in favour of the site of *his* choice. Legends of this kind are very common throughout Europe and they usually tell of a building, planned for one site, being removed by some supernatural agency to another, often more outlandish, one. It is believed that the truth hidden in such tales concerns the ancient conflict between the new faith,

Christianity, and paganism, for in those early times the people were still drawn to their age-old sacred places and crept to them by night to worship the old gods in secret. By establishing the new church or chapel on the old temple site the Christian missionaries outwitted the Devil at his own game!

The difficulties of building on such a hilltop must have posed great problems - and what a sweating of men and belabouring of beasts there must have been; to the peasants of the workforce, toiling up and down with materials and supplies, the instigator of the project must have seemed to them to be in league, himself, with that legendary Devil!

Quite simply, the answer may be that it was built on the top of Chosen because there was a place of worship already there - one which had fallen, perhaps, into a ruinous state, or was deemed unworthy as the central church of the archbishop's lands in the Southern Province.

Extensions to the fabric were made in the 13th and 14th centuries, notably the south aisle and the north porch. The former became known as the *Hucclecote Aisle* because it was specifically for the use of the parishioners of Hucclecote which was then part of the same parish, as it continued to be until the 19th century.

Incised head on interior wall, north porch; thought to be mediaeval and to represent one of the persons of the Trinity, possibly Christ.

The north porch is perhaps the most interesting part of the church; on the walls inside the entrance a number of examples of mediaeval 'graffiti' can be traced and there is also at least one votive cross to be found. Going on pilgrimage was quite a popular feature of mediaeval life and these marks were carved by pilgrims to show they promised thank-offerings should they be granted safe return from perilous journeys. Although seating inside churches was minimal, or non- existent, at the time St.Bartholomew's was built, there are stone benches against the porch walls; these were necessary because the porch was very much a place in which people gathered before the start of the service, many worshippers having walked from the farthest points of the parish.

Above the entrance is what is known as the *Priest's Room* because here, it is believed, the visiting canons from the priory lodged while serving the parish in the office of priest. The room, which contains cupboard recesses and a fireplace with external flue, is entered from the church by a narrow winding stair. The doorway at the top is slotted for the insertion of a defensive beam, indicating the use of the chamber as a 'strong room' in which church and parish valuables were stored; as there is a window overlooking the nave, it may also have been a 'watching chamber' for the safeguarding of the interior of the church.

By the standards of the time this lodging seems to have been designed with some consideration of comfort and security, but it must have been lonely indeed for the occupant as he kept his vigil on long winter nights.

The Priest's Room, interior showing east wall and fireplace

The Priest's Room, interior showing west wall, and doorway in which slots for security bars can still be seen.

The cottage in the churchyard, now known as the *Sexton's Cottage* is certainly ancient and perhaps almost as old as the church itself. It is built of hill stone and originally consisted of two dwelling, built back to back and possibly with stabling. It has been suggested that it may have been a shelter for workmen, a lodging for paupers and poor imbeciles, or have served as a leper house, but there is no contemporary documentation to confirm any of these ideas.

There are grounds for thinking that Archbishop Walter de Gray, whose primacy of York spans many years in the first half of the 13th century, may have initiated, or overseen, some at least of the additions to the original fabric of the church for he visited Churchdown many times, often even in winter and continuing into his old age. There are a number of references to transactions by the archbishop while residing in the barony, several headed *Chirchedon* or *Chircheden*. These are in the *Register of Archbishop Gray*[31] and the following are but two examples:-

'Confirmation of grant made by William, Prior of St. Oswald's, and his Convent to Juliana, the anchoritess of Sandehirst.' (1231)

'A letter to the archdeacon, to whom the care of the spiritualities had been entrusted, to deliver them up to him.' (1255)

The Church (Sexton's) Cottage near St. Bartholomew's Church,
from an old photograph.

(We also know from these entries the name of the bailiff at 'Churchedon' in 1251 - he was 'dom Ric(hard) de Cumpton,' Compton Abdale being then part of the barony).

In the Preface to the Register we are told that the Archbishop 'exerted his influence to secure the erection of chapels' in the large parishes of his diocese.[32] Many of these chapels, the writer says, became distinct or separate benefices, or became completely non-existent except for lingering reminders in such names as 'chapel field' or 'garth'. Did the archbishop extend these building activities over the wider area of his jurisdiction; is it possible that *he,* and not Aethflaed, as has been popularly supposed, built a chapel on Chapel Hay in Churchdown? Gray's 'taste and munificence' is also attested to in this Preface, the buildings for which he was responsible being in the Early English style of architecture, as are the additions made to St. Bartholomew's.

The present chancel dates from about the 15th century but it is not known if it replaced an earlier one or who was responsible for its building. The archbishops of this later time seem to have taken less personal interest in their Gloucestershire estates than did their predecessors and there is no evidence of their having initiated local building projects.

By church tradition the holder of the rectory is responsible for the maintenance of the chancel, the rest of the building being the responsibility of the parish. In the case of St. Bartholomew's the 'rector' was the Priory of St. Oswald (which was also under the jurisdiction of the archdiocese of York) but as the priory by the 15th century was in straitened circumstances it would be surprising if this house of religion was in a position to undertake any expensive project.

The chancel is out of alignment with the nave, being off-centre and inclined to the right, which may be due to inaccurate surveying but is more likely to be because of the difficult nature of the site; the ground falls away sharply to the east/north-east and the subsoil is unstable - possibly the reasons for the Normans not planning a chancel extension.

The building of St. Bartholomew's and of the subsequent additions to the structure were, no doubt, matters which proved both exciting and disturbing for the people of Churchdown, and this would be especially so when there was an influx of itinerant craftsmen ('foreigners' by the extreme parochialism of the time). The circumscribed pattern of manorial life, however, was surely most violently disrupted when one of the archbishops, accompanied by his impressive retinue of attendants, made one of his periodic visits. The accommodation and provisioning necessary on these occasions no doubt stretched the resources of the manor to their limits and alarming inroads were made into stores of foodstuffs and fodder.

The Visitations and Jurisdiction of the Archbishops

It has already been seen that the archbishops made frequent visits to Gloucestershire and most of these are recorded as having been at 'Chirchedon' or 'Otington' (Oddington).[33] The Register of Archbishop Walter Gifford (1266-1279) contains several references to 'household expenses' incurred in Churchdown; for instance, Hugh de Babington was to be paid £14 for these in 1269, and 'J. bailif of Cherch' was instructed to reimburse Master R. de Fangefosse £95. 8s. 4d, and then a further 114s.4d for the same outlay, while, in 1270, £918.11s.4d., was paid with an extra £32.7s.8d. for wine.[34] These seem large amounts, so do they reflect the size and state of the archbishop's retinue, or over-liberal entertaining? Sometimes the visits were over the Christmas period as was the case in 1265 when £26.15s. was paid to Stephano de Munden *pro jocalibus emptis et receptis in festo Natalis apud Churchedon* (for entertainment provided during the feast of Christmas in Churchdown), and instanced again in 1293 when Archbishop Romeyn celebrated the festival in the village.[35] Much of the provisioning was probably supplied from the estate, as, possibly, was, too, some of the wine, for this was still produced locally to some extent. (Payments to the vinegrower of Churchdown of 33s.6d., 36s.6d. and 39s.4d. are recorded in the Pipe Rolls in 1185, 1189 and 1190 respectively.[36])

In 1269 Archbishop Giffard, who was extremely attached to his sister, Alice de Mandeville, paid the expenses (33s. 4d.) of her journey from Guildford to Churchdown, where she presumably joined her brother[37]

In 1309 Archbishop Greenfield made a 'searching visitation of the jurisdiction in person,'[38] but a more surprising entry is recorded in the previous century when a notification was issued in the king's name (Henry III's) to the barons of the Cinque Ports to the effect that a truce for five years had been agreed between the king and the king of France - and this is recorded as having been sent from *Churchdown* on 6th April, 1243.[39] Two days later the document shows a more domestic matter being dealt with - but still from Churchdown; all merchants coming to the fair of St. Ives are notified that the king is sending Roger de Haverhaull, clerk, and Jordan de Aynho to 'make prises and purchases of cloth in the fair to the use of the household of Edward, the king's son, against Whitsunday.' (n. 39 above) Why were such matters, one, apparently of considerable national importance, dealt with from Churchdown? One can hardly imagine the king himself being present in the village (although he was frequently at Gloucester) so had the officers of the Chancery (the court of the Lord Chancellor) somehow found themselves in Churchdown, perhaps while en route for somewhere else? If so, where, when they came, were all these important persons, including visiting archbishops with their entourages, accommodated?

There is record of manor houses or 'courts' at Pirton, Parton and Elmbridge, but of a residence of similar size and importance in Churchdown itself there seems to be no record whatsoever, at least, none so far discovered; surely though one must have existed and, if so, a guess might be hazarded that it would have been on the site of the present (miscalled) 'Manor House.' This was previously named 'The Great House,' but the building cannot be traced back farther than the 17th century and no evidence of an earlier structure has yet been found. There is, however, a length of wall foundation between St. Andrew's Church and the church hall which may have formed the boundary of an important property; only the footings now survive and these are protected by the flagged path which runs a few feet away from the north wall of the present hall. It seems amazing that a building, suitable for housing such lordly visitors, should have vanished so completely without trace - nevertheless, if one did exist, this seems to be the case.

There were a number of sub-manors in the Churchdown area of the barony, Pirton, Parton, and Elmbridge, mentioned above, and Brickhampton a little farther away and all these were held by the process known as *subinfeudation*, that is the holders of the estates paid homage and rendered service to the lord in exchange for their lands. This was the basic principle of feudalism but, while at the villein level the service took the form of working the land, the holders of properties, provided the service of *knight's fees.* We are told, for instance, that Churchdown was held 'by barony of the king in chief for the service of two knights' fees' and that the sub-manor of 'Perton' was held for one half-knight's fee by Reginald of Perton, and that land at Compton (Abdale) and Brickhampton was held by Thurston le Despenser for 'one third of a knight.'[40] This meant that the archbishop held the barony directly from the king and was under obligation to provide two trained fighting men, while sub-manor holders such as Reginald and Thurstan had either to render military service themselves or provide for another to do so. When estates were divided into small units, as was the case with the Churchdown sub-manors, and the liability thus became a fraction (a third of a knight!) it was often rendered in the form of cash payment known as 'scutage.' Military obligation in the feudal system had been instituted by the Norman kings to strengthen their hold on the country; they were aliens and probably regarded as imposters and tyrants by many of the native English, so their own security, and that of their adherents, was a priority.

The manorial dues owed by the peasantry to the lord are instanced by these examples from the Court Rolls of the Barony of Churchdown[41]:-

'Richard Preste, son of Walter Preste, succeeded to his father's land and gave to the lord as heriot two pairs of sheep valued at 3s.8d.,' and, again: 'William Crouke, who held one messuage and one lundilate (7 acres) of land called Smethes, died. Through his death there falls to the lord as heriot one cow price 12s. And on this account comes Agnes, who was the wife of the said William, and asks to be admitted to the said messuage and land....that she might have her bench (the right of the widow of a copyholder to hold her late husband's lands for life) according to the custom of the manor while she remain single and chaste. And she was admitted to the said form and made her fealty to the lord.'

Law and Order in the Barony

The local archives lift the veil a little to give a few tantalising glimpses of what life in the barony in mediaeval times was really like. Why, for instance, did Edward Townsend of Shurdington, who had cut down 'without licence' an elm tree and saplings and carted them to Cheltenham, also remove the bolts and door keys from the tenement in which he had been living?[42] We read that William Brews was 'presented' (before the court presumably) for having made a brewing, a 'tolcester' of which was due to the lord,[43] and that John Ives was given 'one day before the next court' to get the deteriorated thatch of his barn repaired.

Some cases from the Court Rolls of Dudstone Hundred (of which Churchdown was part) illuminate the state of law and order in the mediaeval years; these indictments were heard before the Abbot of Reading and his 'fellow justices itinerant' in 1221.[44] Murder, it seems, happened all too often and successful prosecution had, not infrequently, to be abandoned. When five persons were killed in the house of Edith, a widow, she herself being one of the victims, three nearby residents were arrested by the sheriff (one of these suspects being 'John, *son* of the priest of Widecumne' (Witcombe)) but they were released on jury acquittal. Edmund le Batur was then under suspicion because he had fled and had been denounced as an outlaw, but, as he was from another county (Wiltshire), had no goods and, being itinerant, was not in frankpledge, little could be done to bring him to justice; Hugo Velator, on the other hand, who had killed his friend, was promptly arrested and committed to prison, where he soon died - an insight, perhaps, into gaol conditions in the 13th century.[45] Stephen Wetecharm, who was held responsible for the death of Adam the Clerk, fled into a church for sanctuary and was subsequently allowed to leave the country.[46] Walter Peverel and Peter de Ponte fell out over the ownership of a sheep and, in the heat of the dispute, Walter felled Peter with an iron bar; Peter survived this blow for twenty-one weeks, after which death occurred, but the fortunate Walter was allowed to go in peace because it was declared by the jury that his victim had died from mortal infirmity.[47]

Accidental death happened frequently and it seems that this was quite often from drowning, as in the case of Robert Sprengehose who lost his life in this way when out riding on horseback. The loss of the horse seems to have merited more concern than the death of Robert himself, for all that the entry then records is that the animal was valued at two marks 'for which Ingelard ought to answer.'[48]

Cases of rape were brought to court frequently but, not surprisingly, were seldom proven; they may, however, have been among 'the crimes and excesses' which, early in the 14th century, Master Peter de Caldewelle, who was rector of Broadway and warden of the spiritual jurisdiction of Churchdown, found during his visitation and was commissioned to correct.[49] Churchdown may have been no greater sink of iniquity than any other similar place - mediaeval reports often paint an over-lurid picture and some degree of exaggeration seems almost to have been expected!

Nearer the end of the period, in 1483, Churchdown found itself municipally engulfed by Gloucester when the Hundreds of Dudstone and King's Barton (the former of which included Churchdown) were ceded to the town by the Charter of Richard III.[50] This king, who had been Duke of Gloucester, visited his Duchy when on progress after his coronation in July of that year and, as a mark of special honour, made Gloucester a county in its own right with jurisdiction over 45 square miles of the surrounding area. How this actually affected Churchdown and the archbishop's jurisdiction over it, is difficult to assess; possibly it only meant that the profits of the Hundred Courts went to the County of the *town* of Gloucester rather than to the county of the *shire* of Gloucester, and so little difference would be made to the way life was organised in the barony.

Social Life

As the years of the mediaeval centuries passed the view of the countryside and village as seen from Chosen would show little major change; the general pattern and layout would, throughout this period, be little different from how it was at the Conquest, or how it was even before that in the later Saxon years. The flat area of the old camp and the promontory of Tinker's (or Rabbits') Hill to the north-west were still common pasture, although invaded then, as now, by gorse (valued as a fodder crop) and scarred by quarrying and by the digging for marl, a naturally occurring mixture of clay and limestone used as fertiliser. Rabbits, which were introduced by the Normans, delighted in the light sandy soil - and, no doubt, found their way into many a peasant's cooking pot, although the taking of wild animals and birds was regarded as poaching, such creatures being, officially, the property of the owner of the land.

The flocks and herds were taken down into the fields after harvest to graze the stubble and fertilize the land with their droppings, manuring being essential for revitalising the soil. The number of animals kept on the demesne lands seems to have been considerable as a document of 1283 decrees that 502 oxen, 54 horses, and 1,000 sheep should always be maintained 'for the profit' of the archbishop and 'the good of the church of York.'[51] In addition 'in the bailiwick of Chirchedon' there were to be 2 cart horses with a cart, and 36 oxen with 4 ploughs and their gear, with 18 oxen and 2 ploughs at Norton. (63 oxen, 7 ploughs, 4 cart horses and 2 carts, in all, were also to be kept at Shurdington, Cerney, Compton and Oddington, all manors in the Barony at that time). The manor tenants had their own animals (with the necessary ploughing and carting equipment) and these are not included in the list, which makes for a considerable head of livestock to be herded, pastured and generally cared for, involving much movement of beasts between pasture and village.

From the vantage point of the hill the countryside presented a vast swathe of strip-patterning with hedges marking only the boundaries between the great fields or the definition of parish limits.[52] There were, too, the carefully-conserved areas of woodland, the hay meadows (mostly bordering the streams) and the ley pastures, the latter probably enclosed to contain the animals which grazed there. The relative values of these different areas of manor land are instanced by an inquisition taken in the reign of Edward III on the demesne of John of Pirton.[53] The sixty-eight acres of arable were worth only 3d. per acre (old currency) whereas one and a half acres of meadow were worth 12d., one acre of pasture being 8d., but one and a half acres of 'mead' were valued as nothing because there was 'no underwood or pasture.'

It would have been possible to discern the numerous roads and trackways serving the area, although there is little evidence of these

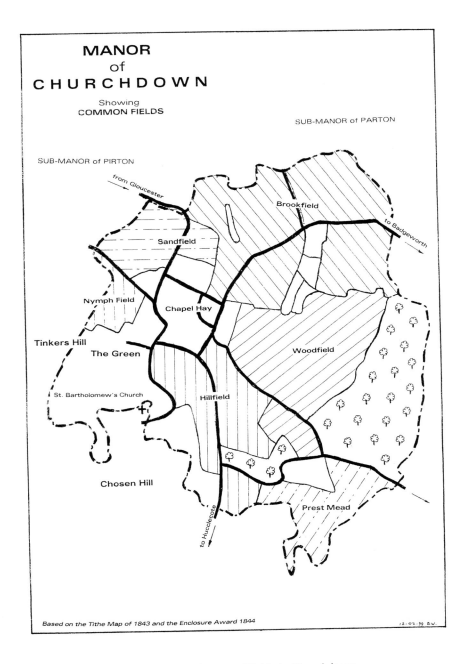

Plan showing Common Fields in Churchdown

mediaeval routes today. Where an existing road lies between deep banks, as does the one which ascends the hill from The Green to the path through the pine plantation, it may be assumed to be a very long-established way; similarly, the bridle path from the present metalled road to the south entrance of the churchyard may be ancient, and, in this case, possibly much older than mediaeval. Roads that take a tortuous course are usually following time-honoured routes, and often show right-angled bends where they once followed the defines of the great fields. All such highways and byways are surfaced now, with only the occasional farm track and bridle path giving any indication of the condition of such roadways in past centuries - that is, muddy and rutted in winter and dust thick in summer. The 16th-century traveller, John Leland, when journeying from Cheltenham to Gloucester, found 'muche low grownde, subjecte to al sodeyne rysinges of Severne; so that after reignes it is very foule to travayle in.'[54] Churchdown itself would not have been directly affected by the 'rysinges' of the river but then, as now, flood water would have backed up the water courses and flooded the brookside meadows.

Some of the footpaths existing today may mark the tracks which once went from village to field, or village to wood and pasture, and along these ways the farm carts would have struggled. Old drawings show that these vehicles were usually two-wheeled and rimmed with toothed 'tyres' to facilitate grip on the muddy surfaces; but, despite this practical addition, accidents were frequent as the local Court Rolls of the time reveal: 'Near Hukelingcote Osbert of Hukelingcote was buried under his cart and the township concealed that suit on account of pity. Value of horse and cart, six shillings, for which the township ought to answer.'[55] The horse and cart, being 'guilty' of causing Osbert's death, were forfeit to the lord but the neighbours did not report the matter - perhaps out of sympathy for Osbert's heirs who could not afford the loss.

Several cart tracks must have converged on the tithe barn of the manor, but positive evidence of the existence and siting of this important building seems lost, although, the small, residential development called 'Barn Hay' on the site of the field known by the same name surely reflects the memory of a once very important barn. The payment and collection of tithes was a dominating factor in the mediaeval economy, and it is probably not possible to over-emphasise the importance to the people of this system which amounted, more or less, to a tax on everything produced from the land or by the hand of man.

A tithe barn, a strongly-built and dominating feature of most local communities, has been described as 'an ever-present reminder of the power and needs of the Church,' a tenth part of all 'fruits and produce justly acquired' being owed to God 'in recognition of His supreme dominion over man and to be paid to the minister of the Church.'[56]

The greater tithes were payable on such staples as corn and the products of animal husbandry, and the lesser tithes on fruits and vegetables, honey and other produce from orchards, crofts and yards. Personal tithes were collected from the profits of craftsmanship, business and manufacturing. The proceeds from the collection of tithes were usually paid to the rector of the parish in which the crops were grown or the animals pastured, personal tithes being due to the church in which the man or woman worshipped; quite often these were the same.

The lay subsidies, which were taxes upon moveable property payable to the Crown, were levied on free householders, and a roll of Edward III (1327) records that from the twelve taxable villagers living in Churchdown a total of 9s.7d. was raised, one of the largest subscribers being a woman, Alice de Longforde, who paid 15d.[57] The subsidy, on this occasion, was probably imposed to finance the wars against the Scots.

Houses in Churchdown, as in other valley locations where stone was not easily available, would have been of timber construction using the cruck formation when suitable trees could be obtained to provide the long, curved timbers which, meeting below roof level, supported the ridge beam; this method of building can still be seen in the area today - for instance at Green Farm Cottage in Churchdown; old photographs

Timber-framed cruck cottage in Pirton lane - now incorporated into the modern residence called Chequers.

Green Farm Cottage on The Green, showing timber construction.

also show little cruck cottages dating from about the 15th century in Pirton Lane and in Sandfield Road at the rear of Ye Olde House, itself an ancient structure. The side walls of such buildings were strengthened by timber uprights (studs) filled in with wattle and daub, and some village houses, much later than mediaeval, have, when being repaired or demolished, revealed that, beneath an external brick facing, wood framing with wattle and daub was used in their original construction. Roofs were generally thatched, with an opening left for the emission of smoke from the open fires, and the floors were of beaten earth covered with sand or, if available, rushes; there was no window glass but some form of shuttering was probably used in the rather less primitive dwellings.

These dwellings could be easily dismantled and re-assembled, but they were also easily damaged and complaints about non-repair of properties occur frequently in the court rolls - Henry Broche and Thomas Posth, for example, on being presented for not having repaired their house, were ordered to get this put right before the Feast of St. Michael.[58] Perhaps not surprisingly in view of the universal use of timber, the carpenter was among the most highly paid of all mediaeval craftsmen, rating even higher than the mason in many areas.

Mediaeval peasant life was bound by restrictions, even as to the kind of clothing permitted to be worn, for in those days one dressed according to one's status - in 'hodden grey' or 'cloth of blanket', apparently, if one belonged to the lower orders.[59] The diet of the ordinary villager probably changed little over the years being mostly cereal-based and supplemented by peas, beans, onions and garlic. In the earlier years of the period meat and dairy products were not eaten very extensively by the poorer classes, and, in fact, were not all that easily come by in the winter months, except in salted form, even by the better-off members of the community; eggs, however, were usually more available and provided a valuable source of protein. The wealthier classes fared more liberally and sumptuously, enjoying exotic imports such as oranges, lemons and pomegranates and a rich variety of dried fruits and spices.[60] As fish was required eating on all days of fast, there was a fishpond on many manors but, when fresh fish was not available, the dried and salted alternatives formed part of the mediaeval diet.

Ale, made from barley, was drunk in quantity and drunkenness was the cause of many accidents and quarrels. Food and drink, supplied as part payment for work on the demesne land, was a feature of lordly largesse at times of intensive labour such as ploughing and harvest, and the lord sometimes rewarded his workers with richer and more bountiful fare at the great festivals or in celebration of the safe garnering of the crops. Festivities like these alleviated a little the drudgery of peasant life, as did, no doubt, the annual fair held at St. Bartholomew's-tide. We do not know where this was held - in the churchyard, or, perhaps, on The Green or Chapel Hay.

Daily routine or occasional merrymaking all took place within the confines of the manor; travel was not a part of life for the main body of the populace, although there may have been some permitted journeying between the manors of the barony with selected messengers even being sent to faraway York.

A degree of martial readiness was expected of the able-bodied men of the manor and archery practice was obligatory[61]; this latter must have taken place in Churchdown but where the local butts were situated is not known. There is no record, either, of how much the local people were affected by the wars of the mediaeval period but one writer thinks that, especially in the reign of Edward III, 'the call for men must have affected every village in England.'[62]

Medical treatment was mostly compounded of faith and prayer, herbal lore (which could be efficacious), practices such as blood-letting (almost regarded as a 'cure-all') and a series of taboos and 'remedies' dredged up from deep wells of supersition. Healthy survival in mediaeval Churchdown, as in any other town or village during the mediaeval years, was a very doubtful prospect and few lived to a ripe old age, death being an ever-present spectre even in the normal conditions of life. Then, in the middle of the 14th century, the great pestilence known as the Black Death struck.

The Black Death

The plague began in east Asia, spread across Europe and reached the south-west of this country in 1348, arriving in Bristol in 1349. Gloucester, too, was soon engulfed and we may assume that the surrounding villages were hit at the same time. Estimates of the death rate in the population nationwide have been put as between 25% and 50% and whether the mortality in Churchdown was high or low we do not know. The religious houses, like St. Oswald's, being close communities and committed to the care of the sick, were particularly badly affected, and this inevitably resulted in the parishes they served being deprived of pastoral and medical care.[63] In rural areas cattle were neglected and houses and barns fell into disrepair and we are told that in some places no one was left alive to bury the dead.[64]

The effects of the plague in a small rural community like Churchdown were, of course, on a lesser scale numerically than in the towns but not so proportionally, and they would have been just as devastating. There was little or no understanding of how infection spread, and the afflicted villagers must have felt terrified and bewildered to be so helplessly in the grip of such a mysterious scourge.

When the pestilence subsided, survivors struggled, as they always do,

St. Bartholomew's Church - interior view. The south aisle has been called the Hucclecote Aisle as it was used by worshippers from the Hucclecote part of the parish

to rebuild something approaching normal life, but the threat of a resurgence of the plague did not go away and there were periodic outbreaks of a lesser nature right into the next century and beyond - and neither were the long-term effects of this great mortality to go away.

The first and most obvious result of the catastrophic diminishing of the population was the loss of labouring manpower. Suddenly, the peasants who formed the work force were in short supply with craftsmen being at even more of a premium, so, as a consequence, the ordinary working man now found himself in a position to demand better conditions and more freedom. There had already been a movement towards the acceptance of money payment for rent and wages rather than land service being demanded, and this change was accelerated after the Black Death. Increasingly now villeins attempted to break away from their manorial obligations in order to seek employment elsewhere, and bondsmen pressed aggressively to have their shackles of serfdom removed - in fact, the lord's grasp on the lives of his people was loosening. The long-term economic effects of the plague, and the change in feudal attitudes, were, no doubt, experienced in Churchdown as in most other places, and, perhaps, it was as a result of these that we find the archbishop, in 1399, commuting the labour services of a number of his tenants on the Churchdown estate, although they were still liable for certain duties such as haymaking.[65]

Religious Life

The long-remembered trauma of the shattering loss of life in the plague years shifted spiritual as well as secular attitudes. Deep concern for the well-being of the soul after death led to an upsurge in religious bequests and the endowment of chantries,[66] donors desiring to earn, by charitable giving, some remission of the years they believed they were destined to spend in purgatory. Pious donations and legacies to the Church were very usual and, no doubt, there were many bequests similar to that in the will, dated 1st September, 1483, of Sir William Nottingham who had been Baron of the Exchequer to Edward IV and was a man of considerable standing in Gloucestershire. He held lands in many places, including Churchdown and Elmbridge, and in his will made a number of bequests to local places of religion including 'the Parish Church of Churchdown' to which he bequeathed 'ii torches;'[67] the maintenance of lights was quite a costly undertaking in those days.

The chantry movement flourished strongly in the 14th and 15th centuries, provision thus being established for masses to be said for the well-being of the founder of the chantry, his or her family, and whomsoever else was named in the endowment - which usually included offering prayers for 'all Christian souls.' Sometimes the chantry was founded by a group of persons, such as a guild, and often when this was the case, or when a single donor was very wealthy, an actual chantry chapel was built. Lesser endowments just provided for the offices of a priest to say the required masses, or, if the bequest was more generous, for the provision of an altar specifically for the required celebration.

The discovery, hidden behind woodwork in the south aisle, of a 14th-century piscina suggests that this may have been the basin used by the priest for washing his hands and the communion vessels after celebrating mass at a secondary altar dedicated to the Service of Our Lady. The chantry was dissolved, as were so many, in the reign of Edward VI, so was it then that the piscina was hidden, perhaps with other, so far undiscovered, treasures? This piscina has now been built into the south wall of the main chancel. In this same wall there is a south-side window, (dated as early 17th century and, clearly, postdating the chancel) which may possibly have replaced an earlier opening, a window or a door, which lighted, or led into, a chantry chapel. There is now a curiously blank east wall at the end of the south aisle - was this built to block off an extension which once existed? Churchdown tradition has it that the 'Lady Altar' was at the east end of this aisle, and the term 'Lady Chapel' is often ascribed to this part of the church; the discovery of floor tiles bearing symbols associated with the Virgin, such as the Lombardic 'M', would seem to corroborate this belief.[68]

Great changes were to take place in both religious and secular life during the reigns of the monarchs of the Tudor dynasty in the 16th century, changes which would affect the nation, the church - and most certainly Churchdown.

Chapter 4

'Times of Great Confusion'
The Sixteenth and Seventeenth Centuries

The quotation which heads this chapter comes from the parish records and refers specifically to the years from 1640-1642 when civil war broke out in England, but the phrase could also be applied to the 16th and 17th centuries in general for these two hundred years saw great changes not only political and military in nature but also social and religious.[1]

Village Life.

Well into this period the lord of the barony was to continue to exercise tight control on the lives of the people of his manors. William Whittor, for instance, described as a 'bondman of the lord of this manor,' was found to be at Winchcombe outside the demesne without licence and, as he had not given 'cheraginum' (poll money for permission to leave his land), the bailiff was ordered to bring him back to show why this had not been paid.[2] In another case Edward Hawley, who had held land by right of his wife, Alice, 'as long as he lived alone', had to forfeit his tenure 'by the custom of the manor' because he had remarried, and, in consequence, it was Alice's son who inherited.[3] Similarly, Thomas King was brought before the court because he had married Isola Marden, which was, also, 'against the custom of the manor.'[4] Objection to marriage was often based on the degree of consanguinity (where some degree of blood relationship existed) or in the case of a union being entered into with a partner from another manor without the lord's consent and payment of fee. The lady has a charming name and one wonders whether a strong romantic attachment lies behind the boldness of Thomas in flouting the rules or whether he remarried (he, too, was a widower) for other more practical, but equally compelling reasons.

The court rolls find tenants still offending over the building or upkeep of premises; John Godeswane had not made 'a house of three rooms and his stable of one room as he had undertaken', and Thomas Fforte had failed by not building 'a barn of three rooms.'[5] The rolls include the usual misdemeanours of a farming community - Walter Goodriche, William Jenyns and Chris Solas, for instance, had allowed their sheep to wander over the common pasture on Churchdown Hill - but rather more indicative of a growing threat is the entry which records that the Prior of St.Oswald's had enclosed seven acres of land in Parton 'in which the tenants had common rights every third year.' In another case Rich Gooswayn had enclosed ten acres of pasture land in Brickhampton where the tenants had enjoyed common rights for their animals every third year.[6] At Elmbridge the manorial demesne had been enclosed before 1489 and here the enraged commoners had pulled down several hedges and pastured their sheep and oxen among the crops growing there.[7]

The movement towards private enclosure was gathering momentum and was becoming a source of hardship to the poorer members of the community because, as the above entries show, it often meant the loss of grazing rights. There was a general move towards changing arable land into pasturage, usually for sheep, the sale of wool having become a highly profitable source of income, and so enclosure of the sheep runs was necessary to prevent the animals straying on to cultivated land.

There is no evidence that Churchdown suffered as did many manors from the creation of deer parks or sheep runs but, undoubtedly, a move from arable to pasture did take place resulting in the ridge and furrow patterns becoming 'fossilised', which would not have been the case if the land had been constantly ploughed over all the succeeding years.

Some concern for the less fortunate surfaces in the wills of this time. William Bishop in 1545, for instance, left the quite handsome sum of twenty shillings to the 'Poore Man's bot (box? bounty?) of the Parishe of Churston,' and Walter Theyer, later in 1616, donated three bushels of corn to 'the Poore of this side of the Hill'.[8]

The Church and the parish, both collectively and individually, had always attempted to give relief to the resident poor of their community - that is, the aged, the disabled, the widowed and orphaned - but the increase in able-bodied unemployed posed a new problem and one which was not really confronted until the end of Elizabeth's reign when the Poor Law Act of 1601 was passed. This made the parish legally responsible for providing some form of labouring work or craft for its own unemployed and for giving relief to those genuinely unable to work. A rate was levied on the better-off residents to pay for this scheme; prison, or the House of Correction, still awaited the 'sturdy idle'.

This is the time when the first local records of established charities begin. Giles Cox, who lived in the reigns of Queen Elizabeth, James II and Charles 1st., left by will a bequest to buy property; the money raised from the rental and eventual sale of this was to be divided between twenty-five parishes with Churchdown receiving the largest share of £6.13.4d. The Blunt charity (date unknown) concerned four acres of enclosed pastureland, the proceeds from the renting out of which were to be distributed to local 'poor day labourers and widows not receiving alms.' Early in the next century, in 1704, the Rev. William Stansby instructed that the charity trustees of Churchdown should receive three pounds yearly for the apprenticing, to some trade or occupation, of one or more children of 'honest day labourers', but in no case was this assistance to be given 'to the children of usurers, ale-sellers, or persons of wicked life or conversation.'

The popular 'Merrie England' image of Tudor and Elizabethan England is scarred by this underlying poverty, but it is true that many did prosper during the period which saw the rise of a middle class; in rural areas like Churchdown a member of this social group usually appears in wills and on tombstones as 'husbandman' or 'yeoman.'[9] The wills, at least the earlier ones, do not, in fact, suggest a wealth of possessions but they do reflect the farming nature of the community. Alys Jenyns, a widow, who may have belonged to a more well-to-do family, left to her brother two cows and '2 flytchyns of baken,' and to her grandson, a cow and twenty-six shillings in money, the latter to be given to the poor. Her servant, Hugh Bennet, received a yearling cow and a calf - surely a very welcome and practical reward for faithful service.[10] John Smyth of Hucclecote left to his namesake (possibly his son) all his sheep and all his tools 'apperteynyng to (his) occupatyon' and to other beneficiaries a cow each, two bushels of beans, his bows and arrows, and two coats (his best and second-best.) Every one of his children was also to be given a bushel of wheat which was to be delivered to them at the 'Natyvyte of our Lord cumying twelf monythes.'[11]

This was no 'throw-away' society, clothes, bedding and utensils were hard come by and never casually disposed of. In the will of William Bishop already referred to (see p. 56 n. 8) we find his wife receiving, in addition to a modest sum of money which was to be paid to her in instalments, his best bed with the coverings that were made when they 'cam to dwell together, with the Apptenances (appurtenances) that doe belonge to that Bede, and one cowe that is called hir cowe, and ye best breadinge Pigge, also (a) sowe that I have.' Robert Bishop bequeathed a 'pottle' and a couple of cows, with other fortunate recipients also receiving, individually, a velvet coat, two russet coats and a fustian doublet.[12] William Vynor's godson was given 'a braysyn pott, a cesterne querne (a hand mill for grinding corn) and the coborde (cupboard) in the Hall,' with an ironbound wagon with yokes and 'strynges,' while his son inherited a cow, and Elizabeth and Margaret Coston a 'cowe betwixt them both,' as well as a pair of sheets each.[13] John Little donated to his daughter, Isabel, two quarters of wheat and two of barley, the 'best brazen pot save one, and the worst,' a 'chafron' and 'skettle' and 'al her mother weryng gere' (clothes).[14] Katerin, the daughter of Henry Gelf, however, seems to have been the recipient of only her father's flockbed.[15]

From this sample of legacies it is possible to get some picture of the lifestyle of Churchdown people in the sixteenth century which is seen to be frugal, uncluttered and very practical. Those who worked on the land toiled long; in summer the working day, which began at 5 a.m., lasted until 7 or 8 in the evening, and, from mid-September to the following March, every 'artificer and labourer' was to be at his work 'at the springing of the day,' (as it is rather charmingly phrased), his duties then continuing until nightfall.[16]

Churchdown Houses of the Period.

There are a number of buildings in Churchdown to-day which date from the 16th and 17th centuries but some like The Manor House (previously known as 'The Great House') and Pirton, Parton and Draggett's Courts, which are Tudor or pre-Tudor in origin, are now disguised behind façades of later periods. Timber-framed buildings were erected by the 'pre-fab' method - that is, much of the framework, a kind of wooden skeleton, was assembled on the ground and hoisted into position by communal effort. Even such a large building as The Manor House shows evidence of having been built in this way and part of the original wattle and daub infill has been exposed on internal walls both here and at Ye Olde House in Sandfield Road. Smaller dwellings were still based on the old cruck structure.

There was quite a building boom in the 16th century, but, perhaps, it would be more accurate to call it a re-building for some properties may pre-date, even long pre-date, the period. Both Pirton and Parton Courts, for instance, are known to have been moated, (in Pirton's case double-moated) and this indicates very early origin, perhaps Norman or even Saxon, but both these buildings now very successfully hide their ancient lineage behind later reconstruction, the earlier of which may have been carried out in Tudor times, but little of this can be seen to-day. A recent study of Pirton Court[17] describes blackened roof beams which suggest the original existence of a main hall with central hearth from which the smoke escaped through an opening in the rafters in the typical mediaeval manner. The upper part of this hall was floored over in the 17th century in order to provide bedchambers for there was a movement, well established by this time, towards creating more privacy, at least in sleeping quarters. Structural alteration such as this was now possible because the fireplace could be moved to a side wall against which a high brick chimney was built reaching to above roof top and warming the upper storeys through which it passed. Hillside Cottage, in Payne's Pitch, and Dunstan Cottage in Chapel Hay Lane are good examples of smaller dwellings with an external chimney built on to the side wall. This latter property is listed as being late 17th or early 18th century but

Pirton Court, an ancient, moated building, with Tinkers Hill beyond.
Photograph taken after recent renovation.

there has been much renovation and extension of the original two-bay structure.

The owners of Ye Olde House think this may date from the 16th century,[18] while the Old School House on the Green, Mulberry House, and The Olde House at Home in Brookfield Road may be a century later. It is not possible to fix a date for the building of these properties as no really early deeds exist. The owners of The Olde House at Home believe it to have been once part of The Great House development and probably built at about the same time, that is from the mid-16th to mid-17th centuries. The Great House stood in a 'large enclosed ground with an entrance in Brookfield Road'.[19] The Olde House at Home is constructed on a 3-bay, one-room-deep, plan with a bakehouse extension; later in its history ale and cider were sold from these premises and the cider press remains to-day.

Draggett's Court in Chapel Hay Lane may be one of the oldest surviving houses in Churchdown, possibly even 15th-century, although, as usual, there has been so much alteration that it is difficult to date its construction. It is brick-built for the most part but with some use of stone; there are heavy wooden beams and timber door supports which are rough-hewn, even bark-covered in one case, and apparently very old; variations in floor levels and ceiling heights pose interesting questions as to the original plan and use of the building. No evidence has so far come

The Old House at Home in Brookfield Road, from an old photograph.

to light to account for the name, Draggett's Court, also called The Homestead, a usual term for a farm, but a family called Draycot are recorded in the parish register as living in Churchdown from the end of the sixteenth century, so Draggett may be a corruption of this name.

The Old Elm Inn, which features in old photographs, stood to the front of the site of the present Bat and Ball in the centre of the village and was completely demolished when the new inn was built. It has been suggested[20] that the older tavern was built by Thomas Thache in 1695 but it may be that it was *rebuilt* about then and was the second inn on the site. If this was so, the present Bat and Ball stands near where a hostelry has long existed, perhaps from the Middle Ages. Does this mean that this is where the 'heart' of the village was sited, the tavern being situated where it best provided amenities for travellers coming to the important baronial centre of Churchdown?

From the 17th century onwards there is more direct evidence, from records, wills and buildings, of what it was really like to live in Churchdown. We know some of the houses in which the people lived, we know where they were placed (scattered rather haphazardly it seems) and we know something of the possessions the inhabitants valued.

We have record, too, of a royal visit which took place in 1535 when the king, Henry VIII, and his queen, Anne Boleyn, passed through the outskirts of the parish. They were given a right royal welcome; the king's

The Old Elm Inn (now demolished).

break with Rome in the previous year and his establishment of himself as head of the Catholic church in England had, seemingly, not affected his popularity with the common people.

The royal party had travelled from Tewkesbury and were met by the Mayor and Corporation of Gloucester, wearing their best scarlet gowns and velvet tippets, at the 'grene at the hether ende of the lane athisside Brickehampton's brigge.' This is reported in the records of the borough[21] and begins: 'Howe owre most dreade Soveraign Lorde Kyng Henry the VIIIth, by the grace of God of England and Fraunce Kyng, Defender of the Faith, Lorde of Ireland, and in erthe Supreme Hedde of the Churche of England, and his most dere and entierly beloved lawfull wiff Quene Anne, at ther first commying to Gloucester....was resceyved......' The courteous formalities are then recorded and describe the town maces being presented and kissed with gifts being given and graciously received.

It is not easy to fix the point where this ceremony took place; Brickhampton, which was, of course, part of the barony, was in the area between the present Innsworth Lane and the main Gloucester-Cheltenham road, perhaps near Staverton Bridge - near enough for the people of Churchdown to walk to on this memorable occasion. They must have been agog to see, in all their splendour, 'the Kynges grace and the Quene with all the ladies and gentilwomen following them,' and they were probably still remembering and retelling the wonder of it a year later when word came that the King's previously 'most dere and entierly beloved lawfull wiff' had been beheaded. Hardly had this astounding news been assimilated than an event of greater significance for Churchdown took place - the Priory of St. Oswald was suppressed.

Changes in Administration for St. Oswald's Priory and for the Parish and Barony of Churchdown.

It seems that the priory had reached the nadir of its existence by 1536 when this happened and was reduced to a penurious state barely able to support the surviving seven canons and eight servants.[22] The last prior, William Gylford had been receiver of the Barony of Churchdown and King's Chaplain and was awarded a crown lease of the 'manor of Perton with the chapel or rectory of Chursden, and all tithes, etc., thereto belonging....last belonging to the dissolved Priory of St. Oswald...'[23] The king, however, retained the manorial rights and the 'great timber' for twenty one years, and made himself responsible for overseeing the repair of the woodwork and the tiling and slating of buildings, the tenant, for his part, carrying out thatching and other necessary repairs - for which work he was to have sufficient hedge wood. The king was also to discharge and pay all 'quit rents, procurations, pensions, etc.'[24]

There is a rather cryptic reference to the transaction in a letter from Edward Lee, Archbishop of York, to Thomas Cromwell in 1538 which reads: 'where you require me to take no grief that Sir William Jenyns, my late surveyor of Churchden, is come to your service without informing me; I am very glad he has done so, and glad that I have any fit to serve you.'[25] Is this just a courteous exchange between two men of influence or is there a hint of political time-serving here?

When the king created the new diocese of Gloucester, making the Abbey church of St. Peter its cathedral, he appointed John Jenyns, who was a member of his household, as first dean.[26]

Exactly what the grant to Jenyns (Jennings) of the 'chapel or rectory of Chursden and all tithes' really meant is something of a mystery; he cannot have held these acquisitions for long for the churches which had belonged to St. Oswald's, including St. Bartholomew's, passed into the King's hands after the Dissolution and became part of the diocese of Gloucester when it was founded in 1541.[27] Apparently, the Archbishop of York raised no objection when this happened (no doubt realising it was politic to keep on good terms with such an unpredictable monarch as Henry VIII) but he *had* registered a protest earlier when St. Oswald's was about to be dissolved, inevitably to no avail.[28]

Some of the rectorial tithes and other dues (known as the 'spiritualities') were sold into private hands, Edmund and Kathleen Thame seemingly being the main beneficiaries of these.[29] (The rectory of Hucclecote was included with Churchdown's.[30]) The rectorial responsibilities, however, including the advowson (the right to appoint the priest) were vested in the Dean and Chapter of Bristol.[31] Churchdown became an ecclesiastical parish in 1550, a perpetual curate being appointed, but the first priest actually recorded in the parish register is John Simons in 1563.[32]

With the loss of links to the Priory and the loss of the spiritual jurisdiction which the archbishops had exercised over the appropriated churches and their parishes for the past five centuries or so, Archbishop Holgate of York seems to have been prepared to relinquish what remained to him of the barony - that is his manorial rights and dues (known as the 'temporalities'). He received in exchange 'certain rectories, churches, advowsons and lands in Yorkshire;' it could be that his far distant demesne in Gloucestershire had become more of an inconvenient liability to him than a profitable asset.[33]

Thus Churchdown's age-long association with York was severed, although 'severed' seems almost too strong a word for what appears to have been a very low-key arrangement. The manor of Churchdown, itself, seems to have remained in the King's hands for some while. A court held in Churchdown in 1547/8 names the monarch as 'in lands of Church of England and Ireland supreme chief *in his barony of Churchdon*'; whereas, three years earlier, when, one, John Symonds of Norton was found guilty and hanged for attacking William Hale 'with a stick called a padelstaffe' and killing him, the court is titled as being the 'Court Baron of Edward, *Archbishop of York.*'[34]

In Edward VI's reign, in 1552, the manor was granted to Sir Thomas Chamberlain who was a diplomat in the King's service, 'an able and far-sighted politician and Treasurer of the Mint at Bristol.'[35] Smaller portions of land and properties in the barony were acquired by various persons (John Broxolme of London, for instance, obtained the Priory's manor of Norton), but the beneficiary of the most valuable assets, apart from those of Churchdown itself, was, Sir John Jennings, to whom, in 1545, the King had granted in fee for £236.7s.6d., the manor of 'Perton with appurtenances in Perton, Chursedon and of all other possessions of St. Oswald's Priory in these places.'[36] Exactly how much he had acquired is rather vague because the 16th-century spelling 'Perton' strikes an unhelpful ambiguity between 'Pirton' and 'Parton.'

The request by Sir John for the purchase of the manor is followed by a note to the effect that the trees growing about the site and in the hedges *enclosing the fields* would be insufficient to supply the wood necessary for carrying out repair work.[37] There seems, here, to be an admission of enclosure which gives some added corroboration to the belief that this was already happening in the Churchdown area.

The Pirton/Parton property was inherited from this Sir John by his son, also John, and it then passed through the female line to Robert Kemp, husband of Joan Jennings, and, on his death, to John Wright who had married Agnes, their daughter. In 1618 the estate was purchased for

William Craven who, upon reaching his majority in 1627, was created Lord and Baron Craven. The manor continued to be held by the Craven family until 1842.

The Chamberlains were lords of the manor of Churchdown until the 18th century, although they resided at Oddington and, never, it seems in Churchdown itself. When Sir Thomas first obtained the properties of the barony, at the end of the reign of Edward VI, it may be that he had been angling for some time for territorial advancement - to satisfy his 'lust for loot' as one writer describes it[38] - for in a letter, dated 17th July, 1545, he alludes to his friend, Richard Pates of Lincoln's Inn, as one who could 'shortly spy something meet to purchase from the king.'

The Church and Parish Life.

At the same time as these administrative changes were taking place unprecedented religious changes were coming about but, although in the reign of the young king, Edward VI, the Reformation really got under way, it is obvious from the wording of extant wills that the traditional teaching and customs of Catholicism still held sway as late as the mid-16th century. William Vynar[39] bequeathed 4d. to the 'Hyghe Alter, a bushell of whete to the Rood Lyght' and 6d. to each of four priests who were to preside at his burial, during which obsequies four tapers were to be burning. In another will of the same family the testator submits his soul to God and to 'oure lady Sayncte Marye and to all the company of Hevyne.' He donates a cow to 'Our Ladyes Servyce' and he, too, desires to have four priests with six tapers and two torches on the day of his burial.[40] Alys Jenyns of Pirton[41], who was probably a wealthy widow, wished for a priest 'hawlf a yere at the Church of Chursden to syng for me and myne and all Chrystyens and he also that he kepe my twelfmonythe mynde thorough the yere,' while John Lyttle[42] in his will 'written at my mansyn hous at Chursdon' (where was this, one wonders?) similarly commends his soul to God and Our Lady, leaving 8d to the Rood Light and expressing the wish to be buried in 'the churchyard of Saint Bartholomey at Chursden.'

There is little evidence of Lutheran Protestantism here, although it was steadily advancing on the Continent, but there is a hint of it in the Lewys will of 1544.[43] The testator here abjures any intermediaries between himself and his Maker and requires no sung masses or lights (such as Tyndale would call 'superstitious practices'), putting his faith completely and directly in the 'saving grace of Chryste my Savyour,' in the best Protestant tradition.

Even before Edward VI's reign ushered in a general iconoclasm many of the rich church trappings to which the people had so long been accustomed had begun to disappear and now anything which could be considered to be associated with 'superstitious practice' was got rid of. During the excavations in St. Bartholomew's churchyard in 1994, fragments of mediaeval glass were discovered crushed into the ground. The people of Churchdown were, no doubt, distressed to lose the treasures of their church; there is, for instance, some evidence that the parish officers were very unwilling to give up the endowments of the chantry - but did this reluctance stem from devotion or more from materialism? The reign of Edward VI saw the suppression of all chantries, although founding of these had continued right up until about 1547.[44] When it came to the turn of Churchdown's 'Our Lady Service' to be abolished the 'proctors and substantial men' of the parish made out a case for keeping hold of everything that had been bestowed upon the chantry, swearing on oath that all possessions shown in the church inventory belonged to the parish church and not to the chantry.[45] It seems the parish may have succeeded in holding on to these until the reign of Elizabeth for an entry in the Patent Rolls (1569-1572) grants lands to various tenants, these properties having been chantry lands 'bequeathed by John Mathewe for an obit in the church in Chursdon and Hatherleye Meade in the county of the city of Gloucester.'[46] They had been given for a stipendiary priest to celebrate service in honour of St. Mary the Virgin 'in one part of Chursdon Church by the warden of the said service called 'Our Ladye proctour.'

When in 1551 John Hooper was enthroned as bishop of the diocese he promulgated his fiercely Protestant convictions with unrelenting vigour. In his burning desire to rout out all vestiges of the old religion he swept away any remaining embellishment and imagery in the churches of his diocese and St. Bartholomew's was, no doubt, included in this purge. (In the modern 'Bishop Hooper' window in St. Andrew's Church the local priests are shown remonstrating at the seizure of their church valuables).

The accession of Mary I. in 1553 brought a return to Roman Catholicism and this meant that parishes, already very pressed economically in many cases, were bound to attempt the restoration of such features as the roods which had been removed in the previous reign. As a result of all this upheaval the upkeep of churches suffered right through the Elizabethan period and into the succeeding years. Several local wills of the late sixteenth century and early seventeenth include donations towards the repair of St. Bartholomew's; William Blunt of Wood Hucclecote bequeathed 3s.4d. for this purpose in 1589, and Richard Blunte of Churchdown in 1614, made a gift of 20s. 'toward the Buildinge of the Arche that is decayed beetweene the channcell and the Churche' the first item in his will.[47]

In 1563 the churchwardens complained that 'the bodie of the cherche and churche yeard are not decentlie kepte as the ought to be. Also the churche house is in the lyke decaye. No sufficient curat but a Reder onely, the benefice beinge worth Cli. a yere.'[48] In 1571, when the church was again reported to be 'in decay and to lack the bible in the bigger volume,' the churchwardens were admonished to repair the building by the feast of All Saints and to procure a Bible by the feast of St. Bartholomew.[49]

Amongst other changes a parish register was also now to be kept and the first 'Register boocke of Chursdowne' is dated 1563 and opens, appropriately, with two baptisms, those of Gyles Bishope and Alice Malverne. (There were only six burials in that year). The parish priests are listed from this year onwards, John Simons being the first to hold the office.

The registers, for the most part, are a straight record of marriages, baptisms and deaths but there are some entries which are less conventional - why, one wonders, was John Danvers' listed both as 'gent.' and as 'wayfaring man' when he was buried in 1615? There are, too, several baptisms of illegitimate children, 'Elizabeth, a basd. child, the dr. of Julian Boule,' and 'Margery, the daughter of a wayfaring woman' being two of these. The 'servant of John Blunt' was interred in 1614 and is nameless in the register, he only merits entry, apparently, as a domestic appendage of his master.

The churchwardens, assisted by such officials as the Overseer of the Poor, the Constable and the Surveyor of Highways, were now playing an increasingly important part in the affairs of the community. The holders of these offices were elected at the annual parish vestry which was 'a veritable parish parliament',[50] but there was often considerable reluctance among the eligible laity to accept these posts for the duties were onerous and often resented by fellow parishioners. The church wardens were assisted by 'two or three discreet persons' (sidesmen) and, according to this rhyme in a seventeenth-century parish book, discretion was, indeed, sometimes required of them for they were to: 'ken and see and say nowt, to eat and drink and pay nowt; and when the wardens drunken roam,' their duty was 'to see them home.'[51]

We know the names of the churchwardens of Churchdown in 1563 - John Daunser and John Theyer - for they brought a complaint that 'William Thomas and family dothe not come to the parishe churche as the ought to do for the space of one yere last past.'[52] The Act of Uniformity had stated that: '...all and every person and persons inhabiting within this realm ....shall resort to their parish church...upon every Sunday and other days ordained and used to be kept as Holy Days, and then and there to abide orderly and soberly during the time of Common Prayer, preachings or other service of God there to be used and ministered'.[53]

In 1575 the wardens reprimanded William Vyner for profaning the sabbath, which he denied saying that 'in cause of necessity and before prayers,' he had only gone out 'with a forck to batt out a little meat for his pigge.'[54]. In the same year Richard Bysshopp, who was admonished because he had not received the holy communion at Easter, was ordered to receive it within a month and to certify that he had done so.'[55]

The wardens were also the guardians of public morals. When William Bubb, in 1572, was reported to have fathered Agnes Willcock's illegitimate child, (which he denied,) he was ordered to 'purge himself on the next Wednesday- which, accordingly, he did with Thomas Smythe and John Cosenn acting as his 'compurgators' to affirm his innocence. The young woman, Agnes, was commanded to do public penance in the parish churches of Churchdown and Badgeworth and also in the public market-place (presumably in Gloucester).[56]

The inhabitants of the parish were subject to strict regulation; every landowner, for instance, was responsible for supplying equipment for the repair of roads and the villagers were enforced to work on their upkeep for six days every year.[57] Despite this annual effort at pothole-filling and bridge-repairing, roads were all too often in appalling condition. John Leland, when travelling in this country in the sixteenth century, found the environs of Gloucester 'very foule' after heavy rainfall - but the land well wooded and well planted with corn[58]

Supervision of this highway maintenance was the preserve of the Surveyor but he, in turn, was answerable to the wardens who were also responsible for the parish's state of military preparedness, with a store of weapons being kept in good order and archery still practised on a regular basis. Harrison tells us that the 'armour and munition' of every parish was stored in one place and was 'alwaies readie to be had and worne within an houres warning,' adding that almost no village was so poor that it could not equip 'one archer, one gunner, one pike, and a bilman at least.'[59] No doubt as great a state of readiness prevailed in Churchdown as in other parishes when the Spanish invasion threatened in 1588. Although no certain evidence has yet been found of one of the warning beacons having been stationed on Chosen Hill, there is record, in a lease, of land on the Hucclecote side being called 'Ye Fiary Beacon'.[60] As the knoll above this site is still known as 'the Beacon' it seems likely that one of the chain of signal fires was built there.

James I and Charles I (in 1618 and 1632) believed that the people should be allowed lawful recreation on Sundays after Divine Service, but 'disordered and unlawful exercises should not be kept.'[61] A declaration to this effect, known as the Book of Sports, was ordered to be read in all parish churches, but, in 1634, the curate-in-charge at Churchdown, one, William Beele, who was strongly of the Puritan persuasion, was presented in the consistory court for neither saying prayers according to the Book of Common Prayer on specified weekdays nor for reading this Book of Sports.[62] He would not do the latter, he said, 'because he was not satisfied in his conscience.'

The following incident, which reportedly took place in 1634, forms something of a sequel: 'A Miller at Churchdown, neer Glocester, would

67

needs (contrary to the admonitions both of his Minister in private, and generally in publike, yea and that very day, and of other Christian friends) keep a solemn Whitson ale, for which he had made large preparation and provision, even of threescore dozen of cheesecakes, with other things proportionable, in the Church-house, half a mile from his Mill, his musicall instruments were set forth on the side of the Church-house where the Minister and people were to passe to the Church to Evening Prayer. When Prayer and Sermon were ended, the Drumme is struck up, the peeces discharged, the Musicians play, and the rowt fall a daucing, till the evening; when they all with the Miller resort to his Mill; where that evening before they had supt, about nine of the clock on Whit-sunday, a fire took suddenly in his house over their heads, and was so brief and quick, that it burnt down his house and mill, and devoured with all the greatest of all his other provision and household-stuffe. This is confirmed by sundry good testimonies.'[63] This account appears in a pamphlet entitled 'Judgement on Sabbath Breakers, 1634 and 1635.'

Churches were austere enough now, however, to satisfy the most Puritan conscience - having bare, whitewashed walls, plain glazing and the altar a simply-furnished table in the nave, but St. Bartholomew's actually gained, during this period in two respects. In 1601 the new, and present, tower was built and bears this inscription: 'This belhows was buyldede in the year of our Lorde God 1601' and the fine carved oak

St. Bartholomew's Church viewed from the north-west, showing the tower and north porch with priest's room above.

St. Bartholomew's Church - wood carving from one of the 17th-century panels in the Tower Room. The motif of dragon or winged serpent is of ancient symbolism and represents evil; a similar motif is said to have been painted on the nave wall.

pulpit was installed thirty years later, the date '1631' being inscribed on the back panel. Both bells and sermons were approved of by the Puritans; the former were used not only to call to worship but also to give notice of more secular matters such as the start of working hours, the sounding of the curfew, the celebration of occasions of national rejoicing and the marking of local events and anniversaries. The deaths of members of the parish, or times of national mourning, were observed by the tolling of the passing bell. Items concerning the upkeep of the bells, or the refreshment of the ringers, occur frequently in parish records; the wardens' accounts for Churchdown and Hucclecote include the entry: '14 shillings paid for malt and hops for ye Ringers', which seems a considerable sum for those days but, then, it seems the team had their own special brewing![64] Later in the century, in 1678, John Blanton, churchwarden, was ordered at the Bishop's visitation 'to cast the bells and set them in order and to testify by the 25th March.'[65]

Of the present six bells in St. Bartholomew's belfry, the oldest bearing a date is the tenor, cast at Stamford, and inscribed: 'H. Wright. Tobie Norris Cast Me. 1678'. It seems that John Blanton had lost no time in carrying out the Bishop's instructions. Bells 4 and 5 are undated and the age of these is not known. Of the remaining bells of the ring, two date from the nineteenth century (number 2, 1841, and number 3, 1827,) while the sixth belongs to this century, being given in 1933 by the sisters of the poet, W. H. Auden, in memory of their mother who lived in the village.

The pulpit at St. Bartholomew's is very similar to that in the old church at Oddington, the village where the Chamberlain family had their principal residence, which raises the question of whether the Chamberlains were the donors of both pulpits. Both have sounding boards above to increase the effect of the minister's forceful preaching, but Churchdown's pulpit is a stage lower than Oddington's, perhaps having been reduced at some time. Despite this, it is still high enough for the speaker to be seen by all in the congregation and was so even in the days when the high box pews of the well-to-do screened those occupying them from the eyes of their neighbours - and, of course, most effectively, from the vulgar gaze of their social inferiors who were crowded on the benches well behind them.

The ownership of private pews carried considerable status and many were the disputes when the cherished rights of tenancy were infringed. The classic Churchdown case actually belongs in time to the eighteenth century when, in 1718, Freame Windowe of the Great House and the Pumphreys of Evergreen Farm clashed on the issue. The case was heard before the Chancellor of the Diocese of Gloucester, and Windowe was granted the right to 'two certaine seats or seat places situate in the Parish Church of Churchdowne near to the Chancel and the Pulpit,' (a prestigious position), and here he and his family had the right to 'Sitt, Stand and Kneel to hear Divine service and Sermons'. Anyone contesting this right was summoned to 'appear at a certaine time and place and show cause' (if they had any, a thrust, no doubt, at such as the presumptious Pumphreys,) 'why the two seats should not be granted and confirmed to the same Freme.'[66] (By this time Freame Windowe, a modern replacement of whose coat of arms is displayed on the external face of the of the South Aisle above the family vault, was well established as Squire of Churchdown).

The church suffered from an excess of Puritan fanaticism in 1616 when the raised floors of the main and side chancels were levelled as being idolatrous 'high places', being thus, so it was believed, contrary to the strictures laid down in Holy Writ. According to the Rev. Frederick Smithe, who was vicar in the nineteenth century, these pavements were broken up and thrown into a hole in the churchyard. The tiles now displayed in a glass case in the ground room of the tower are probably relics saved from this destruction.[67]

The parish register records the hiatus in ministry which occurred during these times of religious contention; between 1631 and 1638 there was no minister, previous to this William Beale had served as 'curate-in-charge,' and for a period in the latter half of the century, when many clergy were expelled from their livings, Samuel Colereck was appointed to be 'parish register' which post authorised him to solemnize marriages.[68]

After the restoration of Charles II to the throne in 1660 and the end of the Puritan dominated period the Anglican church came back into its own again; the Book of Common Prayer, a little revised, was re-issued in 1662, but the changes and divisions of the previous years could not be healed entirely and so no longer could it be said that one form of worship prevailed, unchallenged, in every parish. The comment has been made that from now on the social/religious divide between 'church' and 'chapel' took root and developed.[69] The Bishop of Gloucester's articles of visitation of 1671 enquire of the minister, churchwardens and 'sidemen': 'Is there in your Parish any person known or reputed to be an Heretick or Schismatick? Any Papist, Familist, Anabaptist, Quaker, or other Sectary, that refuse to come to Divine Service established in the Church of England? Is there any that impugn the King's Supremacy in Causes Ecclesiastical, or the Book of Common Prayer?'[70]

It is from this time that the oldest surviving tombs in St. Bartholomew's churchyard date. The table tomb beneath the yew tree is the oldest *in situ* and on this the wife of Henry Wright (Yeoman) who died in 1700 is commemorated in the style typical of the period:

'Here lies a verteous woman's dust,
Who in the Lord did put her trust.
Worthy wife and neighbour kind,
Her good example therefore mind.
Death comes apace, judgment is nigh,
Read and prepare for thou must die.'

This epitaph reflects the customary requirements of an eulogy - the sure faith of the deceased is recorded, her exemplary character praised, and the observer is reminded of his or her own mortality. Henry Wright, her husband, had predeceased his admirable spouse in 1663, and if he was an old man when he died he had lived through all those 'times of great confusion' which had prevailed earlier in the century.

The carved stone panels now let into the outer wall of the South Aisle come from another table tomb which had collapsed into ruinous state. The inscription on one of these panels, that for John Cummin of Zoon's Court (1689), reads, when translated from the Latin:

'One road and to one bourne
We are all goaded late,
Or soon will issue from the urn of unrelenting Fate.
The lot, that in yon barque exiles us all
To undiscovered shore from which is no recall.'[71]

(The last line echoes Shakespeare's words in the soliloquy spoken by Hamlet, 'The undiscovered country from whose bourne no traveller returns.')

Times of War and Unrest.

It has already been seen that a state of martial readiness was expected of the citizenry of all towns and villages and Churchdown was no exception. *Men and Armour for Gloucestershire in 1608*[72], while listing the eligible manpower, also records the employment and status of at least

71

a section of the inhabitants of Churchdown, 'whereof Sir John Chamberlen, knight, is Lord.' Of the sixty-six men and youths listed, about half are described as husbandmen, ten as servants, three as carpenters, another three as smiths, one a tailor, one a 'shoomaker'' and three as labourers, while Thomas Moore is designated 'yeoman' and Thomas Chamberline, Richard Harmer and Gyles Carter are 'gentlemen.'

The approximate ages of those men, who are all within the range of twenty to sixty years, are also shown (the majority being in the middle year group) with indication as to their suitability for bearing arms; those of tallest stature, for instance, are 'fit for a pykeman,' those next to 'make a musketyer or to serve with a calyvere,' and those who are the shortest (the ' meanest') may be 'a pioneer or be of little other use.' Eleven men are listed as being trained soldiers.

By this time certain family names begin to appear with frequency in the local documents - the Vyners, Bishops ('Bushopps'), Bubbs, Theyers, Hallings, Littles and Malvernes all feature both in *Men and Armour* and in the Parish Registers, being joined in the latter by the Rogers, Draycotts and Holfords. Members of the Holford family are still farming in the village today.

The major conflict of the period was the Civil War when the long-brewing quarrel between King and Parliament finally came to a head. Charles I raised his standard at Nottingham on 22nd August, 1642, and the country was engulfed in civil war, with Churchdown, like so many other rural parishes, being inevitably drawn into the vortex.

Probably the average Churchdown dweller cared little about these quarrels between King and Parliament provided they could continue to grow their crops and get their produce to market.[73]

Going to market would not, for a time at least, have been possible, for, in the late summer of 1643, the siege of Gloucester began.[74] Bristol had fallen to the Royalist army in July, and Gloucester, guardian of the Severn crossing, was the next strategic stronghold to be taken; accordingly, the King's forces moved into position around the city. Accounts of the courage shown, and the hardships endured by the defenders, make a great story but it is the effects of troop movements and military manoeuvres near the besieged city that must concern us here, for these affected quite dramatically the surrounding parishes, and Churchdown did not escape.

It has been estimated that about 30,000 cavalrymen and infantrymen were deployed around Gloucester and its immediate environs; these men needed provisioning and, when supplies did not satisfy their needs, they plundered and looted and ransacked homes, harassing the local people, pressing the menfolk into service and, no doubt, forcing unwelcome attentions upon the women. There were innumerable local skirmishes some of which, it is believed, took place in the Pirton area where fragments of armour and weaponry are said to have been dug up.[75] The

'Soldiers' Walk' on the south-west ridge of Chosen Hill is reputedly so-named because a Royalist outpost was stationed there, the discovery of a number of small cannonballs at the site partly confirming this. Troops were almost certainly quartered in St. Bartholomew's as they were in many local churches.[76]

This is the time of the hiatus in the Parish Register for, in 1641-2 a whole leaf is recorded as missing and then comes the entry 'Times of Great Confusion' followed by the terse comment, 'Rebellion rages.' (The next entry in the Register is not until 1652 when Nicholas Cargill is shown as being the minister).

At what is described as 'the town of Padsworth', which local historians who have closely studied the documents think may be Churchdown's neighbouring parish of Badgeworth, a rally of three hundred local men fought off a Royalist attack killing, it is said, one hundred of the assault force. This bloody encounter may have been the result of attempts by Prince Rupert, the Royalist commander, to extract from the villagers a monthly levy to support the King's cause.[77]

The gentry were, with a few exceptions, for the King, the Chamberlains being almost certainly so, for one of the family, John Chamberlayne of Maugersbury, was accused in 1645 of supporting the Cavalier faction, while William, Lord Craven, owner at this time of the Pirton and Elmbridge estates, a strong Royalist, offered his land for the quartering of the King's troops.[78] The King himself lodged at Matson House on the eastern outskirts of Gloucester but his nephew, Prince Rupert, is alleged to have made his base in Churchdown. He is supposed to have resided at Parton Court but the present owner has been unable to verify this.[79]

Churchdown Hill was probably the site of a manoeuvre engineered by the Royalist officer, Colonel Gerard, as a ploy to draw the defenders out of the city. The parliamentary troops under the Earl of Essex were marching to relieve Gloucester but were making only slow progress. Gerard's ruse was to stage a mock battle on the hill and light warning beacons in the pretence that he was engaged in skirmishing with an advance party of the relieving force, but Colonel Massey, commander of the Gloucester garrison, was not deceived and kept his defenders safely marshalled behind the city walls.[80]

The relieving army actually reached Prestbury Hill on the 5th September and encamped there during a night of torrential rain. They moved down into Cheltenham and then marched on towards Gloucester three days later - to find the royal army had already struck camp and withdrawn from the environs of the city. The siege of Gloucester - 'A city assaulted by man but saved by God' - was over.[81]

The war itself, however, was not, and there were to be further alarms and skirmishes around the neighbourhood but at least the main thrust of the attack was lifted from the Gloucester area and, almost certainly, Prince Rupert moved his troops from Churchdown. The villagers now had safe access to the hill again and were able to set about restoring their church to decent order. There are no records of how much rehabilitation was needed in the parish, or how much damage had been done to houses, farms, crops and livestock - but it was probably very considerable. The following extract throws light on the situation suffered by the county: 'During all these months Gloucestershire was in a sorry plight. Impoverished by civil taxation and military contributions; pillaged now by Massey's hungry and ragged soldiery, and now by Rupert's roystering troopers, till there was not a head of cattle to be found between Gloucester and Cirencester. Its towns captured and re-captured. its churches used now as fortresses and now as prisons. In any village of any size a garrison, and hardly a parish which had not at one time or another been the scene of bloodshed.'[82]

The local gentry were penalised for their support of the Royalist cause; Lord Craven, owner of Pirton Court since 1618, fled to Europe, his lands being confiscated, and John Chamberlayne was forced to appear before the committee for sequestration where, when pleading his cause, 'he displayed so much resource and ingenuity that his case remained undecided for nearly four years.' In 1649 he was summoned to give account of his Churchdown lands which, he declared, he had inherited, heavily burdened with debts, from his uncle, Sir John Chamberlayne of Prestbury. Despite this pleading, his Loyalist allegiance finally cost him £1,246.[83]

At the accession of Charles II, the loyal gentry whose lands had been sequestrated were rewarded with reinstatement, Lord Craven especially so by being created Earl Craven in 1665. The king, remembering Gloucester's past defection, lost no time in inflicting punishment by levelling the walls and abolishing the City's control, (granted in 1483 by the charter of Richard III) over the area known as the 'In-shire' - and of this Churchdown was part; so, accordingly, the parish now passed into the jurisdiction of the sheriff of the shire.

The troubled seventeenth century did not continue with a period of uninterrupted peace and stability. When Charles died in 1685, the succession of his brother, James II, who was reputed to be of the Roman Catholic persuasion, provoked a Protestant rising led by the late king's bastard son the Duke of Monmouth. The local militia were, no doubt, put on alert during the emergency, and it was in this same year that John Chamberlayne was appointed Deputy Lieutenant of Gloucestershire.

The late Mrs. E. C. Brown, one of the owners of The Manor (Great) House in recent years suggested that some of the prisoners convicted of having taken part in this rebellion may have been lodged there for, when some previously hidden panelling was discovered, the words, 'Create in me a clean heart and renew a right spirit within me,' were revealed carved into the wood and under these were inscribed sixteen names - including 'Monmouth' and a date, 1686.

The Great House (now The Manor House).

Churchdown's Great House was most probably built, or rebuilt, during the Elizabethan era and it was, for a short while at least, in the possession of the Raleigh family who, it is generally accepted, were close relatives of the famous courtier, explorer and writer. Exactly what the relationship was is uncertain. Verifiable ownership of the property by the Raleigh family seems to start in 1672 with Carewe Raleigh, of Kenton Park, Middlesex, and Dame Philippa his wife, and it was their son who was the Sir Walter Raleigh whose name heads the indenture of 1698 in which he, and Dame Elizabeth his wife, are stated to have been 'lawfully, rightfully and Absolutely seized of ....the said capitall messuage and scite of the Mannor' (of Churchdown). The property was then sold to Samuel Cockerell by Sir John Elwes, (of St.Martin-in-the-Fields, London) and Elizabeth his wife.[84] This Elizabeth was the eldest of the three daughters of the above-named Sir Walter who, some think, was a close relative, perhaps grandson, of his famous namesake.

Churchdown tradition has it that the Sir Walter famous in history visited the Great House and, of course, planted one of the first potatoes there! Sir Walter is credited with introducing the potato to Ireland in

The Manor House, previously called The Great House.

1584/5, after arriving in that country and landing at Youghal. In order to cross the Irish Sea Sir Walter may well have journeyed to the coast via Gloucester for his embarkation port in Wales, so he *could* have broken his journey by staying with his relatives in Churchdown. The likelihood of there being any truth in such a visit hinges on whether or not the Raleigh family, apart from just owning the Great House, actually occupied it..

The name Raleigh, however, occurs locally as early as 1486 when one, 'Edward Raleigh, Knight,' is recorded in the proceedings of a court at Churchdown, and, again, in 1536, when a 'George Rawleigh, Esq.,' appears in the Court Baron records.[85] The Hearth Tax returns of 1671, however, show the property with the largest number of hearths (seven) as being owned by 'Chamberlen' and the Parish Records record no *Raleigh* baptisms, marriages or deaths but include several *Chamberlayne* baptisms between 1670 and 1673.

Sir Walter himself, or members of the same family, are accredited with the ownership of properties in various parts of the county[86]; the manor of Wheatenhurst (or Whitminster) coming to the Crown on the attainder of Sir Walter.[87]

No document has so far been found to show who possessed the house between 1540 (the suggested date for its building) and 1608 when *Men and Armour for Gloucestershire* shows no Raleigh entry for Churchdown, saying only that 'Sir John Chamberlen' is lord[88]; so, while we know that the Raleigh family *owned* the house in the 17th century if not earlier, their actual residence there, unfortunately for Churchdown, cannot be proved.

The occupancy of the Great House by the family of Windowe (or Wyndowe) is, however, well documented. An early reference to the name appears in the will of Alice Huntleye of 'Churfsdowne' in 1609 when 'Alice Window' (daughter of Thomas Wyndowe) is the recipent of her 'woockeday Petticoate, woolen Apron and Redde Waste cotte,' which suggests that this Alice may not have been of the gentry class to which the Windowe family later aspired.[89] In fact, 'Widow Huntleye' gives Thomas Windowe two shillings and names him as 'one of the Poore.'

By the end of the 17th century the Windowe family were firmly established in the occupancy of The Great House. A fragment of paper found under an attic floor, and dated 1699, concerns 'Mistress Wyndowe's' liability for 'King's Pay' (a kind of tax or rate). This Sarah Wyndowe had married Henry Wyndowe of Gloucester in 1682 and, although Chamberlaine was still lord of the manor, the Wyndowes, as owners of the principal estate of Churchdown, were, from now on, regarded as the foremost local family. The coming eighteenth century was to be very much the age of the squirearchy.

Chapter 5

Times of Great Change
The Eighteenth and Nineteenth
Centuries

The changes to come in the 18th and 19th centuries were to prove more profound and far-reaching than any that had happened since our distant forebears gave up their nomadic way of life and took to agriculture. This period saw the almost total abandonment of the old open field system, a dramatic improvement in farming practice, a great upsurge in manufacturing and technology, and the harnessing of a 'new' source of power - steam. History has named these changes as revolutions, the Agrarian and the Industrial.

The Countryside and Enclosure

A significant extension of enclosure was one of the major changes to take place during the period. In the 18th century the open field system still predominated around Churchdown, although no doubt interspersed by small areas of private enclosure, and field names which include words such as 'Close' or 'Piece' may indicate early enclosure of this kind. A field plan of Parton Court Farm in 1766 shows, among the traditional strips, a number of apparently separated areas - 'Townsend's Close,' 'Pumphrey's Orchard,' 'Dyer's Hay,' for instance, and these suggest private ownership. Where the old methods of communal farming were still followed there was little opportunity for new agricultural ideas to be tried, but private landholders could carry out experimental methods on their own property.

It was not until 1836, later than in many places, that Churchdown became subject to official enclosure which was, basically, the breaking up of the open field strip system, and the commons and waste into consolidated, fenced or hedged, holdings. This was a process that was to affect radically the lives of the people and the appearance of the countryside. The first parliamentary enclosure in the county was that of Farmington in 1713; Brockworth's occurred in 1795.[1]

It is not known why Churchdown held out and remained in the old pattern for so long; was it because an inherent conservatism prevailed among the landholders, or was it because Edmund Chamberlain, Lord of the Manor, who had applied to enclose his Hucclecote holdings (part of the manor and parish of Churchdown) as early as 1727, wished to effect change only slowly, one area at a time? (The manor of Oddington, where he and his family resided, was enclosed in 1786).

Chamberlain sets out his reasons for wishing to enclose at Hucclecote in the preamble to the request document, making these points: 'the several Lands of each proprietor lie intermixed and dispersed over the whole Fields, in small Parcels, which by long Experience, has been found very prejudicial and inconvenient to the Owners thereof, and has often occasioned Disputes and Differences amongst themselves, and by being kept in constant Tillage, and by the great Difficulty and Expense of carrying soil and manure to so many and distinct places, are greatly impoverished, and as they are now used and occupied, are incapable of Improvement' - and thus he emphasises the fundamental issues which made enclosure generally desirable. The strip system, with its dividing baulks and furrows, *was* wasteful of the land available, and, as the many landholders had their individual preferences and abilities, it was difficult, in fact well-nigh impossible, to introduce the new methods and inventions which were coming forward at this time.[2]

Several factors made greater productivity desirable: first, the import of foodstuffs, and of the foreign materials needed by the new manufacturing industries, had become restricted during the Napoleonic Wars (1799-1815); secondly, many people from the countryside were flocking into the towns and cities seeking employment in the rapidly proliferating mills and factories, and all these urban immigrants needed to be fed; and, thirdly, this movement of population from country to town meant fewer workers were now engaged in agriculture at a time when the demand for home-grown produce was greater. It was essential, therefore, to use the available land and manpower to the best advantage and this often meant, not only the abolition of the old methods and farming patterns, but, also, the making of incursions into the 'waste' and commons - both of the latter being important amenities in the local economy.

From the viewpoint of national benefit, enclosure was a very good measure, and it was to prove advantageous to all well-established and prosperous landowners who had the means to buy over the strips of their humbler neighbours, meet the expense of fencing and hedging and invest in the new machinery which speeded farming processes; at the same time, wage bills were reduced as fewer labourers were needed.

There was no deliberate intent to downgrade the humbler tenant; Chamberlain in his enclosure request makes the point optimistically that the new system 'will tend not only to the publick Good, but also to the

The Old Barn (before demolition and re-building). This was in the Village Centre and was a threshing barn; the doors, which faced each other on either side of the barn to allow a cross draught, were high to afford access to loaded carts. The apertures at the top of the side walls were owl holes.

mutual Advantage and Benefit of all Persons concerned therein.' Unfortunately this was often not how it turned out in practice. It was, perhaps, the loss of common rights which hit the poorest members of the community hardest for they had habitually pastured their animals and poultry on the commons and stubble fields and gathered wood and kindling from the waste. The result was that many now fell to the level of paupers and became subject to the provisions of poor relief, a fund which was dispensed by the parish officials and financed through the rate payments levied on the better-off.[3]

How much the inhabitants of Churchdown parish were disadvantaged by enclosure we cannot tell, but there is, however, plenty of evidence in the surrounding countryside of how enclosure altered the *appearance* of the farmlands.

The wide open expanses were now divided into smaller neatly-defined fields fenced, or more generally, hedged with straight-set, well-trimmed quickthorn. The 1843 Tithe Map for Churchdown[4] gives the names of the 'closes', 'pieces', 'orchards', and new 'allotments', and fascinating many of them are - 'Far Alleys,' 'Guzzymoor,' 'Catsbrain Broadacre,' 'Buncroft,' and 'Puck Ridings.' Elms, now sadly decimated by the ravages of the Dutch Elm disease, were planted at intervals and the hedgebottoms became the habitats of small creatures and a haven for wild flowers and insects. In recent years it has been farming policy to remove some of these hedges in order to facilitate the operating of large modern machinery, and so it is now possible, when standing on Chosen, to get some idea (particularly when looking across the countryside on the Zoons side of the hill) of how the area looked in the old, pre-enclosure days of wide open fields.

Local Travel before the Coming of the Railway.

It is unlikely that a rural parish like Churchdown was directly affected by the Industrial Revolution which was, for the most part, an urban phenomenon centred on what became the great manufacturing complexes of the midlands and north. Gloucester was not a major industrial city, Cheltenham had not at the beginning of this era become a place of note, and even when these towns began to grow it would have been well-nigh impossible for the average villager to travel daily to either for employment. Public transport in the early years of the period was non-existent; the first mail coaches ran along the main routes from about 1784, but most of the working populace of Churchdown sought to earn their living within the parish as they always had done. Churchdown, therefore, remained a more-or-less self-contained unit and this it continued to be until the railway came in the 19th century.

Access to the towns was severely hampered by the deplorable state of the highways which were notoriously bad at this time. The herding of livestock to market along the roads and the increase in private coach traffic may have been contributory causes for both of these served to gouge the haphazardly maintained surfaces into deep ruts, and exceptionally severe weather then accelerated the deterioration. It had long been the responsibility of each parish to maintain the stretches of public thoroughfare within its own boundaries but the efficiency of such upkeep was erratic to say the least. By the 18th century the turnpike road was becoming a more widespread feature but the efficiency of maintenance was very much dependent on the conscientiousness (or otherwise) of the members of the trusts who administered the highways. These trusts were composed of local dignitaries who reimbursed themselves for the expenses incurred by levying tolls for the use of the roads.

One such trust was formed in 1756 for the maintenance of the thoroughfare from Gloucester to Cheltenham which passed through the outskirts of Churchdown parish.[5] At first Chosen Hill limestone was used for surfacing, but later slag and stone from Bristol or Chepstow came to be preferred for its greater durability in wet conditions. The tolls exacted under the Act of 1778 were: for horses, 1d per animal - but 3d if drawing a carriage, 10d a score for cattle, and 5d a score for sheep. Wide-wheeled vehicles were usually charged at a lower rate than those with narrow wheels as the latter cut the surface more. Some very local movements of livestock were not subject to toll payment.

That the roads in the Vale of Gloucester were still in a very bad state when William Marshall was writing in 1796 is graphically illustrated in his account of the rural economy of the county.[6] 'The roads of the Vale are shamefully kept,' he reports. 'The Parish roads mostly lie in their natural flat state, with the ditches on either side of them full of water to the brim.' The road between Gloucester and Cheltenham (which by this time had become a fashionable centre owing to the patronage of royalty,) merits particularly adverse comment from him. This highway, which he designates 'now one of the most public roads in the island' is, in his opinion, 'scarcely fit for the meanest of their Majesties' subjects to travel on - and pay for ; and is much less suitable for their majesties themselves, and their amiable family, to trust their own persons upon.' (His Majesty was King George III).

As the coaches of 'The Quality' struggled along the turnpike road it is unlikely that their noble occupants paid much attention to the unremarkable outskirts of Churchdown through which they passed, except, perhaps, to comment on the church on the hill - a noteworthy feature then as now. Even William Marshall seems a little impressed as he writes of the Vale of Gloucester: 'The surface is an extended plain swelling with gentle protruberances; and set with some hillocks of remarkable beauty. Church Down is, in beauty, next to Matson's lovely hillock...'[7] The parish, lying just off the route between the towns, was probably more of a rustic backwater in the eighteenth century than it had been in those heady mediaeval days when it was visited by the great of the land.

Unless the residents belonged to the social class of 'carriage folk' and kept their own conveyances, the journey to town was made on foot, on horseback or by hitching a lift on cart or wagon, and the route taken to Gloucester was probably that which led from the present cul-de-sac by Sugar Loaf Bridge to Elmbridge. This footpath was bisected when the railway was built and survives now as a right of access across the track.

Later, in Victorian times, a hansom cab service was in operation from Pirton Court where there were stables in the block near the road for the accommodation of the horses, the moat serving as a watering place for the animals.

In 1809 the main turnpike road from Gloucester was re-routed to afford a more direct approach to Cheltenham.[8] (Previously it had turned north at Staverton Bridge and joined the Tewkesbury Road at a spot called 'Bedlam' near the present Cross Hands Inn). The condition of the highway was, however, so bad that the Postmaster General ordered the withdrawal of the mail coach service along its length.

In 1831 a public transport system was inaugurated between the two towns when a steam carriage, capable of carrying twelve passengers at a time, left Cheltenham twice daily, at 10 a.m. and 2 p.m., arriving at the Spread Eagle Hotel in Gloucester at 12 noon and 4 p.m. respectively. The *Worcester Herald* of 3rd March, 1831, records that the carriages were 'well filled with passengers, including a great many ladies,' and all, it seems, were 'much pleased' with this novel form of locomotion and found the movement 'remarkably smooth, regular and agreeable.'

In 1831 no accident had occurred but some months later a quantity of large stones strewn across the highway damaged the axle of the vehicle and the service had to be ended; it was suspected that the obstruction had been deliberately planted by the turnpike trustees who objected strongly to the new venture, fearing that it would prove detrimental to their income from horse traffic.

Rail Transport.

The construction of the mainline railway in the nineteenth century was the source of the greatest change to Churchdown and from then onwards the village began to grow considerably, but earlier the Gloucester and Cheltenham Tramroad had foreshadowed the coming of rail transport.

By the beginning of the nineteenth century Cheltenham had become a fashionable watering-place and growing fast. The necessary heavy building materials, and the coal for domestic use which were now being brought into the town in quantity, were transported along the turnpike road and this was causing severe destruction of the surface. The need for an alternative method of heavy freight carriage led to the building of the Tramroad which ran from the quay at Gloucester to Cheltenham with a collateral branch to the stone quarries on Leckhampton Hill. The Act for the making and maintaining of this railway or tramroad was dated 28th April, 1809, the first stone block having been laid in that year and the official opening taking place in June, 1811.[9] This was one of the first railways of its kind in the country. For a short time steam locomotion was experimented with, but for most of its existence the wagons were horse-hauled.[10]

The course of the tramroad passed through the outskirts of Churchdown and the wide verges along the Cheltenham road remain today to remind us of its previous existence. It went behind the Plough Inn (now private premises) where, it is thought, there were stables for the horses.[11]

The new turnpike road to Cheltenham ran on a straighter course from Staverton Bridge to Cheltenham and was laid parallel with the tramroad. Dr. Jenner, famous for the introduction of vaccination, was one of the trustees of this new highway scheme.

There were a number of public houses along the route (probably about sixteen!)[12] and these were well-patronised, sometimes too well, by the wagoners as they waited for clearance of the track ahead before proceeding with their trains. The railroad was intended mainly for the carriage of freight but passengers travelled unofficially - if they were hardy enough to face the rigours of the facilities provided.

The tramway continued for some years passing into the control of the Birmingham and Gloucester Rail Company in 1840. It succumbed finally to the rival power of steam when a rail link was established between Cheltenham and the Forest of Dean enabling coal to be transported by steam freight trains. In 1859 an act for the tramroad's abandonment was passed, the sell-off took place two years later and the track was then taken up.

In 1840 the first steam train ran from Cheltenham (Lansdown) on the permanent way which passed through Churchdown en route for Gloucester; it was one of England's pioneer rail lines. The journey took sixteen minutes, today's average being about nine minutes, and the passengers enjoyed the new system of travelling finding the views 'delightful....the Leckhampton and Churchdown hills being within sight for nearly the whole distance.'[13]

The story of the colossal feats of civil engineering undertaken in the construction of the line, of the complex and often acrimonious negotiations, and the many setbacks which bedeviled progress, makes absorbing reading but can only be touched on briefly here. The venture was started jointly by the two interested companies, the Birmingham and Gloucester Railway and the Cheltenham and Great Western Union Railway; the former operated on standard gauge track (4'-8½'') and the latter on broad gauge (7'- 0¼'') so there was a major problem from the start. This was overcome in 1847 by the laying of a third rail to accommodate rolling stock of both dimensions when using the route.

The construction of the track bed through Churchdown must have been an achievement of earth-moving unrivalled in the history of the village since the Iron Age people of Chosen encircled the hill with fortified banks and ditches. A deep cutting was gouged out between Pirton Lane and Parton Road and the soil thus excavated was carted away and used to form the embankment which continued, from then on, for some distance. Through these earthworks four brick or stone-lined underpasses were made and two bridges were constructed to carry the two roads (Pirton and Parton) above the track - and all this was done by an army of 'navvies' with shovel and pickaxe, cart and barrow! What an exciting, but disturbing, experience it must have been for a little rural parish, this influx of hard-labouring, rough-speaking, hard-drinking strangers, and what a sight it must have been to witness the moving of tons upon tons of Churchdown sand and clay.

Until Churchdown had its own station, would-be rail users had to travel to either of the two main stations, Cheltenham or Gloucester, although there were two halts established briefly, one in Churchdown in

1842 and another near Badgeworth in 1843,[14] but these lasted for only a few weeks as, presumably, they were not used enough to be thought profitable.

Gloucester station was at the very heart of what has been called 'The Battle of the Gauges' for here passengers, their luggage, and all goods had to be disgorged and transferred to another train of the gauge appropriate for the journey ahead. These upheavals afforded occasions of spectacular chaos, but, by the time Churchdown Station was opened in 1874, the broad gauge was no more and both the Midland and Great Western Railways, which were the companies by then operating through Churchdown, were using the same track.

It seems that the Rev. Dr. Frederick Smithe, the eccentric, enterprising and by now resident vicar of Churchdown, was the main initiator of the local campaign for a station to serve the village, but, first, an accident which occurred on the line near Gloucester prompted him to suggest that signalling should be improved on the stretch of track between Church-down and Gloucester. As a result of his efforts a signal box was installed near the Sugar Loaf Bridge; but no sooner had the vicar tasted this success than he instigated another petition, this time asking that certain trains should be halted at Churchdown to pick up and set down passengers. The result was the building of the station which was opened for traffic on Monday, 2nd February, 1874.

Churchdown Station at the turn of the century.

That the travel facilities now available to the parishioners were appreciated and well used is instanced in a communication addressed to the two railway companies requesting the siting of a goods siding in the near vicinity.[15] This 'Memorial,' as it is headed, states: '... the parish of Churchdown is situate on rising ground in the midst of the Vale of Severn, midway between Gloucester and Cheltenham and its favorable (sic) position coupled with its railway facilities by the joint line of the Great Western and Midland Railway Companies make it a very desirable place of residence. No country village anywhere in the neighbourhood is so well supplied with Railway accommodation for passengers, and the present service might still (with very little additional cost to the Railway Companies) be greatly improved. For a small Station the passenger traffic is very large and especially in the Summer months.

'Until the year 1874, there was no Railway Station at Churchdown and up to that time, there had for many years past, been practically no increase in the number of houses or of Inhabitants in Churchdown and the parish was a purely Agricultural one.

'Since the opening of the Station 50 to 60 houses have been built, most of them within the last four years (1884-7) and this notwithstanding the heavy cost of building and other materials, and of coal and other necessaries of life owing to the absence of facilities for goods traffic.. Within the same period (notwithstanding the depression of the Agricultural Interest) the rateable value has increased from £6234 to £9780 and the population has also largely increased........'

The request was turned down as it was not thought commercially viable, but it is obvious from the above that Churchdown was now beginning to become what in modern terms we might call 'commuter territory' and that the nature of the village life was changing. New houses were springing up, as the document says, and many of these, mostly red brick, slate-roofed and bow-windowed villas, are a feature of Churchdown architecture today.

A New School.

The growth in population and the demands of railway staff recruitment were two important reasons for establishing a new school.

By his will made in 1734 the Rev. Henry Wyndowe (later the family name became spelt 'Windowe') appointed trustees to administer rents and profits from his various properties to provide revenue for the setting-up and maintenance of two schools in the village, one for the instruction of poor children of Churchdown and Badgeworth, from the age of six years upwards, in reading, writing and 'casting accounts', and the other for teaching infants under six to read and girls to knit.[16] The schoolmaster for the 'upper' school was to receive twenty pounds salary

The Old School House on The Green, from a local postcard. This is where
Churchdown's first village school was held.

per annum and was to live in the house on The Green which is still called
'The Old Schoolhouse', while the mistress of the infants' school was to
be paid five pounds a year and live in the dwelling house belonging to
John Chamberlayne, situated in the lower part of the village, perhaps, on
the site of 'Summerwell' in Parton Lane. The will of Henry Wyndowe
also directed that the schoolmaster was to conduct his pupils to Divine
Service at St. Bartholomew's every Sunday, and one feels he more than
earned his modest salary! The Wyndowe schools continued in
Churchdown from the time of their founder's death, about 1745, until the
building of the present village school was begun in 1872.

Until then the old school on The Green and the kindergarten classes
held in the cottage in the village were still, as far as is known, the only
places of education in the parish. (Hucclecote is reported to have had at
first two, and later four, privately-run schools from as early as 1819, and
by 1852 had a small National School.)[17]

The view was expressed that 'Doubtless the schools under the master
[in Churchdown] have in their day done good service; and in a district
where female labour is in request for farm-work, the infants' school was
very convenient as a place of reception for the young children until the
toil of each day was over.'[18] The schoolmaster, however, was now 'aged'
and also 'uncertificated' and the schools that had 'afforded an education,
though rough and ready,' but ' sufficient for a carter or a ploughman,'
were found less adequate to qualify men for railway employment.

William Swift. First Headmaster of the
new Village School opened in 1874

The indefatigable Dr. Smithe was again a prime mover in the campaign
for a new school and the successful outcome was, in no small measure,
attributable to his long-sustained efforts, which were given further
impetus by the passing of the Education Act in 1870. The Act was
concerned only with the schooling of children under thirteen years of age
and the education was not free except in the case of the very poorest
families. Under the new education scheme both 'board' schools (which
were controlled and partly financed by local government) and
'voluntary' schools (largely denominational) existed together. The new
Churchdown school was to be still partly funded by the Henry Wyndowe
endowment (with which the investments of a charity initiated in the past
by Mrs. Blunt, a local widow, were now incorporated)[19] and so it was
subject to the Endowed Schools Commission under the act of 1869.

At the first meeting of the Governors (2nd February, 1872) notice was
given to the schoolmaster, John Palmer, and to the schoolmistress, Sarah
Wilkes, that their appointments were to be terminated. The old
schoolhouse was offered for sale and was purchased by a Mr.Newman
who was also the donor of the land on which the new school was to be
built. Funds for the project were raised from the sale of the old property,
from subsidies provided by the Education Department and the Diocesan
Association, and from 'liberal gifts from the landowners and
parishioners.' The plans were drawn up by the architects Fulljames and
Waller for a 'substantial and neat stone building of 14th-century style'
(and this example of 'Victorian Gothic' remains in use as part of the
modern school complex in Station Road.) The building was to comprise

boys' and girls' schools, separated by a partition, a 'spacious infants' school with hall and lavatory,' and a master's residence. There was also to be a room designated for use as a school chapel. The estimated cost of the whole development was between £800 and £1000.

The foundation stone was laid by the Vicar on the 5th July, 1872, and the first pupils, 30 boys and 24 girls, took their places on the 5th January, 1874, under the instruction of a master and an assistant mistress. Children from Badgeworth were allowed to come to Churchdown school if there was sufficient accommodation for them.

The first headmaster of the new school was William Swift who held the post for thirty years; he wrote a history of Churchdown and also kept a remarkable series of diaries which spanned most of his adult life, and these are illuminating about village affairs and written in a style both trenchant and amusing. William Swift was something of a Samuel Pepys for nineteenth-century Churchdown.

'The Scheme for the Management of the Schools founded by Henry Wyndowe in Churchdown' (and 'approved by Her Majesty in Council, 9th August, 1872,') is a statement of the constitution and aims, the first of the latter being 'to give a sound and practical education to boys and girls in the parish of Churchdown.' The Governors were to ensure that the proper requirements for religious education were fully observed and that the Bible was read every day, while the secular subjects to be studied were reading, writing, arithmetic and geography, with, in addition, needlework for the girls. Any money remaining after the expenses of running the school had been met could be used for any, or all, of a variety of benefits including the provision of free places, a library for use by the scholars, prizes for achievement, and 'exhibitions' of sufficient monetary value to induce the parents of promising pupils to keep them at the school longer than would otherwise be the case; it was also possible for scholars of exceptional merit to be awarded an exhibition to a place of higher education. The resources of the endowment could also be used for the provision of maps and scientific apparatus, gymnastic equipment, 'the expenses of military drill,' and whatever was needed for practical instruction in carpentry, gardening, cookery and laundrywork. Apart from the mysteries of 'military drill', this 100-year-old curriculum does not seem very far distant from present-day thinking on education but, in practice, the teaching methods (much of which were by 'rote') would now seem very rigid and class-control over-regimented. It must be remembered, too, that this was not free education, for all. The original document of 1872 states that 'all scholars shall pay such tuition fees as the Governors may fix from time to time; no fee being more than nine pence per week'; but ten years later, in 1882, the state of family economy was being taken into account more specifically. The sons and daughters of 'Farmers, Tradesmen, and others of equal position' were to pay sixpence a week, the two eldest children of 'parents above the position of day labourer;' fourpence per week, with twopence for their younger brothers and sisters, while the children of the 'day labourers' were able to receive their schooling for threepence or less.[20]

One of the conditions to which the Governors had to agree in order to be eligible for a grant from the Education Authority was that the school must be open to official inspection. It seems that voluntary funding, begun perhaps enthusiastically at the outset, had begun to drop off owing, as the Vicar declares in a 'Statement,'[21] to 'the absence of a resident landed gentry or landlords, and the agricultural depression;' in consequence of this the school had been transferred to the Churchdown School Board in 1881 - but with the proviso that the interests of the Church and of the Wyndowe Trust were to be safeguarded.

At the time of this statement (in 1890), the school's reputation had, according to the Vicar, declined (partly as a result of inadequate staffing) and he goes so far as to describe the situation as nearing 'general breakdown.' The report of Her Majesty's Inspector in 1887 could hardly have been more damning for in it he declared that, of the two hundred schools he had visited, four were bad, one being Churchdown. The log book entries, however, do not reflect quite such a grim picture as this as, for instance, only three years earlier it was said, 'The school continues to improve even in the face of difficulties caused by illness among the children and that of the Assistant Mistress. For these reasons the Good Merit Grant is recommended which the actual results scarcely warrant. Reading is generally above the average in intelligence. Handwriting is also good in the Lower Standards, but Spelling in the third and Fourth Standards is weak.' Achievement in arithmetic, however, became poorer higher up the school and grammar in the higher classes was ' by no means good.' An earlier report given only two years before in March, 1885, had been quite glowing: 'A very well taught and well-ordered School, the answering on the Prayer Book was creditable, and a good proportion of the children answered well on the Scripture subjects...'

The later report, in March, 1887, does reflect the problems to which the Vicar had alluded for it seems that the need for 'a stronger teaching staff,' which had been stressed by the Inspector, had gone unheeded, and matters had deteriorated as a result. Help, however, was at hand as the Vicar, having been appointed Chairman and Co-optative Governor of the school, was now in a position to lead the governing body and carry out the recommendations of the Inspectorate which he was going to do 'with unremitting energy' in order to ' whip up the School from this low state to a more satisfactory condition.' The Vicar's optimism about imminent improvement seems to have been justified, at least by the comments he chooses to cite in his 'Statement', for the inspector's report for February, 1889, commends the school for having passed 'a highly successful examination,' and goes on to say, 'If it continues to improve as it has done during the last two years I hope next year to be able to recommend the highest merit grant.' In actuality the school had its normal share of both commendation and criticism in the years that followed.[22]

By the end of the century the school's summer break was still called the 'Harvest Holidays'; the log book records that on the 4th September, 1899, several children had not yet returned to school and this was, presumably, because they were helping in the fields. There was still an agricultural basis to village life in Churchdown and any alteration in this respect came slowly.

Religious Life and the Church.

While great changes were coming about in secular society, the established church remained rooted in conservatism and tradition, and it lacked the vision needed to meet the challenge of these new developments. One of the general problems, and this certainly applied to Churchdown, was the lack of a resident vicar in the parish - a situation which lasted until the end of the nineteenth century. The spiritual needs of the people had to be met by a series of 'perpetual curates' and these ministers were poorly paid.

At a meeting of the vestry on Boxing Day, 1704, a complaint was put forward and sent to the bishop of the diocese that 'the minister has no house, orchards or gardens...no glebe lands, and all the tythes, both Grate and Small belong to the Impropriator.'[23] These produced an income of £220 per annum but the minister received only the small stipend of £20 a year, which, they protested, 'is a very Scanty allowance in proportion to the Impropriation.' Accordingly, they begged the bishop to allow a better remuneration but this, seemingly, was not forthcoming, the only concession made being that he was given permission to teach the children of Brockworth - and, presumably, earn a little from doing so.[24]

The minister at the time was John Sommers who seems to have been something of a rebel[25] for, in his indictment for certain breaches of church regulations, he is described as a 'Priest in Holy Orders Instituted to the Vicarage of Badgeworth who also Suppliest the Cure of Churchdowne,' who had 'for Severall years last past Attempted to serve in Churchdown... without admission or Examination of the Ordinary of the Diocese'. He had also preached sermons in St. Bartholomew's without 'making Subscription and Declaration as the Act of Uniformity requires,' and had been at fault by publishing the banns of marriage in a church where he had 'no lawful authority to hold any ministerial office'. Despite his misdemeanours Sommers appears to have remained in office until 1712 but without any improvement in stipend, and it was not until many years had elapsed that the income of the minister, his successor Obadiah Dunn (or Done), was augmented by the rents from glebe lands. Dunn was rector of Cranham but also curate of Churchdown and, although his memorial tablet in Cranham church records that he had been 'a pattern to his people,' one wonders how much pastoral attention he had been able to give to his cure of souls in the nine-mile distant parish of Churchdown.[26] When the Rev. Henry Wyndowe was licensed to serve as curate in 1742[27] he presumably resided in the village as the Wyndowe family occupied The Great House. (This was the Henry Wyndowe who endowed the first school in Churchdown.)

That the religious provision in the parish sometimes left much to be desired is instanced by the provision of two charities, one set up by Jeremiah Michel in 1721 and the other by William Smith in 1785.[28] The first took the form of an annuity of thirty-six shillings to provide for the administration of the sacraments at St. Bartholomew's nine times annually. The Eucharist at this time was being celebrated on only three occasions during the year, and even then, apparently, was poorly attended, as the bequest stipulated that if 'no persons of discretion' should be present to receive the sacrament' the value of the bread and wine was to be given to the poor. William Smith, by his endowment, left provision to cover the costs of administering the communion once every calendar month.

Irregular attendance at Divine Service may well have been due in part to the custom of charging pew rents which, combined with inadequate provision of free sittings, discouraged those lower in the social scale from church-going. An entry in the Gloucester and Bristol Diocesan Calendar for 1860[29] reflects a state of affairs which had been in operation since the seventeenth century: 'In very many Parishes the Free Sittings for the poor are lamentable and shamefully inadequate. The large pews of the upper and middle classes, which have been so truly described as "the eye-sores and heart-sores of our Churches" have usurped the space intended originally for the benefit of all classes; and the lower class have ceased to be church-goers in great measure, because their wealthier brethren have driven them out of the church'.

Such a state of affairs was, to some extent at least, likely to have existed at St. Bartholomew's. We know that the Wyndowe family and the Pumphreys quarrelled over their seat rights and, no doubt, the better-off farmers were anxious to assert their increasing prosperity by paying their way into superior pews. In 1815, although there was accommodation for three hundred worshippers in the parish church, there were only 16 'open' (free) seats.[30]

It is against this background of inadequate ministry and acute social division that the upsurge in breakaway religious sects can be placed and, in 1746, the first application for permission to use a private house for worship occurs in the diocesan archives.[31] The request is directed to 'Dr. Martin Benson, Lord Bishop of the Diocese of Gloucester' and continues,'These are to certify your Lordship that some of his Majesty's Protestant Dissenting Subjects do intend to hold a meeting for the worship of God in the Dwelling House of Thomas Smyth, shoemaker, situate in the parish of Churchdown, in this County, and desire that this may be registered in the Bishop's court, according to the Act of Parliament of William and Mary. Witness our hands this 26th day of May, 1746. John Harman: John Summers: Richard Jones.' In 1790 a similar application was made to use the house 'set apart for that purpose' of John Dance in Hucclecote,[32] and further requests of the same kind occur in the 19th century from 1814 to 1833.[33]

In a survey of the diocese in 1743 Churchdown is shown as having a population of 460 of whom five were Quakers while, seven years later (the population having dropped by ten), there were seven 'papists' and five presbyterians.[34] When Jane Pumphrey, a spinster, died at the age of 94 she was described as a member of the Society of Friends. The Pumphreys were at this time prominent members of Churchdown society.

Non-conformist sects were by now established in Churchdown and foremost among these was Methodism. George Whitfield, an associate of Charles and John Wesley, preached his first sermon in Gloucester in 1736, and from then on frequently addressed meetings in the Gloucester/Cheltenham area. It is possible, therefore, that Churchdown people had the opportunity to hear him, and it certainly seems that Methodism became established in the parish quite early in the nineteenth century.

An entry in a return by Charles Hardwick (curate of Churchdown for a short time in 1821) records: 'Two Meeting Houses: Wesleyans and Lady Huntingdon,' as existing in 1815.[35] The Methodist Circuit Preaching Plan for 1849 indicates the existence of a Wesleyan Methodist church but where this was is not known and two years later there is no mention of it.[36] In 1884 a barn at Drews Court Farm , 'in the occupation of Mr. Alfred Champney and used by him for the holding of religious services' was rented by the local Methodist worshippers as their meeting place.[37] The building, now business premises, at the junction of The Piece and Sandfield Road was originally a Primitive Methodist chapel which existed from the end of the nineteenth century until 1925.

It is apparent that by this time Protestant Non-conformists were generally tolerated and allowed freedom of worship, but Swift makes his feelings very clear about the activities of a new dissenting sect which was establishing itself in the parish - the 'Ranters' he calls them. 'The Chapel opened today by a man named Hunt,' he writes, 'and our people came to show their colours as church people in opposition to the Ranters.'[38] (The Chapel he refers to may have been the Primitive Methodist Chapel in The Piece). Seven years later, in 1884, his attitude to any form of worship other than orthodox Anglican is still decidedly illiberal, and this time his satire is turned upon the meetings in 'The Barn.' (This was probably the barn at Drew's Court in which for some time the local Methodists held their services). 'All those inside the Barn were 'saved,' he tells us, 'and those outside lost.' (Swift and the Vicar were, undoubtedly, in this last category). 'After this comfortable thought,' Swift continues, 'the missioner amongst other matters prayed for Dr. S. that he (Dr. S.) might come amongst them.'[39] It is highly unlikely that in this instance the missioner's prayers were fruitful.

The vicar, the Rev. Dr. Frederick Smithe, was, so Swift tells us in his diary, 'very disheartened at the present state of the parish, the want of a proper church feeling in it and so on,' and adds that he tried to cheer him up.[40]

Another problem for the vicar was the growing feeling in the parish that, in times of bad weather, it should be possible for services to be held in the village rather than on the hill. Swift writes of this in his history[41] and of the use of a room at the school for this purpose: 'Though most persons would admire, as a picturesque object, the old Church of St. Bartholomew on the summit of the hill, 580 feet above sea level, yet it must be acknowledged that this position is the cause of much inconvenience in bad weather and at evening time for at least eight months of the year. Then again, it is at all times inaccessible for the infirm and aged. To remedy this, Evening service was held in the schoolroom for over 30 years.' (Some of the sacraments, baptism for instance, were also administered in the schoolroom). Why this sudden disinclination to go up the hill to church? (If it *was* sudden; attendance, it seems, had often been poor in the past). Had the condition of the ascent lane deteriorated badly? Were wet top hats and bedraggled crinolines now too much of a problem? Or was it that newcomers to the parish, being mostly from the towns, were less prepared to attempt the muddy trek up Chosen?

In time the villagers from the main road end of the parish came to feel that they, too, needed a more convenient place in which to meet for worship, (St. Bartholomew's was an arduous mile and a half away even by the shortest route across the fields,) and so, in 1888, a room was rented near the present Hare and Hounds Inn over the forge of Mark Dancey, the blacksmith. Here, for sixteen years or more, a Sunday evening service and a Sunday School were held under the supervision of Mr. Champney, a solicitor from Gloucester; from this small beginning the new ecclesiastical parish of St. John, Churchdown, was, eventually, to grow - but this did not happen until well into the next century.

Dr. Smithe became the first resident vicar of the parish when the vicarage was built in 1859; by this time Hucclecote was a separate parish, which it had been since 1851, and thus was severed the last remaining link of the ancient barony.

Despite the vicar's misgivings about the quality of religious life in his parish, the sentiments expressed on the memorials in St. Bartholomew's churchyard seem to bear witness to a community that was still God-fearing - but the pious hopes, were expressed more economically than in earlier years. Now the rustic, hand-carved headstones, 'with healthy, well-fed cherubs trumpeting their victory over death and winging into the hereafter with a smile and a tune,'[42] are replaced by more austere and professional-looking memorials which often follow a set pattern with 'I.H.S.' carved at the top and 'R.I.P.' at the base. A sentence of scripture, rather than several lines of verse, now confirms the hope that ills which have been endured with fortitude on Earth will be redressed in Heaven. 'I reckon the sufferings of the present life are not to be compared to the glory that shall be revealed to us,' are the words inscribed on the tomb of Thomas Billingham who died in 1886, but it is to be hoped that not everyone suffered as much in transit as did the unfortunate William Beale of 'Hucclecoat' who had died in the previous century; his epitaph reads:

> 'Pain was my portion
> Physick was my food
> Groans my devotion,
> Druggs did me no good.
> Christ my Physician knew which way was best
> To ease my pain and sett my Soul at rest.'[43]

At the top of the Billingham slab the popular funereal design of a drooping plant is carved but the symbol most favoured on these late nineteenth-century graves is that of a draped, classic urn. An example of the latter heads the stone of Charles and Elizabeth Mouldey and this memorial carries a longer inscription than that of most of their contemporaries. Elizabeth died in 1870, predeceasing her husband by eleven years; he chose the following epitaph for her: 'Death is a debt to nature due.

> Which I have paid and so must you.
> She's gone the one we loved so dear
> To her eternal rest;
> She's gone to heaven we have no fear
> She is for ever blest'.

Premature death was a familiar source of grief to the people of Churchdown as it was in most places; tuberculosis and cholera were the plagues of the 18th and 19th centuries (and remained so at the beginning of the present century) and childbirth took its toll among young women. Mary Herbert died at the age of 27 years in 1811 and the inscription on her tomb is witness to the stoic acceptance of such a tragedy:

> Husband and children you agree
> To serve the Lord and follow me,
> For I'm not lost, forbear your tears,
> I am but hid till Christ appears.
> God thought it best to end my time
> And cut me off just in my prime'.

94

Memorial in St. Bartholomew's Churchyard (1833) to John Durett 'An Honest and Faithfull Servent'.

It was, of course, only the rather more well-to-do parishioners who could afford to erect headstones in memory of their departed relatives but there is at least one interesting exception to this in St. Bartholomew's churchyard. On the right of the path leading to the south door (that is, in one of the 'best' positions) is the following gravestone:

In memory of
John Durett Who
died Aprill the 9 1833 Aged 60 years
An Honest and Faithfull
Servent.

Another memorial worth noting is that of Mary Windowe who died in 1877, aged 84 years, and of 'Robert Her Son - *Roadman'*.

Was this Mary a member of The Great House family? If so, it is a little surprising that her son was employed as a roadman. It seems there could be a story rich in human interest here.

The Wyndowes were firmly established as the chief family of the village. The will of Sarah Wyndowe, drawn up in 1757, is extant and in this, among other bequests, she leaves £20 to the poor and £100 and £10 respectively to her servants Elizabeth Oakes and William Stephens. The will concludes with Sarah's wish 'to be buried in the same grave with my late husband, Henry Wyndowe, in as plain and private a manner as possible.'

Robert Windowe's services were called upon when the road leading up the hill needed clearance so that access to the hill could be made easier,[44] and this was, no doubt, part of the great scheme for improving the church and its approaches which took place between 1880 and 1889. Swift, in his history of the village, gives an account of this work and of the state of neglect into which St. Bartholomew's had fallen. He describes the interior of the church as being 'a scene of squalor and desolation,'[45] the chancel being in a particularly bad state. The brick floor had become worn into deep ruts and was badly affected by damp, two rusty girders spanned the roof space between the north and south walls, and access to the sanctuary was restricted by the obtrusion of 'four tall ugly pews' and by high oak railing around the altar. The Vicar persuaded the Vestry committee to agree to the removal of these obstructions on the grounds that, 'females, owing to the prevailing fashion of dress, had considerable difficulty in squeezing themselves into the spaces north and south of the altar respectively.' Rows of hat pegs in the nave and in the chancel were, Swift considered, a disfiguring feature and when, during Divine Service, these were 'occupied by cloaks, umbrellas, hats and the like' the 'general aspect was grotesque in the least.' The gallery at the west end was also taken down, having probably, like so much else at St. Bartholomew's, fallen into disrepair.

By the beginning of the last decade of the century important discussions regarding the parish church on the hill were taking place and, at a meeting in May, 1890, what was called its 'disadvantageous position' was discussed. One of the problems was the deterioration of the access road which had yet again become impassable and overgrown with thorns and briars, worshippers now having to make their way to church by climbing the steep field path through Ashfurlong. Funeral corteges could 'lack a general want of sobriety in the presence of death' when the incline was wet and slippery for all coffins had to be 'shouldered' up to burial on the hill,[46] and, in winter, when Chosen was in the grip of ice and snow, the dead remained unburied for weeks.

The church and churchyard also suffered, then as now, from vandalism and supervision to prevent this was difficult. The problems of litter and 'other wanton acts of certain tourists and visitors who were in the habit of carving their names or initials on the walls,' were discussed. In view of all the problems connected with the old church a very radical solution was put before the meeting - should a new church be built down in the village?

Money had been quite lavishly spent during the past nine years on improvements to the ancient building, and upkeep was always likely to be an ongoing financial commitment. One suggestion was that St. Bartholomew's should be abandoned as it was 'ridiculous to throw away £400-£700 upon the old building when the sum would form the nucleus for a new one.' The vicar was vehemently against such a drastic step; 'If we agreed to abandon the old church,' he declared, ' we should be the laughing-stock of all sensible people....of all who had a taste for antiquity or who had friends and relations lying in the adjacent churchyard.' The situation improved a little when the road was repaired and gravelled in 1893, which Swift said now made going up to church 'very pleasant,'[47] but the debate continued for the rest of the decade without a final decision being made and it was not until the new century that the plans for a second church were to come to fruition.

People and Houses

The historian, Sir Robert Atkyn, writing in 1712, tells us that there were 100 houses in Churchdown parish, with 400 inhabitants and 20 free-holders.[48] Samuel Rudder, over fifty years later, records 131 households with 630 inhabitants and comments, 'these numbers show that the place is remarkably healthy for a vale situation, as only one in 47-8 upon an average dies every year; and the population increases very considerably.'[49]

A number of the sturdy cottages, often brick-built, which are a feature of the village, may date from this time, although most, like the residence on The Green, now known as Chosen Hay, which is a conversion of three cottages, have been modernised. Brick-making, where a suitable supply of clay existed, was, in a number of areas, a small local industry and there was a brick-pit in Churchdown at the Barrow Hill end of the Brockworth road.

It was probably around this period that The Great House received its new Georgian frontage; the extensions now known as 'Caledonia' and 'Meadows' seem to have been added about 1740 and 1780 respectively; it has been said that 'Meadows' was originally a dairy.

The Village Green

Churchdown, undoubtedly quieter and more healthy than the towns, was now being promoted as a desirable place of residence particularly to be favoured by the up-and-coming middle class. When the estate of William Singleton was disposed of in 1786 the 'Messuage or Farm Place of the manor of Parton,' (which included meadow and pasture land 'partly inclosed and partly in the Common Fields and Meadows of Churchdowne'), is described as being in a 'very Eligible Situation, being about four miles from Gloucester, and six from Cheltenham; and near the Turnpike Road from Gloucester to Cheltenham.'[50] Another lot comprised 'A very valuable Freehold Estate delightfully situate at Churchdown on the slope of the celebrated Chosen Hill, about Three and a Half Miles from the City and thriving Port of Gloucester, and the same distance from the fashionable Town of Cheltenham.' These distances must have been as the crow flies! The sale included 'An Old Manor House (fit for the residence of a Gentleman).[51]

Earning a Living
The Census returns for 1851 and 1881, which record Churchdown (excluding Hucclecote) as having a population of 585 and 686 at these dates, show that most of the needs of the inhabitants could be supplied very locally. William Arkell of Brookfield, a farmer, was the only butcher, but several residents give 'baker' or 'grocer' as their occupation. One, Charles Pearce, lived in the Sugar Loaf Bridge area in 1881 where there was a little enclave of about forty-three people; the inn or alehouse called The Sugar Loaf which was in this same area was probably well-patronised by parishioners using the field path to Gloucester which began close by. The General Stores was in the Chapel Hay Lane part of the village, William Taylor being the proprietor, but by the end of the century Theophilus George Baker is shown as being at The Central Stores which may have been the same business by a different name. In old photographs the name 'Elias Baker' appears above the shop at the corner of Chapel Hay Lane.

There were four shoemakers (or cordwainers), a similar number of carpenters, two smiths, several gardeners, a thatcher, a sawyer, a wheelwright, dressmakers and needlewomen, all offering their services. Three women are listed as laundresses or washerwomen and a wash-house is known to have existed in a cottage on The Green. William Price was a builder and there were three bricklayers and, no doubt, some of the sixty or so labourers who appear in the Census were working either for him or in the brickyard at the top of the Brockworth road near Barrow Hill. A number of these men may have been employed on road or ditch maintenance, but it seems that the upkeep of the village roads left much to be desired for the lane going up the hill frequently became almost impassable and Parton Lane little better, while Pirton Lane was no more than a footpath or, at best, a bridle path.

There were one or two persons of independent means but only one resident is actually described as being of the gentry, Jane Thomas, Gentlewoman, who lived at 'The Cottage' and had come originally from Peterborough. By the turn of the century the lordship of the manor of Churchdown had been sold to Major Selwyn Payne[52] by the Chamberleyne family who resided at Oddington in the county.

Most of the people living in the parish in the second half of the nineteenth century had been born in the immediate locality, few were 'imports', but a number of residents who stated their occupations as 'draper,' 'general dealer,' or 'timber, corn or iron merchants' probably conducted these businesses in one of the towns.

By the 1881 census the number of men employed by the railway companies had shot up from nine in 1851 to twenty-nine, and their positions ranged from stationmaster (Nicholas Adams), through signalman and clerk to platelayers and rail labourers.

About thirty-five persons, mostly women and girls, are described as servants and many of these will have had situations in the seventeen farming households. Most families in the upper social bracket employed a servant or servants - there were two at the Vicarage, for instance, and a 'Mrs. Roberts' (who may have been one of the charwomen listed as living at the Grotto) worked for the Swifts.[53]

The nineteenth century was a time when class snobbery reached a peak; servants belonged to the 'lower orders' and, in town houses at least, were banished to the basement or isolated in the attic when not performing their duties. A rather less rigid social barrier may have existed in Churchdown, which was a very close-knit community, but, no doubt, the quarters of the 'domestics' were shut off from those of the family by the inevitable green baize door.

The earlier census shows Churchdown still very much an agricultural community with farmworkers predominating among the working population; by 1881 the number had dropped but, with the general labourers, they still formed the bulk of employed persons. In 1833 The Gloucester Association for the Encouragement of Deserving Labourers and Servants had been formed and in 1868, £3 was awarded to a Churchdown man, John Saunders, a shepherd employed by Thomas Lawrence of Parton Manor in whose employ he had been for fourteen years. The certificate he was given records that John Saunders had reared that season 145 lambs from 114 ewes 'with the loss of one lamb only and not having lost an ewe the last four years.'

Although the rising costs of foodstuffs during the Napoleonic and Crimean conflicts (of 1799-1815 and 1853-56 respectively) and the effects of loss of common rights after enclosure undoubtedly caused hardship to the poorer people, it is difficult to believe, that living conditions for the labouring class in Churchdown in the 18th and 19th centuries were quite as black as some of the chronicles of the time have reported them as being in the nation more generally. The farm cottages that remain seem sturdy enough and if any of the broken-down, damp hovels which they describe existed they have long since gone. The farmworkers' cottages which are said to have existed on the hill did, reputedly, fall into neglect and were pulled down and there is no trace of them except where garden fruit trees, now grown wild, stand as evidence of lost gardens.

In 1871, following a poor harvest, food prices rose again and in that same year legal recognition was given to a new movement which had risen in the country - the National Agricultural Labourers' Union.[54] By the following year membership of this was spreading in Gloucestershire and in 1874 farmworkers from 'the villages round Gloucester' are said to have joined.[55] Swift records that the Liberal candidate for the Tewkesbury division, addressing a local meeting before the General Election of 1885, spoke of a proposal made by his party that, should they be returned to office, an Act would be passed to form local boards with the power to acquire land for letting out to the labourers. The 'little remaining common lands,' the candidate said, should be allowed to the poor.[56] Despite these promises the Conservative candidate was elected - which is all the more surprising in view of the fact that for the first time in history the labouring male populace over the age of twenty-one now had the right to vote.[57]

Poor Relief.

As has already been said, there was some parish provision for those in the community who had fallen on hard times through unemployment, disability, old age or widowhood.

To help provide housing for women who were both widowed and poor, Richard Holford, in 1748, gave four acres of land at Parton as a source of revenue for the maintenance of four cottages on Churchdown Green.[58] These almshouses have been pulled down this century.

The accounts of the Overseers of the Poor, who administered the poor relief, exist for Churchdown from 1808 onwards.[59] (Money was collected 'by Rate' and supplemented by donations.) These records give insight into the conditions of life among the humbler members of the parish and also indicate a seemingly commendable degree of care and concern by those responsible for the distribution of the charitable funds - but how effective the system really was we cannot know. That payment of a villager's rent had sometimes to be made is instanced by John Triggs receiving two guineas for this, and there are also many entries concerning the distribution to poor cottagers of coal, the fuel most used for heating and cooking by this time. This coal may have been brought from the Forest of Dean mines by wagon or, alternatively, from wharves on the Severn where it had been off-loaded from Midlands barges; it was then carried by cart to the village, but, in either case, haulage must have been both difficult and expensive.

The Almshouses on the Green, now demolished.

Clothing and footwear were frequently given to the needy; Sarah Hopkins received two guineas 'to Cloath her children...and for a pair of shoes.' Ann Dondley's 'shift' cost four shillings but when, very soon afterwards she died, a shroud was supplied for her at six shillings. These prices seem quite high, bearing in mind that, according to Marshall, a labouring man might earn only a shilling a day. The shroud may have been made of wool probably spun and woven locally for there were mills at Stroud and still some weaving industry in Gloucester; the 'shift' was perhaps of linen, for cotton was still something of a new product and, despite the inventions which were to revolutionize the textile industry, cotton was not yet the cheap material it would later become.[60]

Some hapless parishioners were forced by their personal problems to be a drain on the relief system. Charles Perkins received four charity payments, three of four shillings and one of seven, plus a quarter of a ton of coals, and then, when shortly afterwards his death occurred, Sarah Bunt was paid thirteen shillings for attending to his 'lying-in.' 'For the men to carry him to Burial,' a further nine shillings were also disbursed. Burial was in the churchyard on Chosen Hill and the coffins were 'shouldered' up what was called 'the funeral path' through the fields to the summit.

The doctor's fee for attending Mary Scrivens was five shillings, and the wooden leg for John Townend cost two pounds; expenses such as these would surely have been beyond the means of the ordinary villagers had there not been help available from the charitable funds.

There are miscellaneous outgoings such as the twelve shillings given to Charles Arkell 'for ringing the Bell at Harvest' (a seemingly generous remuneration for what would appear a not unduly onerous duty), while a similar amount awarded to Jonah Coopey, the Constable, for 'meeting the High Constable four times' was, presumably, to cover his travelling expenses. When Betty Robberts had to be conveyed to Little Dean Prison the hiring of the 'horse and Gigg' cost one pound - so she was seen off in some style![61]

In 1851 fifteen parishioners are recorded as receiving parish relief while there are two or three persons listed as 'pensioners', either 'Greenwich' or 'Chelsea,' one of these, Emmanuel Lees, being married to a lady named Frances who was a 'stocking knitter.' This Frances surfaces again in the local records when, in 1895, she (apparently a widow by then) applied for admission to one of the Holford Charity almshouses on The Green. Her request was granted but only after some discussion at the Parish Council meeting regarding her suitability, her chastity being in question as she had been living as housekeeper to one, Will Davis.[62] 'Fanny' Lees, who lived to the age of 88 years and died in 1913, seems to have been a well-known figure in the village, dressed in her bonnet and shawl, and always observing the old custom of bobbing a curtsey on meeting.

Local Administration and Law and Order.

The Overseers of the Poor were officially appointed by the Justices of the Peace, as were the other principal officers of the parish such as the Surveyor of Highways and the Constable, but, no doubt, the members of the parish vestry suggested suitable candidates. Only those members of the community who were ratepayers were eligible to serve and vote on this committee and so, in a small village like Churchdown, this meant that the onus of parish government lay heavily on a select few. The churchwardens' responsibilities were many and varied from supervision of clergy duties and of the parishioners' morals, to the control of vermin. The local churchwardens' accounts for 1714 include 5s. 'paid for the taking five foxes,' and 10d. 'paid for taking five hedghoggs.' These harmless animals were unpopular because they were believed to steal milk from the udders of cows.

The Justices of the Peace set the parish rate and enforced the support of the disabled and unemployed, controlled the constables and were responsible for apprehending those who had committed crimes; they also issued licences for the holding of fairs and for the sale of alcohol. The squire of the village (and in Churchdown the reigning Windowe of the day assumed this role) was usually one of these Justices, his local knowledge being of value on the Bench, and so, consequently, he wielded considerable power in his area.

The Justices, in their turn, were answerable to the county High Sheriff and to the Lord Lieutenant of the shire. It was the latter's duty to raise the militia in times of national emergency. In 1704/5 Edmund Chamberlain, who was then High Sheriff of Gloucestershire, was given permission to reside outside the county, provided that he made adequate arrangements to cover his absence.[63] It is doubtful how much actual authority the Chamberlains now exercised as Lords of the Manor, for county and local officialdom had taken over many of the responsibilities which had anciently belonged with the title, and it was now the local minor gentry such as the Windowes and Pumphreys who figured prominently as leaders of Churchdown life. It is possible, though, that a manorial court still operated as the records of Quarter Sessions for the period 1781-1827 contain no entries whatsoever for the parish and, as it seems unlikely that the inhabitants were so remarkably law-abiding, offenders may have been tried and punished by local court[64]

In 1894 the Local Government Act led to the setting-up of parish councils which were democratically elected and women were both allowed to vote and be elected; women, in general, however, still had only limited suffrage at this time and there was to be a long and bitter struggle before they obtained equality of franchise with men.

Resistance to any form of change seems to have been endemic in rural Gloucestershire for earlier in the century, in 1840, considerable protest had been registered to the establishment of a police force in the county. In one area[65] the view was expressed that not only was the proposed measure 'exceedingly expensive' but that it was also 'absolutely unnecessary and useless', the habits of the population being allegedly so peaceful that no such watch upon their actions was required, and neither were any checks needed upon their 'innocent amusements'. When (of course only *very* occasionally) any persons were guilty of some misdemeanour, 'a single admonition from their Masters and Employers had always been found a sufficient corrective without the aid of a constable.' Churchdown's petition[66] echoed similar sentiments, but with an additional expression of concern for the feelings of the Yeomanry 'whose loyalty and promptitude in assisting the civil powers' had always been found sufficient 'in the most turbulent times for the suppression of outbreaks.' It was considered that, when any case of 'popular commotion', occurred 'the good and loyal feeling of the great Majority of the Inhabitants, combined with the assistance of the military Force,' would always be 'found sufficient to preserve the peace.'

There is no doubt that the nub of the protest was the fear of an increase in the county rate which would be the inevitable result of the provision of a police force - but was there also concern that official surveillance would throw a little too much light on some of those 'innocent' rural activities.

By 1859 a county force was in existence but whether it operated in

Churchdown is uncertain; later, in 1883, Swift mentions in his diary that he was summoned by a *policeman* to attend an inquiry on the death of an illegitimate child.[67] Such an officer seems to have been uniformed for when Swift heard a disturbance in his fowl house one night he found the matter was being investigated by a man 'who proved to be a policeman by the flash upon his buttons.' The culprit upsetting the hens turned out to be 'a hedgehog which the constable helpfully killed and was duly rewarded with some beer and sixpence.

Lawless behaviour was certainly not unknown in nineteenth-century Churchdown; in 1891 a party of youths from nearby Longlevens burst open the door of The Old House at Home (where beer and cider were sold) because drink had been refused them. After this act of vandalism they continued down to the Hare and Hounds Inn where they smashed the front door, broke the jugs and maltreated the landlord. He was eventually rescued by Constable Morris who, it was felt, should now be equipped with a uniform - such heroism should be clothed with authority.[68]

The will of James Nicholls (1897) names 'The Police Station' as being among buildings on his land in the Chapel Hay Lane area,[69] but Smart's Directory of 1902 records 'Carter, A. J., Police Constable' as living at 'The Police Station,' and residing, according to the Electoral Roll, at 2 Cotteswold View, Sandfield Road, Churchdown; it was at this address that the local police station was sited for many years with another police station existing at the Cheltenham Road end of the village from 1908.

The picture of rural peace described in the anti-police-force petitions hardly accords with the state of affairs which emerges from some writings of the time. The Diocesan Calendar for 1859,[70] in a commentary on behaviour at Harvest Suppers, refers to 'the yoke of vicious habits under which the labourer has too long bowed - habits which show in their grossest forms at these ancient feasts.' The writer attributes much of this disorderliness to the lack of those recreational facilities which would provide an 'outlet for the animal spirits of our working classes,' whose lives he sees as just 'work, work, work.' The remedy he suggests is encouragement to take part in what he calls 'the manly and truly English game of cricket' which could provide 'a first advance from degrading habits and pursuits, and thus be a means of starting them on the way towards a thorough reformation of principal and conduct.' To see sport (even cricket!) as a remedy for social ills was a little simplistic but the writer was making a valid point about the need for some leisure provision and his views reflect a growing awareness at this time of the need for reform in many social issues. William Swift and his close associates, though, despite being well-intentioned in many ways, were very suspicious of 'liberalism' whether in politics or society; when for instance, Home Rule for Ireland was discussed 'with other tax collectors' they were all dead against this 'although several were Liberals.'[71]

It was very important in the thinking of the time that the conventions of decorous behaviour should, at least, appear to be observed, but there *were* unfortunate lapses - as when Mr. Swift heard that 'Mr. Lawyer Smith's wife had gone off with a *dissenting minister.*'[72] (William Swift himself was, of course, a staunch Anglican!) In 1896 the Parish Council were much concerned when it seemed that even in the quiet confines of the almshouses on the Green these standards were being breached, for 'persons were living with the widows'; it was necessary, therefore, to ensure 'that any occupation was consistent with propriety and what is desirable.'[73]

Despite the moral high tone ostensibly adopted, Victorian society was subject to many problems, illegitimacy was by no mean uncommon[74] and drunkenness was rife - in Churchdown as elsewhere. On a summer's day in 1884, as Swift records, the church choir with some other members of the parish went on an excursion by train to Weston-super-Mare.[75] 'The greater part of our expense,' he writes, 'consisted in beer, beer, beer!' Several of the party became intoxicated and either succumbed to alcoholic stupor or behaved in embarrassing or foolhardy manner. Swift was 'very glad to get out of it at about 10.30' - and this was a church-sponsored outing!

Health and Hygiene.

Churchdown enjoyed an enviable reputation as a healthy place in which to live and one where the risk of contracting cholera or typhus was less than in the crowded towns, but the village was not without its problem areas. A number of deaths had occurred in, or near, the small development at the station called 'The Grotto' where there were no sanitary conveniences for the residents of the cottages, and where, also, a foul ditch contributed to a most unhygienic situation.[76] The authorities were asked to look into these matters, and also into the insanitary state of properties near the Sugar Loaf Bridge and in the Avenue.

The state of the public pond near the Hare and Hounds Inn and the main Gloucester to Cheltenham road was also a perennial source of trouble, and a topic which could always be relied on to fill a vacant space in the agenda whenever the local council met. This pond frequently became polluted and so was unfit to be used as a watering place for the animals of the riders, coachmen, carters and drovers who used the highway, sheep and cattle being driven to Gloucester market 'on the hoof' in those days.

For domestic purposes most people still relied on wells and, seemingly, were content to do so, for when, in 1895, a committee was appointed to see whether a public water supply could be obtained 'at moderate cost' there was 'not much inclination on the part of the parish to consider the matter,'[77] The scheme which had been put forward was to pipe the spring at Duns Elm (on the slopes of the hill) which ran 1,500 gallons a day to a storage tank which could hold three months' supply.

The cost of such a project, which would have included a mile of pipes and twelve standpipes, was estimated to be £1,500 and, not surprisingly, such a scheme alarmed all concerned, but in the following year there was severe drought and the subject of water supply came forward again. It was finally arranged[78] that a well twelve feet deep should be dug on the property of a Mr. Nicholls and that this well should be connected with the old well at Draggetts' Court. A pump was to be set up on a platform with steps and be suitably fenced, but despite this precaution, complaint was registered in the Council minutes that stones were being constantly put into the barrel of the pump; vandalism, it seems, is not just the curse of the twentieth century![79] Churchdown was not connected to mains water until about 1914 and it took some time for a piped supply to be laid to every part of the village.

When the parish was threatened by the possibility of a smallpox outbreak, Swift was one of the main supporters of the pro-vaccination campaign. A serious epidemic erupted in Gloucester in 1895-6 with some 2,000 people suffering from the contagion and over 400 deaths occurring, with the consequence that the city and its inhabitants were shunned by the outside world. An entry in the Minute Book of Churchdown Parish Council at this time states: 'That every endeavour be made by vaccination and otherwise to keep smallpox out of the village.'[80] Dr. Prance, who visited patients in Churchdown (travelling by dog cart from Cheltenham)[81] offered to vaccinate free of charge. There was much alarm, naturally, when a case of smallpox was reported at Parton Farm, and then, a little later, on The Green, and so an extraordinary sitting of the parish council was called in April, 1896. This meeting, which seems to have taken place in Mr. Swift's own home, was duly reported in his diary.[82]

Mr. J. H. Jones, a prominent member of Churchdown society, was in the Chair and opened the debate by affirming the advantages of vaccination but, after this suitable beginning, opinion was so much divided that, it appears, the meeting degenerated into something of a 'free for all!' 'The din was deafening,' writes Swift, 'my head ached with the noise. At one time it looked as if Bubb and Harris would have fought. I trembled for my lamp in the middle of the table.' At last, a resolution was passed suggesting that Dr. Washbourne, the public vaccinator, should be invited to attend at various centres in the locality to carry out the programme of immunisation. Rancour had not died, however, and Swift adds: 'It appears that the dispute and high words were carried out on the Road afterwards and that the next morning Morris and Mr. Jones had another altercation in which Mr.Jones called M. a bigoted fool.'

The motion that the Board of Guardians should be requested to put compulsory powers into force to compel all parishioners who had not yet been vaccinated to receive treatment was finally carried by four votes to three.[83] At the end of the campaign Swift was able to record with some pride that, in all, 500 persons had been vaccinated out of the population of 750. At one point, during the peak time of alarm, an isolation hospital or tent for the village had been proposed but this does not seem to have been necessary for by June, 1896, the epidemic appeared to be contained and congratulations were expressed to all who had contributed to the stemming of the outbreak.[84]

Communications
When his young son was ill, William Swift tells us he *telegraphed* (that is he probably sent a telegram) for the doctor to come from Cheltenham, and, in response, Dr. Prance came out on his bicycle, prescribed castor oil and pastilles for the patient and advised that a mustard plaster should be applied to the heart if the condition continued.[85] If Dr. Prance's surgery had been connected to the telephone system, Swift could have *telephoned*, for, at least by 1897, there was a call box at the Central Stores in the village.[86] There were, however, few private lines at this time and the first in Churchdown was installed at the home of Dr. Moore in 1904 when Churchdown had its own resident doctor.

Another incident which Swift records was the occurrence of an earthquake which was felt over most of England. In his usual graphic style he describes how he was awakened from a sound sleep just after five that morning 'by a tremendous blizzard or whizzing-like noise as if someone was very quickly and loudly agitating sheet iron at the bedroom door. Then came the shock when the bedstead was tilted from the left to right.'[87]

William Swift read of the far-reaching effects of this startling occurrence *in the papers,* but he does not say whether the newspapers were on sale in the village, brought out from town, or delivered by post; a postal service was in operation by this time although exactly when it began is not documented. There is reference in 1856 to a wall letter box being by the gate of The Manor (Great) House in what is now Church Road, and a statement made in 1858 says that the postmaster at Hucclecote (on Ermine Street) was responsible for the delivery of letters to Churchdown as well as in his own locality.[88]

The mail arrived by 'messenger' and, in 1867, the holder of this office, Edwin Lea, was appointed to a direct round from Gloucester to Churchdown. The story is told that, before the railway came, the postman walked from the city, possibly via Twigworth and other villages en route, and arrived at Churchdown in the late morning. Here he would rest and refresh himself at 'Granny Hunt's' cottage at the Grotto. Upon hearing the tune played on his horn, the villagers would run out and give him their letters which he then took back with him to Gloucester.[89]

After 1874, when the station had been opened, there was a demand for an improved postal service and the first village post office may date from this time although there is no actual mention of this until an entry in the Post Office list of 1st January, 1879. The 1881 census records the name

The Post Office in Church Road, about 1907.

of 'George Preece Garness, coach-builder, carpenter and postman,' and it was he who became the parish's first sub-postmaster. When he died in 1886, his wife, Anna Maria, was appointed in his place and she operated the post office services from 'Homeside', 46 Brookfield Road. Her daughter, Susannah Maria Garness, succeeded her mother in 1907 and held the position until 1937 but by this time the office was based at The Stores in Church Road.

There is a Victorian pillar box outside the library in Parton Road but this is not 'native' to Churchdown; it came originally from the Great Western Railway station at Gloucester and was put in its present position in 1934.

The Cheltenham Road end of the village did not have a post box until 1897 when one was placed on the premises near the forge. The first post office came in 1923 and was run by Mrs. Hilda Smith, who, with her husband, kept a small general shop called The Black and White Stores, at 77 Cheltenham Road East.

Social Life and Events.
Towards the end of the century the hill was becoming a favourite spot for picnickers (some of whom offended by leaving the remains of their picnics in the 'shape of orange peel, broken glass, paper and the like'),[90] and a trip out to Churchdown was a popular excursion for people living in Gloucester or Cheltenham. Teas were served on the hill and on The Green but it seems there was some rivalry between the 'tea ladies.' 'John Davies,' Swift tells us, 'had filled up the Mussell Well at

the instigation of his mother to prevent Mrs. Berry having water for her tea parties.'[91]

The Hare and Hounds is probably Churchdown's longest-established inn, and Swift says that the Court Leet used to be held there in the past.[92] The Rising Sun pre-dated, perhaps in name only, The Elm (later called The Old Elm) which was on the site of the present Bat and Ball; Swift recalls The Old Elm being put up for sale in 1896 and being sold on that occasion for £3,550.[93] An elm tree, renowned as a village landmark and said to be 178 years old, grew near the Vicarage and may have been commemorated by the name of the inn.[94] The landlord of the Rising Sun from 1841-1851 was Charles Tidman; the landlord of the Elm in 1861 was Thomas Price, and of the Old Elm in 1881, John Paterson. An hostelry built, or rebuilt, by 'Thos.Thache' may have existed from at least 1695.

The Old House at Home (now 5 Brookfield Road) sold only beer and cider and possessed its own cider mill. In 1895 George Henry Garness applied for a licence to conduct this public house and the vicar (Dr. Smithe) gave him a glowing testimonial saying that Garness , who was a member of the church choir, had much self-control and 'the power to maintain that order and discipline without which a public house is simply a public nuisance.'[95]

The Chosen Hotel was built at the end of the century (E. May being proprietor in 1902) but was not at first licensed, being termed a 'Temperance Hotel;'[96] it was, however, used for concerts and these seem to have been quite a feature of the social life of the parish. A 'Concert Room' had existed in the village before the Chosen Hotel was built and Swift attended a function there in 1887 and so we have a record of the programme on this occasion.[97] It opened very patriotically with 'Rule Britannia', and closed, of course, with 'God Save the Queen' after a selection of recitations, pianoforte and harp solos and other suitably decorous items. 'Comic Songs' were also included by way of light relief - one of these being cryptically entitled 'The Bulls Won't Bellow'.

William Swift tells us of another social occasion he attended, in this case a wedding. The bridegroom was Edwin Redman who had been employed at Churchdown Station for two years and had acquitted himself so well in the performance of his duties that he was presented with 'six guineas in an old-fashioned purse.'[98] The gift (a wedding present?) was accompanied by a letter in which his 'kind, steady and attentive conduct' is commended and continues: 'so...we ask your acceptance of this slight token of the value set upon your merits and from it to learn the moral that a kind, straight-forward, obliging, cheerful and ready endeavour is never lost in the path of life but is duly appreciated by all conditions of men.' (Admirable, but typically Victorian sentiments!)

The wedding breakfast was held in one of the cottages and there was quite a crush when all the guests had assembled so that William felt 'very

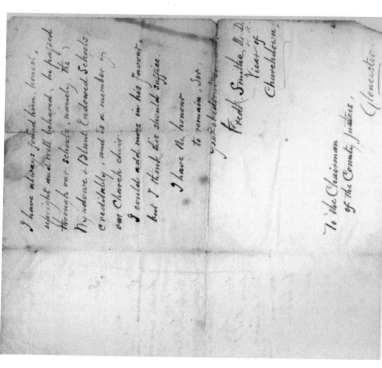

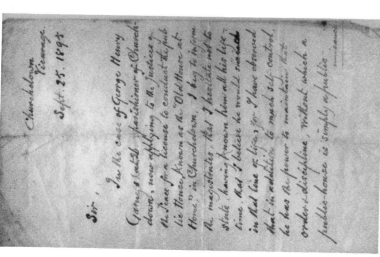

Reproduction of letter from the Rev. Dr. Frederick Smithe, vicar of Churchdown, regarding appointment of a licensee for the Old House at Home.

The Chosen Hotel (now demolished) where concerts were often held.

awkward, with overcoat, stick, umbrella, and present in the shape of a bread board and knife.' An impressive spread was provided: 'a prime piece of beef, ham, chickens, leg of mutton, plenty of beer, sherry and port, wedding cake, etc.' When the festivities became rather jolly, 'Mrs. Lucas,' who was wearing her best lavender silk, 'held her dress so high that her lack of undergarments and her striped stockings were distinctly visible.'

William Swift seems to have been quite a stylish dresser himself for, later in his diary, he tells us that he bought 'a pair of light trousers for 10/6, a russet cord coat for 5/6 and a straw hat for 2/8. The fare to town to buy these articles was 1/- and the glass of beer he bought to help him cope with making the purchases cost 3d.[99] (William was by no means averse to alcohol, and when, in 1901, he bought a bottle of gin for himself it cost 2/5d. and half a pint of whisky for his wife 1/3d.)

The two really memorable social occasions of the latter end of the century were, of course, the celebrations of the Royal Gold and Diamond Jubilees in 1887 and 1897 respectively. In Churchdown the former, marking the 50th anniversary of the Queen's accession, featured a parish feast, held in a tent erected in the field opposite The Manor House, and the presentation of commemorative mugs to all the children - but the Diamond Jubilee which followed ten years later was an even greater event.

At the Annual Parish meeting held in March, 1897, it had been unanimously agreed that 'an endeavour be made to celebrate Her Majesty's

Diamond Jubilee in the Parish as a day of real rejoicing,' in recognition of the loyalty due to our beloved Sovereign, our common nationality, and our splendid heritage throughout the world.'[100]

Tuesday, the 22nd June, the day on which the Jubilee was to be celebrated, dawned fine 'with light clouds and a pleasant breeze,' and the festivities got off to a rousing start with the ringing of the church bells at the early hour of 4 a.m.[101] The Parish Dinner was held at one o'clock in the tent on Chapel Hay; Swift approved of the meal for the 'meat was good and there was plenty of salad', but there was a deficiency of what he calls 'drinkables,' - the assemblage being kept 'fairly supplied with beer,' however, by 'Josh Yeates,' who had been 'put in command of it as the only means of keeping him sober.' Yeates wore a dress coat with brass buttons and, apparently, 'behaved with great decorum,' the vicar, in his 'stove hat,' carved the meat 'with great energy,' and 'Squire Bubb,' evidently entering into the spirit of rustic celebration, 'arrayed himself in a clean white smock frock with his felt hat turned down.' The proceedings concluded with a speech by Mr. Jones who again recounted 'as we had heard in the two sermons on Sunday, the material progress made in the last 60 years,' and then all sang *God Save the Queen* as they were to do at frequent intervals during the rest of the day.

In the afternoon there was a 'Negro Entertainment' and a programme of sports which included, as well as the usual races, a '240 yards Pipe Lighting Handicap'. This was followed by teas for the children and then for the adults, the water being boiled in 'a kind of portable furnace.' Medals were distributed to the children and each of the more junior young people received, in addition, one of the '100 Japanese figures' which had been supplied. During these events the band played at intervals. The prize-giving, which took place on the stage, was 'presided over by Mrs. Stokes...with great stateliness,' but the fact that 'H. Goodwin' appeared on the stage in *tights* warrants an exclamation mark in the diary!

From 6 p.m. onwards there were 'Old English Games, a Variety Entertainment, and dancing, etc.;' then, as Swift says with perhaps some relief, 'at last the Company left for the hill and for the bonfires.' There were two of these, one located so that it could be seen from Hucclecote and the other sited in good view from Churchdown. As darkness increased a starting rocket was fired from Great Malvern and then all the forty-five beacons on the hills around blazed into light. Twenty-five rockets went up from Chosen and coloured lights glowed among the trees creating, in Swift's words, 'a romantic effect' that 'could not be described.' What must certainly have been one of the most memorable days in the whole annals of the village, ended with the children on the hill cheering, with guns firing from the valley below, and with the final singing of the National Anthem by all who were present on this great occasion. In July the Parish council accepted with gratitude the offer

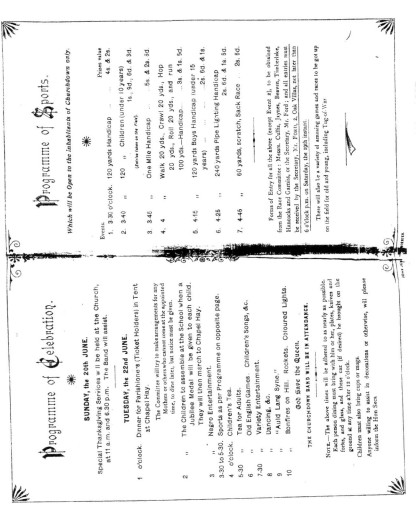

Programme of Celebrations of Queen Victoria's Diamond Jubilee, 1897.

113

made by Mr. J. H. Jones of a piece of his land on the steep northern side of the hill to be used as a recreation ground for the Parish. The area was planted with the fir trees which border the ascent steps to-day and seats were placed at suitable vantage spots, the whole project being designed by Mr. Jones in part as a family memorial, but also, in commemoration of the Jubilee and 'as a reminder of the benefits which flow to this country from our grand Colonial Empire and our kith and kin beyond the seas.'[102]

The nineteenth century seemed about to end on a fine, triumphal note but, far away, in South Africa, trouble was brewing. In his diary for the 16th September, 1899,[103] Swift reports that *'The Citizen'* (the local newspaper)' speaks of war being imminent with the Transvaal' and the entry for 11th October states tersely: 'Boers begin war.'

And so, as the nineteenth century slid into the twentieth, a century shadowed by two major wars, the transition was marked prophetically by the outbreak of conflict.

Chapter 6

Time of Growth and Conflict
1900 -1919

A New Century and a New Reign

The twentieth century, which was to see both amazing development and unprecedented destruction, opened with a burst of frenetic national rejoicing as the country went wild with joy at the relief of Mafeking, Churchdown joining wholeheartedly in celebrating the good news from the war front in South Africa with a whistling of railway engines and the exploding of detonators. When, soon, Pretoria, too, fell, Swift hoisted the school flag to mark this sign of a turn of fortune in the Boer conflict[1] and the children were given a day's holiday, which they may have appreciated more than the lecture by Mr. J. H. Jones on the heroism of the defenders of the beleaguered cities; any diversion from the normal routine of school life was, however, probably welcome as the curriculum was usually strictly adhered to. In the Inspector's report for the first year of the century the advice is given that the infants should be taken out into the front garden of the school and allowed 'to walk sedately around and watch the flowers grow' as a means of affording them 'a recreational break.'[2] The same report notes that a sprinkler was required for cleaning the slates, and Swift adds, 'to prevent the children using the moisture which nature provides'.

The New Year, 1901, saw the nation now plunged into mourning. The old Queen died on the 22nd January and in their Minutes the Council 'desired to place on record their sense of the great loss sustained...and the great service rendered by her to the nation during her unexampled reign of sixty-three years. The Council had the fullest assurance however that King Edward VII would follow in his Mother's footsteps'. Swift's report of the real sense of loss felt in the village was probably a reflection of the sentiment nation-wide. 'We felt on hearing this,' he writes, 'a feeling as if a relation, or a personal friend, was taken away.'[3] Victoria had reigned for so long that she had become the focus of the nation's identity, and had stamped her personality so indelibly on the era, that there was now, perhaps, a sense that the old order of things was changing and would never be the same again. On hearing the sad news, Swift immediately lowered the school flag to half mast, which, during the Mafeking and Pretoria celebrations, had flown 'higher than anyone else's.'

The Memorial Service for the late monarch was held on the 2nd February and Swift tells us that the Church 'was almost quite full - and all (nearly) in black.' The pulpit was draped in mourning and the service began with the Funeral March.

At a meeting of the Parish Council[4] it was affirmed that the coronation of the new king, Edward VII, should be celebrated in 'as loyal and hearty a manner as possible so that all might join in the festivities'; these, however, had to be postponed because of the King's illness and a service of intercession for his recovery was held. The following message was sent to Buckingham Palace: 'To Their Majesties The King and Queen. The parishioners of Churchdown, assembled in accordance with the King's expressed wish, beg to render their heartfelt sorrow at His Majesty's illness and their earnest Hope that the Coronation may be celebrated at no distant date.'

This took place on 9th August 1902, and was marked by the customary bonfire on Chosen Hill which was the usual culmination of celebrations in Churchdown. Harry Brown was thanked 'for erecting the arch' and George Yeates for 'erecting the copper' and organising the supply of boiling water, as liberal potations of tea were, apparently, an essential part of the loyal proceedings.[5]

New Churches

Two major projects were undertaken in Churchdown during the early years of the present century: the building of two new places of worship. At the time St. Bartholomew's was still the only Anglican church (with the schoolroom available for supplementary services) and the Wesleyan Methodist congregation were continuing to meet in the Drew's Court barn, but this was proving inadequate for the growing population. At the Cheltenham Road end of the village the Mission Room was providing worshippers in that area with what Swift describes as 'a nondescript sort of worship.'[6] He was very traditionalist in his religious outlook and did not approve of the freer, more or less undenominational, form of service practised by the Champney/Dancey team and their young lay readers. The Primitive Methodist chapel at the corner of The Piece was still meeting the needs of a small congregation and this it continued to do for some years until, eventually, declining numbers caused its closure in 1925.

On 10th May 1901, the local Wesleyan Methodists held what was called 'A general Conversation' at which the feeling was strongly

Primitive Methodist Chapel in The Piece. This later became the Village Hall, then a branch library and is now business premises.

expressed that the time had come to 'Arise and Build.' Plans were begun immediately and a building fund opened with a promise of £101. A trust was set up in September and a circular appeal for contributions to the building fund was sent out.

On St. Andrew's Day (30th November) in that same year, a parish meeting was held to discuss the building of a new Anglican church which should serve, for some time at least, as a chapel of ease while St. Bartholomew's remained the Parish Church. The funds of the new Building Committee were immediately boosted by the promise of £400 5s. from local donors and circulars were distributed asking for further donations. In the opening statement of these it was stressed that 'the picturesque old Church' on Chosen Hill, which was 580 ft. high and 'away from the people,' did not meet the needs of what was, undoubtedly, a rapidly increasing community; it was impossible of access for the aged and infirm, and, in bad weather, it also became so for the congregation in general. The schoolroom, which seated only 130 was proving quite inadequate for the population of the parish which then numbered about one thousand. It was added that the Building Committee were convinced that the only way in which the spiritual needs of the parish could be properly provided for was to build 'at all events, part, of a substantial Church' which might if necessary eventually become the Parish Church.

In the following year a tremendous boost was given to the building schemes of both churches by gifts of land donated, with admirable ecumenical even-handedness, to the Anglicans and Methodists alike by the Churchdown Land Company the owners of extensive property and land in the parish. The sites were in the Chapel Hay area, that ancient space in the centre of the main village where, later in 1924, the remains of the chapel-like building, with burials around it, were uncovered. In 1902 these discoveries had not, of course, been made, but there was even then a well-established local tradition that some early place of worship had existed, probably in the field suggestively called '*Chapel* Hay.'

By now the Methodists had got off to a head start as their plans, drawn up by the Gloucester architect, J. Fletcher Tew, had already been approved and by July 1902, work, under the direction of the builder, W. Jones of Gloucester, had actually commenced, the foundation stone being laid on 15th October by Mrs. E. A. Jenking of Cheltenham.

It had been decided that designs for St. Andrew's, the Anglican church, were to be submitted on a competitive basis and so matters moved forward more slowly, but the designs of the architect, W. B. Wood, were finally chosen and the first sod on the church site was cut in March, 1903, the contractor being A. J. Dolman of Gloucester.

The Methodist Church was now actually ready to be opened and this ceremony took place on Thursday, 30th April, 1903. The *Gloucester Citizen* reported the event in these words: '....The building is erected in a

Churchdown Methodist Church

picturesque orchard. The design is early Gothic and is carried out in Painswick stone and Bath stone dressing. A stone tower is erected over the entrance porch....'. It continued: 'After singing hymns and being led in prayer, Mr. F. Cullis, jun., on behalf of the Trustees, presented Mr. R. A. Lister' (a well-known Gloucester businessman) 'with a silver key with which to open the Church door. The company then entered the building when an encouraging and congratulatory address was delivered by Mr. Lister. The Rev. T. Rippon preached at a short dedicatory service.'

A reception held in the Barn, the previous meeting place, was followed by a large gathering in the new Church for the evening service, during which the Choir sang its first anthem: 'O Lord how manifold are Thy works.' It was recorded that the collections taken during the day amounted to over £86[7] which was then a considerable sum of money.

By July the laying of the foundation stone at St. Andrew's was able to take place, the ceremony being performed by Sir John Dorington, Bart., the local Member of Parliament, and watched by an impressive gathering of clergy, choir and splendidly-hatted parishioners.

William Swift was, of course, well to the fore (carrying the processional cross in fact) when the Dedication took place on 25th April 1904.[8] This form of service was held instead of the ceremony of Consecration, the Bishop of Gloucester being unwell and unable to attend, and the Archdeacon of Gloucester, The Ven. E. C. Scobell, officiated in his absence. The opening took place at 2.30 in the afternoon

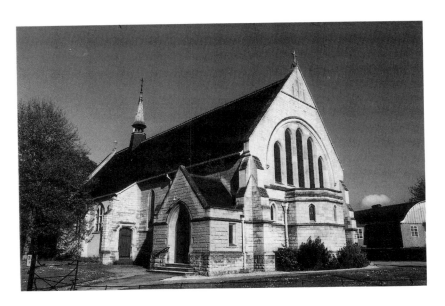

St. Andrew's Church viewed from the north-west.

and was followed by tea at the vicarage; evensong was celebrated at 7.30 and the singing was led by the combined choirs of Churchdown and Hucclecote - 'which made a splendid body of sound,' Swift tells us, as they gave spirited renderings of 'Onward Christian Soldiers' and 'Now thank we all our God.' He adds with some satisfaction that 'All passed most heartily and without a hitch,' and that the village was 'prettily decorated,' with the flag from the tower of the old church on the hill floating 'proudly...as if to remind all that though supplemented it was not superseded or disestablished.'[9]

At the first Patronal Service, on St. Andrew's Day, 1904, the address was given by the Dean of Bristol. He spoke of the 'infidelity' to the Faith that he had seen in France and of the 'rationalism' that was spreading in Germany, but said that he felt belief was still sound in Britain - to which, of course, he felt the building of a new church bore witness. Unfortunately this first part of the service seems to have taken so long that a number of those present had to leave without hearing the performance of 'sacred solos and quartets' which followed in order to catch their trains[10] - visitors from the towns, apparently, having joined the congregation for this occasion.

The actual Consecration by the Bishop of Gloucester took place a year later on the 29th November, 1905 at the 10.30 a.m. Communion service. In giving the Blessing the Bishop concluded with the words: '...grant that in this place, now set apart to Thy glory, Thy Holy Name may be worshipped in truth and purity to all generations....'

On St. Andrew's Day two years later the Building Fund Committee were able to report that all costs had by then been fully met and all accounts settled. The new church had been most generously furnished by many gifts from individuals and group donors. The schoolchildren, for instance, had collected sufficient money to provide the oak sanctuary rails and the parishioners had responded well to the suggestion that they should each donate a chair (at a cost of 3s. old currency).[11]

Both St. Andrew's and the Methodist Church are pleasantly proportioned buildings in an unostentatious, uncluttered and fairly traditional style. The two churches, so contemporary in many ways, have co-existed now for nearly a century and the relationship between the congregations continues to be most co-operative and friendly.

Social Life.

The construction and opening of two new places of worship were such important undertakings that these projects must have been subjects much discussed in the village during these first years of the century, but a happening that Swift calls a 'rowdy dow' must also have been a topic of considerable entertainment value.[12] This took place about nine o'clock in the evening of the 23rd April, 1901, and was in the form of a demonstration by a large body of parishioners against the co-habitation of a local woman with 'one, Harvey, who had left his wife and children for the purpose.' Effigies representing these two offenders were paraded through the village to the accompaniment of a 'rough band,' the members of which made a great deal of noise by banging on tin trays and similar 'instruments.' The effigies were then burnt with 'speechifying, yells and so on' by the morally-outraged villagers. Churchdown in the early 1900's was no permissive society and attitudes to social morals were certainly not, to use a modern expression, 'liberated'.

It was always desirable that social morality and decorum should be observed, especially if one was female. Swift was rather upset by a school entertainment where 'some big girls danced - and the scene was very vulgar owing to their short frocks;'[13] but he no doubt approved of the essay subjects set to the first class in 1905 for the boys wrote on 'Their Future Occupation' and the girls on 'A Christmas Pudding.' When, much later, in 1913, he reports that an act of arson had been committed by suffragettes in Cheltenham he makes no comment![14]

Women could be admitted to the newly-formed Churchdown Golf Club and were allowed all the privileges of membership except the right of voting. They, like prospective male members, had to be proposed and seconded in committee and their names, if approved, were then posted up in the club room for a fortnight; if no ballot was called for during this time, the applicant could be considered duly elected.[15]

The golf links on the hill provided an amenity which was enjoyed not only by, duly elected, local members but also by players from Cheltenham, Gloucester and elsewhere. In 1903 there were 113 members and three years later over 200. The links were two miles in circumference with nine holes: The Gate, The Spinney, Oystershell's Green, The Saddle, Spion Kop, Rabbit's Hill, The Crab, The Railway and Home - but where some of these were sited it is not now easy to discover. The 'Etiquette of Golf' had to be strictly observed and rules governed most of the eventualities and hazards likely to be encountered during play on a distinctly rural course such as that at Churchdown; a ball landing in a dung heap or on a molehill, for instance, could be dropped without penalty, and any dirt adhering to the ball when lying on the putting green could be removed. Swift, who does not seem to have been a member (he was a partial cripple) records that the covered way up to the Camp had to be cleared 'for the convenience of the golf players who (were) continually losing their balls in the bushes.'[16] During the First World War the course was closed and some of the area ploughed for food production.

Another venture begun early in the century, the Churchdown Flower and Horticultural Show, has become an annual feature. Swift, as usual, was actively involved in this and reports that at the first Show, which

Fishlock's Tea Gardens on Chosen Hill, a popular venue for local people and visitors from the towns.

was held in 'Mr. Harris's field, near Mrs. Nicholls' shop,' over one thousand people attended and he and George Davis took £23.15s.7d. at the gate in entrance money.[17]

Well patronised, too, particularly at weekends in the summer, were the places where refreshments could be obtained in the village and on the hill. There were two such venues on The Green, one at the Old School House and another at Green Farm, but refreshments were also supplied at Bakers' in Chapel Hay Lane, at The Pines, and at Brookfield in Brookfield Road. The tea gardens on the hill were those probably most frequented by the many visitors from the nearby towns and villages, especially when they had toiled all the way up Chosen. A local resident remembers walking from Hucclecote to have tea at Fishlock's Tea Gardens where 'Mrs. Fishlock served teas - lovely bread and butter, jam and cakes - at wooden tables with wooden seats in the grassy, tree-filled gardens.' 'After tea,' he adds, 'there were the hens to look at, and Mr. Fishlock's donkey (Sam).' (This donkey was used to carry provisions up from the village in panniers strapped to his back).[18]

Health Care.

In 1900 Dr. Reginald Moore took up practice in Churchdown and became the parish's first resident doctor. In 1904 he was joined in partnership

Chosen Bakery, Village Centre, from an old photograph taken after 1903.
The newly-built Methodist church can be seen mid-right and St.
Bartholomew's top centre.

with Dr. J. J. Foster (and in 1919 by Dr. H. S. Lowry). The two doctors drove motor cars at a time when these were still a source of local amazement and Swift thought it worth recording that when the Rev. H. E. Hodson, went to see his wife in Cheltenham he was 'conveyed in Dr. Moore's motor car.'[19] Cars were less reliable in those days than now and starting the engine could be particularly tricky, so if one of the doctors saw a flag run up as he approached his home he knew that he was called to visit another patient and should, therefore, not switch off the engine. With so few vehicles on the road in those days it is surprising that a tragic accident, caused by a car, should have happened in the village when, in 1907, a six-year-old local child was knocked down and killed. Swift records this, adding that the parents of the dead child were paid £30 by the driver (unnamed) as a 'payment of expenses.'[20]

It seems that, by 1903 at least, there was no dentist practising in the village for 'Mr. Fox' had to be fetched from Cheltenham to extract a tooth,[21] and it was not until 1908 that Churchdown acquired the services of its first district nurse.

Health care in the village was gradually improving but the epidemics of childhood, including such contagions as impetigo and ringworm, spread rapidly among the school population and greatly interrupted the children's education; an entry in the School Log Book in November, 1902, shows that there were seventy pupils absent owing to 'the prevalence of ringworm and mumps,' and two years earlier the school had actually been closed from the 20th February until the 19th of March because of the measles outbreak.[22]

Hygiene conditions still left much to be desired. In 1904 the school playground was described as being 'at times little better than a swamp', and lavatory accommodation, as revealed by an entry in the school records, was most inadequate - 'There are only four closets for nearly 125 children and these are immediately under the window of the classroom.'[23]

There was no mains water supply in the village at this time although Dr. Moore launched and maintained a dedicated campaign for its provision. In 1909 he proposed a local request should be made to Gloucester Rural District Council for a 'pure water supply,'[24] and in 1910 it was agreed, reluctantly, that this was necessary.[25] Dr. Moore pressed on, and the Parish Council Minutes state that, although the Rural District Council 'had no desire to incur outlay', there was 'practically no alternative course' as the requirements of the Public Health and Local Government Acts could mean that matters, if taken out of local hands, could be more expensive.[26] It was not until 1914 that the scheme was completed and the village connected by six-inch pipes to the twelve-inch main in Hucclecote Road, but many wells continued in use for some time after this and pumps still operated to provide a local supply. Sewage piping was in process of being gradually laid through the parish during this second decade of the century.

The population of Churchdown in the early 1900's was just under one thousand, income tax was proposed at 1/3d in the £1 and coal, in 1907, cost 1/3d a cwt. This was the year that William Swift retired as headmaster, a post which he had held for thirty-three years.. He left the schoolhouse and took up residence in one of the two cottages in The Piece which he had purchased, with adjoining land, for £475 in 1891.[27]

In July, 1909, he records in his Diary: 'A. Bleriot crossing the Straits of Dover in a monoplane,' and then on 24th March 1913, he writes, 'Saw aeroplane for first time'[28] - presumably flying over the local area. In 1911 King Edward VII died and the Coronation of King George V and Queen Mary was celebrated in the parish on 22nd June by the granting of a holiday. The usual loyal telegram was sent to Buckingham Palace and the customary bonfire built on Chosen Hill. Unfortunately the weather was very unco-operative, rain poured down at the time of the lighting of the fire and the planned firework display had to be postponed.[29]

By 1913 gas mains were being laid in the village and had reached Station Road, while, shortly afterwards, they were being installed down 'our Dirt Piece', as Swift calls the road in which he lived. (The Piece, was then, and for many years, unsurfaced and very muddy.) There was some considerable disgruntlement felt by gas users in the parish that they were to be charged at 2/6d for 1,000 units as against only 1/10d which was the cost in Gloucester; they were informed that this was because of the distance involved.[30]

CORONATION FESTIVITIES AT CHURCHDOWN, 1911

Coronation Bonfire on Chosen Hill, 1911.

Another cause of complaint was the condition in which roads were left after the trench-digging which had been necessary for the provision of all three main services. There was reluctance on the part of the Council to expend money on improving road surfaces until all the contracting work was finished - but by now this was 1914 and infinitely more serious matters were looming.

The First World War and its Effects.

The Editorial in the Parish Magazine for January, 1914, seems worth quoting in full for the insight it affords of the feeling then prevalent in the country. There was no awareness, of course, of the far worse horrors to come and yet there is a strange sense of foreboding: 'The past year has been an eventful one; and perhaps will be memorable for sad reasons, namely, for the number of disasters on land and sea, in the air, and in the mines; at least we hope that there will not be a more memorable one for these reasons. From other causes the year has been an anxious one. The country has been face to face with many complex problems, and we enter upon the year 1914 with a political situation anything but clear. The two contentious Bills, Home Rule for Ireland, and the Disestablishment and Disendowment of the Church in Wales, are still hanging in the balance. The labour unrest is as serious as ever. These and other difficult questions have to be settled, and no one seems to know quite how it is to be done. Meanwhile, party spirit is running high, and discontent is rife. Never probably was there greater need of true patriotism, never greater need of prayer to the great Father of Nations for guidance than now.'[31]

Comment on the local scene, however, ends on an optimistic 'high' for, although Churchdown had not been without its troubles as sickness had been prevalent, especially among the children, and all had 'experienced great discomfort from the drainage scheme', the writer expresses confidence that 'time and patience will doubtless put this right, and - if reports be true - we shall develop, before long, into a Garden City!'

On the 25th July Swift's Diary entry just says, rather laconically, 'Austria has declared war against Serbia,' and then, on the 5th August, 'Four territorials have left.'[32] Sadly, this fateful year of 1914 was also to be the last full year of his life; he died, aged 73, on 10th February, 1915.

By the 7th September over sixty Churchdown men had enlisted in the Forces. It will be remembered that there was no compulsory conscription at this time. In the autumn Swift seems to have been still well enough to visit London and record his impression of the city by night which was 'not at all pleasant, the lamps being obscured or not lit on account of the Zeppelin aeroplanes which might be mischievous.'

The first entry in the Parish Council Minutes, made in the year following the actual outbreak of hostilities surely, ranks as a classic understatement: 'The Great War broke out on the 4th August, 1914, and this has more or less interfered with everything.' The Minute continues: 'few things have been done which it was not necessary to carry out. Hence no Council Meetings have taken place since the 7th April, 1914.'[33] It is also recorded that Dr. Moore had offered his services to the Army and an expression of admiration of such patriotic action is added with the earnest trust that 'victory in this great war may soon bring him back to Churchdown.'

At this same sitting of the Council, a resolution was passed to the effect that: 'this Meeting of Parishioners of Churchdown in Annual Meeting assembled express their deep regret on the loss of their old and valued Parishioner, Mr. T. W. Swift, (sic.) ('W.T.' were the initials he preferred to use) and their sympathy with his sons on their bereavement' - a simple and dignified epitaph for the man who had given so much to the village, and who, as diarist, has brought it so delightfully to life.

'An Appreciation' written at considerable length and in far more emotive style, was published in *The Spectator* of April 24th, 1915.[34] In this William Swift has been given the pseudonym of 'Mr. Martin' and the village is named 'Thor.' ('Thorsdown or 'Thorsdune' once enjoyed some popularity as alternatives for 'Chosen'). 'He has left us,' the writer says, 'and we are the poorer...We have buried him on the hill-top, near the church whose every stone he knew and loved...A dozen khaki-clad men (ex-pupils of his), come over from their billets in the neighbouring

Churchdown Home Defence Corps in 1914.

town, followed behind the coffin. Thor has given most of its available sons to the King's service - a strong, hardy lot.. So the men of war followed the old man of peace....'

One of the last entries in his diary records the forming in 1915 of the Churchdown Home Defence Corps.[35] A war footing was now becoming established in the village, but, despite this, local matters still commanded the attention of the councillors when assembled in meeting and it was a matter of some considerable indignation that the course of a footpath had been altered without due consultation.

The first edition of the Parish Magazine to be published after the outbreak of war records that there was now one thought dominating the hearts and minds of all: 'War, terrible War!'[36] The struggle ahead is referred to as 'titanic' and one which would tax the resources of every person and every institution to the utmost. Every call that the country would make on its citizens would have to be responded to - and the help of God sought earnestly in prayer. By October it is reported that the parish had responded well to the call for men and that the total number serving was by then seventy, with more names soon to be added to the list.

The necessity for the country to be as self-sufficient as possible in food production was a pressing concern and a pamphlet to this effect, sternly admonitory in tone, was issued to all local councils, including Churchdown.[37] This clarion call declared: 'The first thing is to stir up the wills of all in the district who have anything to do with land, gardens or otherwise, to feel that it is as much their duty to produce food, as of our sailors or soldiers to fight for their country. That production this next year should not be a nicely calculated selfish question of profit and loss; but a matter to be taken in hand with courage, as well as wisdom, in his Majesty's service. Our ultimate success in the war depends on 'enduring to the end' and in this respect what every acre is doing is of interest to the nation.' The services of women, who were now needed as war-workers on the Home Front in many capacities, were often employed on the land in semi-rural areas such as Churchdown.

It was hoped that every garden and many allotments could be used for the rearing of a pig, and in 1916 it was recommended that a committee be set up to consider this suggestion and also to see that all existing pig sties in the parish should be made usable.[38] Unfortunately, the drainage from Elias Baker's pig sties (which he had patriotically put into use) was discharging towards the parish pump and creating a nuisance about which complaint had been lodged. This pump was badly in need of repair with water being wasted and running over the roadway; many of the roads and public amenities of the parish were by now suffering badly from neglect.

Most village activities were focused on the war effort. The school-children had joined the 'League of Young Patriots' who were engaged in fund-raising for the War Relief Fund and were employed in making articles 'for the comfort of our soldiers and sailors.' A concert in aid of the provision of a rifle range for the Volunteer Training Corps was held at the Chosen Assembly Rooms and the audience were entertained by Mr. Mott's Glee Party and by the Misses Whittaker (how one misses Swift's observations!) Girls 'of all classes' were invited to join the Girls' Friendly Society in which women and girls could band together 'for mutual help, sympathy and prayer.' The second stated object of the Society was: 'To encourage purity of life, dutifulness to parents, faith-fulness to employers, temperance and thrift.'[39]

In February, 1916, the first Military Service Act came into force and unmarried men between the ages of 18 and 41 were liable for call-up. There is little record in the parish archives up to this time of war casualties, except for the mention, with regret, of two local men having been wounded. A committee was formed in March, 1917, for the purpose of canvassing residents who were eligible for National Service and an appeal was addressed to all men between the ages of 41 and 60 to enrol - presumably for non-combative duties as, in a partly agricultural community as the parish still was, quite a number of men would be able to claim exemption on the grounds of being engaged in essential food production.[40]

A War Savings Society was started in the parish and sixty-nine people joined this immediately in response to the declared aim which was 'To develop in all the feeling of responsibility for the welfare and needs of their country, and to assist in the work of building up the country after the war by the combined efforts of all classes.'[41] Few could deny such an appeal!

The vicar, The Rev. J. D. D. Cooke, opened the Easter Vestry in 1916 with a prayer asking that the issues of the war should be decided according to righteousness, and that mercy should be given to all the wounded 'our own and of the enemy.' The matter of the insuring of the two churches against air raid damage was then discussed as enemy action from the air was now a possibility although not one of pressing concern in a rural area like Churchdown.[42] The newly-installed organ in St. Andrew's, however, had only narrowly escaped destruction during its construction at Wolverhampton when the factory was bombed in a Zeppelin raid.

As the years of conflict wore on the euphoric confidence of the early days gave way to realisation of the grim knowledge of what war really meant - the sodden quagmires of the trenches, the wholesale slaughter at the Somme, the tragically mounting casualty lists, and the realisation that there was nothing glamorously heroic about lice and trench fever and gangrene. Increasingly deaths had to be 'regretted' at Vestry Meetings, deaths of young men well-known in a small community like Churchdown and remembered as classmates, workfellows and members of local teams and organisations. There were severe losses at sea, enemy air raids were more frequent and more damaging, and the German offensive seemed unstoppable. Panic food-buying led to the introduction of rationing in 1918 and home-production had to become even more a priority; as a consequence there was demand for allotments in the parish and these were eventually acquired in the Parton Road area (more or less where they are today.) Meals were provided twice weekly for the schoolchildren by lady volunteers 'in order to save bread,' and forty-six pupils were fed at a cost of 2d. a head. The School Logbook, 5th July, 1917, also records that the headmaster, F. Phillips, was 'absent today for Guard Duty at Quedgely.' This was an ordnance depot and some Churchdown women worked there, probably travelling the nine to ten miles from Churchdown by train; there was a special platform at the Depot so that workers could alight from and board the train at this point.

At the Parish Council Meeting the chairman, J. H. Jones, emphasised the duty everyone had to grow and save at 'this time of national crisis' and to keep up cheerfulness and hopefulness under the great national stress.[43] At the Easter Vestry in 1918 the Vicar in his address described the British Army as 'fighting with their backs to the wall, ' and spoke of reinforcements being hurried across the Channel and of the Americans being urged to muster their armies to Europe. (On 6th April 1917, the U.S.A. had declared war on Germany). He concluded with the belief that, despite all the hardships and setbacks, 'the country remained steady.'

And then, that summer, the fortunes of war changed suddenly. 'It was not until July, under the sole leadership of Marshal Foch, that the tide turned, and thenceforth the constant successes of the British and Allies were unexampled in the world's history.' This statement, from a circularised publication called 'General Notes after the Cessation of the Great War, was read out at the Churchdown Parish Council Meeting on the 19th March, 1919; 'On the 11th November 1918, at 11 o'clock, an Armistice came into force and the long war seemed over as far as actual fighting was concerned. It was an immense relief, but the sudden removal of the pressure that had kept the nation to the urgent war tasks for over four years, could not but have some ill effects. The general anticipation was that war would end in 1919, so the cessation of hostilities in November, 1918, found us unprepared.'

On 28th June 1919, the peace treaty with Germany was signed at Versailles and the national celebrations began, the 6th July being appointed a Day of Thanksgiving. A 'Peace Bonfire' was lit on Chosen Hill and, no doubt, the village celebrated as it had done on other occasions of general rejoicing; but now the long process of rehabilitation and readjustment had to begin - and it was not to be easy.

Chapter 7

Between the Wars

The Aftermath of War

Three quarters of a million men from the United Kingdom had been killed in the war, and of the two hundred Churchdown men who had enlisted twenty-eight had died as a result of active service; but, also, there were among those who came home many adversely affected by their war experiences, physically or emotionally. Most ex-servicemen returned expecting the promised 'land fit for heroes' but they found a nation tired from the anxieties of four years of conflict and a people dispirited, debilitated (the Spanish 'flu epidemic had taken a severe toll) and curiously out of joint. Churchdown suffered from this malaise as much as did the country in general.

Among those who did return to the village was Dr. Moore and there was a sense of reflected glory and great pride in the Military Cross which had been awarded to him. He had been given this decoration for tending the wounded on the battlefield while under heavy shellfire and without seeking shelter for himself. At the Parish Council meeting in March, 1919, his devotion to duty and the cheerfulness with which he inspired others were spoken of with affection and great admiration.

He was, however, not quite so popular when he championed the cause of a disabled soldier who the doctor felt could be employed in the post of assistant overseer and rate collector for the parish.[1] 'Here we have a young man,' he said, 'who received a very severe wound in the right arm; his disability being such that he will never be able to earn his living by hard manual labour.' There was no seconder to the doctor's suggestion, and an appointment was made of a man who was already experienced and able to begin work immediately. Dr. Moore, although he upheld the Council's decision, still maintained that such work, and any tuition necessary, should be given to disabled ex-servicemen.

In the December Dr. Moore tendered his resignation as Chairman of the Parish Council[2] - was this because he felt at variance with them or was it for some private reason? A petition was addressed to him begging him to reconsider his decision, 'his wise leading and kind service,' being needed more than ever, it was felt, in 'these days of stress,' but he remained adamant.

There was a sense of great grievance felt by those returning servicemen who, expecting to be given smallholdings to farm in fulfilment of promises made to them when they enlisted, found that this was not the case. One man, who had applied six months previously for such an allotment of land, had already invested in livestock; this he had to sell because no firm decision had been made as to whether land would be available for him or not. One councillor addressed the meeting about what he considered the injustice of this situation and spoke in no uncertain terms: 'The present conditions,' he declared, ' are turning the most splendid loyalty to King and Country into Bolshevism.'[3] The Clerk was instructed to write to the Smallholdings Commission about the matter.

In March the urgent need for housing was raised at the council meeting.[4] Many marriages had taken place during the war years and the young couples were now wanting to set up home and raise their families. It was hoped that there would be a building programme (presumably of council housing for rented tenancy) and that each house should stand on sufficient land to form a small holding. There was also a strong expression of feeling, it seems, that the new homes should have 'Parlors' (sic.)

Among other matters discussed locally during this first year of peace was the anxiety felt by the parishioners regarding the presence of German prisoners (probably internees) on Chosen Hill.[5] It was urged, not surprisingly, that they should be kept under strict discipline and control and, as it seems they were engaged in quarrying and were detonating explosives, the alarm of the residents can be appreciated.

It was during 1919 that J. H. Jones (so often mentioned in the village annals) acquired for the price of £250 the lordship of the manor of Churchdown and the 'rights, royalties, privileges, fines, heriots, members, appurtenances and other emoluments... of Churchdown, Hucclecote, Norton and Shurdington'; these carried little financial benefit by this time being of little more than historical interest.[6]

In the years immediately following the end of the war, cities, towns and villages all over the country set themselves to create permanent memorials to their war dead and decisions had to be made as to what form these should take. The first suggestion put forward in Churchdown was that the Chapel Hay field should be acquired as a recreation ground. The cost of purchasing this would be £1,000 and so the Parish Council felt that all ratepayers should be circulated so that their views might be assessed. Accordingly 330 notices were sent out and 58 replies received; one respondent offered £100 towards the cost of the scheme and other offers varied from £25 to 2s. There were five refusals to make any contribution and, in all, it was felt there was no great enthusiasm for this idea. It was now generally felt that 'an old-fashioned village cross' would be the most popular choice and one strongly favoured by the bereaved relatives; the most suitable site was considered to be one fronting the road but in St. Andrew's churchyard. There was a little feeling about the choice of Anglican territory but a suggestion that the memorial should be put in the middle of the crossroads was over-ruled as impractical - as indeed it was! An amendment suggesting an obelisk, erected on neutral ground, received only two votes, one from the proposer and one from the seconder. A consensus of opinion having been finally reached, the designing and erection of the memorial now went ahead, but nearly two years were to pass before it was ready for dedication. The names of the war dead of the parish, however, had been commemorated already on an oak tablet placed in the old church on the hill.[7]

Most impressive of the several private memorials placed in the village churches is the splendid East Window in St. Andrew's. This was given by the families of Capt. Eric Cardew, M.C. and Capt. Ralph Streatfeild-James, D.S.O., young men who were both killed in action. The central light is a gracious representation of Christ calling the two disciples, Simon Peter and Andrew; the side lights are more militarist in theme and show two warrior saints, Michael and George, martially clad in impressive armour. At the heading of the window, below Christ in Majesty, is a rather nationalistic row of flags, Belgium, Britain, France and Serbia, tactfully arranged in alphabetical order.

The needs of the returning men for somewhere to meet socially led to the building of the Churchdown United Services Club (now called the Churchdown Club). There is a strange story concerning its inception. Dr. Moore was attending a delirious patient, a victim of malaria cont- racted during his war service, and in his fever the young man kept calling for a village club. On his recovery he remembered nothing of his disturbed ramblings but he told the doctor that he did indeed think there was a real need for such an amenity. The local response was immediately enthusiastic; the Churchdown Land Company, who had earlier donated the site for the two new churches, gave a plot of land, donations came in from organisations and individuals and funds were raised through an enterprising series of activities. The newly-formed British Legion contributed generously as they had also done to the War Memorial Scheme.[8]

The village Memorial was finally ready for unveiling on the 3rd April, 1921; the day was 'brilliantly fine' and there was a 'large concourse of people' according to *The Citizen* newspaper.[9]

In his address at the memorial the Vicar, the Rev. J. J. D. Cooke, spoke of matters which for some time had been a cause of general concern: 'The danger of the foreign foe overrunning their homeland was past,' he said, 'but what had they at home? Unrest and strife were with them; things seemed to be turning out so differently from what they had hoped two years ago. It seemed as if they would never settle down again.' The

Present day view in Station Road by St. Andrew's Church with War Memorial
left centre.

root of the trouble, as he saw it, was a lack of goodwill among the populace who were all too 'inclined to stand out for their petty rights and privileges and forget the common weal.'

The Methodist Minister, the Rev. F. W. P. Hicks, echoed the same theme, urging more self-sacrifice and more devotion to the service of Christ and to the nation. He wanted every man, woman and child present to dedicate himself or herself to 'live for England' as the men they were remembering had 'died for England.'

Social Conditions

Employment, either the lack of it or the poor pay and conditions within it, was the major issue. In the same week as the memorial ceremony was held the coal miners were on strike. It was a matter of urgency that stocks of coal should be conserved for most households were dependent on coal for heating, and in some cases for cooking; coal was essential also for gas production and, of course for the running of the trains. No coal was to be delivered to any household where there were already 5cwts. or more in store. *The Citizen* described the situation as causing the greatest anxiety as the action of the mineworkers was likely to be highly infectious to other large industrial groups - a threat which did not, in fact, materialise. The rail workers called off a supporting strike and the miners, as a consequence, were finally forced to return to work on terms most unfavourable to them.[10] The problem of industrial unrest had certainly not been tackled with justice or compassion, and the basic underlying causes of resentment which had not been solved were to prove ongoing. As has been seen from the remarks made by the two ministers, Churchdown was certainly not immune to these problems.

The malaise of discontent and apathy was eating away at the heart of society in the parish as elsewhere and unemployment was as much a local concern in Churchdown as it was throughout the country. When the new allotments needed fencing it was suggested that this work could be given to some of the unemployed men[11] but the Minutes state that members of the Council 'undertook to attend to this themselves.' Does this mean they tackled the job personally, or that they employed the men who needed work? Even as late as 1933 the local unemployed were protesting that the Labour Exchange were sending men from Gloucester to carry out work in the village.[12]

There was much maintenance work badly needed in the parish. By the end of 1921 Sandfield Road was still not repaired, and the road up the hill, which had been in a bad state since 1902 and 'inconvenient for funerals' in 1911, was still, by 1923, in poor condition. (This matter was again the cause of a letter to the County Surveyor as late as 1932.)[13]

A local resident who recalls Churchdown as it was in his boyhood has written down his memories of the post-war years. In his account he mentions grass growing up the middle of Pirton Lane and the ditches full of 'revolting black mud which would bubble in the hot weather and stink till there was a good storm.' He had good cause to remember these foul ditches because, on one occasion, he fell into one and was unable to return to school until his clothes had been washed and dried as he did not possess a second set.

His account tells us of the road repairers, many of whom were unemployed ex-soldiers 'who had never used a pickaxe in their lives.' He describes the weather as being so very hot that the men took off their shirts, but by five o'clock in the afternoon they were, he says, 'red raw and their hands covered with blisters; they could get no dole unless they were prepared to accept such casual work as came along.

He writes, too, of the dozens of tramps who came up the lane with their billy-cans and encamped on spare land by the Sugar Loaf Bridge. Here, as this observant boy noticed, they had a fire so frequently that 'the ashes were never cold'. He also watched them searching the ivy and hedge-bottoms for snails which he believed they ate. These men were vagrants many of whom were psychological misfits with war-damaged minds and battle-scarred personalities which could no longer be bent to the conventions of society.

Village Life between the Wars

Up the local roads, too, came the itinerant vendors, the rag and bone men with their two-wheeled carts and the fishmonger in his pony trap 'with the flies queuing up to settle on the fish!' The baker, butcher and grocer called on households to collect orders and deliver goods, and the travelling hardware shop 'sold everything', including paraffin which was essential in many homes, while petrol (10½d-11d. a gallon) was delivered by horse and cart in two-gallon tins secured with a lead seal. Cows and sheep were driven to market on Saturday mornings and 'caused mayhem if anything was coming in the opposite direction' - to the delight, no doubt, of the watching children.

There was little traffic on the roads but this did not deter the writer of the memoirs and his sister from following the current craze for collecting car numbers (which they recorded in little books made from pages of old calendars sewn together.) They would sometimes see no more than six cars all day but they enjoyed sitting on the bank among the abundant wild flowers, 'red and white clover, 'hens and chickens,' cocksfoot, henbane and moon daisies,' - Churchdown was delightfully rural in those days. From his fund of memories he remembers Mr. Daniels who became the sexton and lived in the churchyard cottage . He says he will never forget this man describing his feelings when, having been home in the village on leave, he had to face returning to the battle front. "The sun was

A rural scene in Churchdown, about 1927 - haymaking at Upper Pirton Farm.

136

shining, the birds were singing and the blossoms were all out, and I had to return to that hell on earth. Please God, I said, let me come back and see and hear them again.' He did, and was fortunate enough to obtain employment as a gardener at the Vicarage, and also as sexton and bell-ringer.

Churchdown was a pleasant place in which to live, but in the 1920's and 30's there was much poverty in the area. In his autobiographical account the writer says that as a small child he was very puzzled to see the friends his mother was visiting drinking tea out of jam jars, the reason being that they possessed only one complete cup and this was given to his mother as she was the guest. His own family's standard of living was not quite so stark but the ancient thatched cottage in which they lived was extremely draughty, the water supply was pumped to the kitchen sink, clothes (and the Christmas puddings) were boiled in the copper and, as was still common, the lavatory was sited outside.[14] It was a tied cottage belonging to the farm where his father worked and 'one morning,' he records, his father came home 'put his arm round Mother and they sat crying in the chair; he'd had the sack.' This meant the family would have to leave the tied cottage and that they and all their furniture would be, as he says, 'put on the side of the road.' The situation was saved, however, by his father going 'cap in hand' to beg for his job back and succeeding in being reinstated.

This man earned £1.50 for a 55-hour week, with only a few hours off on Sunday, and in the haymaking season he would be up at 4 o'clock in the morning, get the horses ready to start mowing at daybreak, and then work on till ten at night. In 1930 he bought a chimney sweeping kit and the money he earned as a result (1s.6d for house chimneys and 1s. for those of bungalows) added about another pound to the household budget; this was a very welcome addition, but it meant his working late into the evenings after the day's toil on the farm was over. His son, when he was twelve, was able to earn a little extra money too by delivering the evening newspapers every night for 'the princely sum of fourpence'. Most cottagers grew fruit and vegetables in their gardens, many kept poultry and perhaps a pig or goat, and, if they worked on a farm, as this boy's father did, could obtain milk cheaply; this helped to ease their straitened circumstances.

Despite a very frugal way of life, and living conditions which were decidedly spartan, for this boy 'Life was good! We had no radio, no gramophone and T.V. was unheard of, but we were happy.' There was so much to be observed in the countryside around, the fields to roam in and the hill to explore; there was, too, the occasional treat such as, in his case, a family outing, when petrol could be afforded, in the motor cycle with sidecar which his father had bought in 1929.

The charm of rural life was, however, to some extent offset by the state of local sanitation. In 1921 it was still being urged that the village school should be connected to the main sewer and also a number of other properties in the village which were unconnected.[15] The living conditions at the small development by the Station known as 'The Grotto' were decidedly squalid; in fact, in 1934 this was designated a slum area and the cottages were ordered to be pulled down and the occupants rehoused. That old enemy the malodorous pond at the Hare and Hounds was still holding its own on the Council agenda but was about to be finally vanquished as there was now public demand for it to be filled in; it was believed that the offending stench was caused by seepage into the pond from the cesspit at the inn.

Churchdown was beginning to catch up with the amenities of modern life but it was still quite an event when, in 1924, Dr. Foster and others gathered in the United Services Club to hear the election results broadcast over the *radio*, for it was not until the next decade that a wireless set in the home became commonplace. In 1928 electricity came to the village but the progress of domestic connection was gradual and some residents preferred to keep their old, familiar methods of lighting for some time to come; many years were to pass before the parish roads were provided with street illumination. The Silver Jubilee of the reign of King George V and Queen Mary was marked by the building of the usual celebratory bonfire on the hill, but on this occasion it was lit by J. H. Jones from a switch in his study down in the village. 'Everyone thought it was marvellous,' our chronicler reports in his memoirs,' that he could flick a switch and start a fire.'

Another advantage enjoyed by the villagers in the 1920's was a local bus service. Early in the decade the blue buses of the Bristol Tramway Company began operating their service No.49 along the main road from Gloucester to Cheltenham; by the end of 1923 this was supplemented by the 49A service which ran up Parton Road, and, proceeding to Cheltenham via Up Hatherley, provided an hourly link through the village.[16] The single fare to Gloucester from The Old Elm in the centre of the parish was fivepence, and to Cheltenham sixpence, with children travelling at half-fare.

A timetable for the year 1933 shows three buses an hour leaving Worcester Street in Gloucester for Churchdown, and, in addition, the four buses a day which travelled to Bristol via Gloucester could be boarded by Churchdown passengers at a stop on the Gloucester to Cheltenham main road. It was not until 1950 that the alternate service up Pirton Lane was introduced. Churchdown and its hill now became even more popular with visitors from the two towns and more desirable still as a place of residence. The Parochial Church Council Minutes in 1926 contain this entry[17]: 'The Council recognises that the character of the Parish is quickly changing. With the modern conveniences of water, drainage, gas and motor transport, there has been a considerable increase in the population, and the increase is likely to be more rapid. Even today Churchdown is no longer a small country parish; this means that a great responsibility rests upon Church people during these times of change, the future happiness and welfare of the Parish to a large extent rests with them, and they pray that the present goodwill and fellowship will go on growing, that a hearty welcome will be given to the newcomers and that the new Churchdown will be even happier, and a more prosperous parish, than the old.'

Local inhabitants do seem, indeed, to have held the village in great affection. Winifred Mills, writing of her memories of life in Church-down in the 1920's and 1930's, says: 'I can't imagine a better place for a childhood than Churchdown as it was then. Like most villages at that time, it was an innocent place. Children could roam at will over fields, up trees, yes, and under railway embankments without any of the fears that would be felt for children nowadays...In those days literally everyone knew everyone. Boots passing down the road in the dark of a winter's morning were the railway gangers, and you heard these same boots in the small hours of a foggy night, on their way to put fog signals on the railway line.' Both the late residents whose memoirs have been quoted remember the great excitement when the ancient burials, already referred to, were discovered in the Chapel Hay field in 1924. Mrs. Mills describes the occasion as follows: 'One day a delicious rumour reached our excited ears, that they (the men working on the site behind the Club) had dug up a skeleton, and another and another. Naturally we were mad to see this thing, but the good men of the village judged that this was no fit sight for children, and firmly kept us off. All we could see, from a distance was a sort of pit with the skeletons sitting round, as though in friendly conversation. Experts, who came post-haste, decided that these were the victims of a visitation of the Plague, buried in a sort of mass grave. Before their decision, all sorts of interesting theories had been put forward.'[18] It is actually still an open question whether the remains, which were subsequently re-interred, are mediaeval or much earlier.

School treats and sports usually took place on Chosen Hill but, later, there were more ambitious outings such as when forty-three children, with forty-five adults and staff, travelled to Whipsnade Zoo by motor coach.[19] An occasion to be looked forward to was Empire Day when schoolchildren were given a half-holiday for the spirit of patriotism was fostered and flourished. At 11 a.m. the schoolchildren assembled in the playground, sang the National Anthem, and then marched past saluting the flag, the girls wearing home-made costumes in the patriotic colours and the boys sporting red, white and blue favours. In his memoirs the writer, previously mentioned, describes his sister and himself collecting buttonholes of wild flowers, red clover, blue cornflowers and white moon daisies. 'At that time (1935),' he writes, 'we reckoned this country owned or governed half the world; we were so proud of every bit of red on the map which belonged to us or was governed by us - we were so proud to be British.'

139

Both the writers who have given us the benefit of sharing their happy memories were well aware of the darker side of life in the village for there was evidence of poverty more severe than any we know of today. Some of the Badgeworth children were very poor and, on cold, wet mornings, having walked to school in Churchdown in inadequate footwear, their feet were soaked and chilblained. The teacher allowed them to sit round the blazing fire in the classroom grate to dry their boots and warm their feet. When blackberries were abundant these fruits formed the only filling of their lunchtime sandwiches.

Walking to school must have been particularly unpleasant in May, 1924, for this had been an exceptionally wet month with 6.02 inches of rain falling above the normal average, the local roads, consequently, being turned into 'torrent streams' and much damage done as a result.[20]

There was at this time no school in the lower Parton Road area and the children had to walk to school in the main village, which was a long trudge for the infants, as it was for the older pupils, too, when the weather was bad.

The village school was now classified as 'Junior Mixed' and, from 1931 onwards, the pupils over eleven years of age were able to continue their education either at Longlevens (to which school they were transported by bus) or to one of the town Grammar Schools. To gain admittance to the latter it was necessary to pass what was colloquially called 'the Scholarship,' or more correctly, 'the Special Place Examination.' Some pupils won places which were entirely free while others were awarded part fee assistance, and the funds of the Wyndowe Charity were drawn upon to help in some especially deserving cases.[21]

In 1925 the Chapel Hay field was acquired for the parish from the Churchdown Land Company for use as a public recreation ground, the very moderate sum of £100 being paid for the site. A children's play area was equipped and funded by private donations.[22] The Vicar was now able to write of his 'great satisfaction that Churchdown had this good open site in the centre of the village...for the benefit of Churchdown, just where it was most needed.' Recalling the antiquity of the site (and in view of the recent discoveries of ancient burials and of what was possibly a chapel) he described it as being 'a recreation ground where children can play and old folk sit and rest,' thus making it, 'what we believe it used to be, a Haven of rest for Chosen People.'[23]

Not everyone took quite such an idyllic view for, popular and attractive spot as it undoubtedly was (and still is), dedicated sportsmen lamented the unevenness of the ground. Their ambition was to have a really good playing field with level pitches and adequate facilities for sporting functions; and so began a long campaign for such an amenity.

In 1938 parish feeling on this subject ran so high that a public meeting was held which *The Citizen* reported under the headline 'Playing Field Storm.'[24] There were three hundred people present on this occasion and there were 'heated scenes' and so many frequent interruptions that, at times, it was difficult to hear the speakers. The proposition put before the meeting concerned the acquisition by the Parish Council of land in Parton Road for development as a playing field. The cost of buying this particular land, it was contended, would raise the rates from 11s.8d to 11s.10d and it was said that people were finding the former amount a burden, as indeed many were, these being very difficult times. Few subjects can be guaranteed to raise the ire of the inhabitants of any place more than the threat of an increase in local taxation. The headmaster, Mr. H. A. Lane, brought to the notice of the meeting the neglected state of the Chapel Hay field and spoke of its general unsuitability as a venue for serious sport (adding that he believed the trustees never met!) The meeting then pledged itself 'to provide playing fields for both sides of the parish', but this was, necessarily, going to be very much a long term project, involving, no doubt, vigorous and sustained fund-raising. However, like so many schemes in the late 1930's this, too, was doomed to be shelved because of the increasing gravity of the international situation.

Another matter which, four years earlier, had raised equally strong feeling was the question of street lighting. In his memoirs the writer makes the point that newcomers to the village, many of whom had been town-dwellers used to well-lit streets, were the prime movers in pressing the Council to provide lighting for the roads of Churchdown. The Council could only offer to supply eight lamps, and as there were nine miles of roadway these would be rather inadequate. It was finally agreed that a vote should be taken and the result was overwhelmingly against the scheme, but a notice pinned on a cart positioned outside the meeting hall, declaring in crude terms that the rates would be raised from 10s.6d. to £1, had no doubt influenced the decision. One affluent resident who wanted street lighting - and was very unpopular in consequence - found that 'some wag,' as the writer tells us, had put a candle in a jar and hung it on his gatepost!

This incident serves to indicate that, although class distinction was diminishing during these years between the wars, some division and conflict of interests still existed between the wealthier minority in the community and the less comfortably-circumstanced majority. On the whole, though, Churchdown was following the general pattern and becoming a much more egalitarian society, one reason for this being the multiplication of local clubs and organisations which were open to all who were of appropriate age and inclination. The local Girl Guides association began in 1925 and the Boy Scouts had been formed before the First War. In 1930 the 'Women's Pleasant Hour' was inaugurated and the Churchdown branch of the Women's Institute was founded in 1932.

There was need in the parish for a meeting hall in the main village and,

141

in 1926, the old Primitive Methodist Chapel at the corner of The Piece was rented for this purpose at £15 per annum, which meant that local associations now had a place in which to assemble.[25]

During these years the Parton/Pirton end of the parish was becoming more and more a community in its own right; a sub-post office which had been opened in a small general shop called the 'Black and White Stores' had been transferred to the Sandycroft Stores in 1931 (the small group of shops at Pirton Corner came a little later in the decade) and Sandycroft Social Club had been instituted to provide a meeting place where local functions could take place and clubs organise their activities; thus, step by step, this part of the parish was becoming increasingly self-sufficient, and at the end of the decade, in 1939, the Vicar, the Rev. T. H. Jupp, stated, 'there is no doubt that the new end of the parish is now substantially the larger.'

In the late 1930's the news circulated in the main village that the days of the Old Elm were now numbered. This was greeted with dismay by many local people for the ancient inn had been a popular meeting place for as long as could be remembered. It was learned that the brewers, Flowers, proposed to build a new inn farther back from the road because there was a plan at the time (the late 1930's) to re-route the Gloucester to Cheltenham highway through the village. In order to keep the continuity of the licence the old inn had to be maintained in use until the new one was completed - which it was in 1938. In his memoirs, the writer says,

The Bat and Ball Inn, completed in 1938.

142

'We always reckoned the day they pulled the Old Elm down that finished Churchdown.' It did not, of course, but perhaps the loss of this ancient hostelry, situated as it was in the very heart of the village, did emphasise the changing nature of the community.

The Local Churches

A matter of considerable concern for the parish during the post-war period was the discovery that extensive repair work was necessary to the fabric and footings of the old church on the hill. Perhaps St. Bartholomew's had been rather neglected during the years of war and their aftermath, maybe it had suffered from some lack of attention during the time that the new church was absorbing so much parish effort, but the trouble was thought to have resulted largely from the drying-out of the subsoil during the long hot summer of 1922.

On the 20th March, 1923, the report of the Diocesan Architects, Waller and Son, was studied at a Council meeting. The initial cost of the repair work was estimated to be £500 which was more than the parish could raise immediately, but in response to the crisis vigorous fund-raising began at once. Within a short while a substantial number of straight donations had been received and the Dean and Chapter of Gloucester had undertaken to cover the cost of the chancel repairs which were their responsibility. Collections were also made throughout the parish by an indefatigable and very determined band of church workers. The tender of Merrett and Son of Churchdown for £599.7.0d., which covered the whole project including the chancel repairs, was accepted and the minutes of the Parochial Church Council meeting record that 'it gave them all great pleasure to place the work in the hands of respected parishioners.'[26]

The renovation that had to be undertaken was formidable; the roof was in a particularly bad state, the stonework of the walls, windows and tower was in need of considerable attention, and the foundations at the east end of the chancel were also giving cause for concern. The ivy on the exterior of the tower had acquired such a stranglehold on the masonry, and had formed such a dense, thick growth that a falling stem was heavy enough to fracture the collar-bone of Thomas Merrett when he began stripping the plant away.[27]

The question of the advisability of holding services in St. Bartholomew's while the repair work was being carried out (and, in fact, during the winter months at all times) was discussed at a parish meeting at which the Bishop, The Rt. Rev. A. C. Headlam, was present - and the debate generated much heat. The Bishop himself toiled up the hill to assess the situation and his conclusions were expressed in a decidedly two-edged letter published, at his request, in the Parish Magazine at the end of 1923.

In this he is critical of the standard of upkeep and wonders how many of those so anxious that services should be fully maintained at St. Bartholomew's were regular worshippers there. 'Its appearance at present', he writes, 'is perhaps more picturesque than decent'. He ends on a practical note, urging that every effort should be made to have the road up to the church improved as this would make it possible 'for people to go up to the burial ground in a carriage,' and would also facilitate the transporting of the materials necessary for the repair work.

The Bishop stressed that he was not in favour of allowing St. Bartholomew's to be closed entirely during the winter months but he advised that the services should be 'more occasional' and that the emphasis should be on using the old church for special services rather than on a regular basis. The re-opening for worship took place on Sunday, 3rd May, 1925, and a special service was held to mark the occasion. The congregation were able to hear the new American organ (purchased for £42) which now replaced the old pipe organ. This had been installed in 1899 but the instrument had deteriorated by being affected by damp and was sold for the lowly sum of £22.

The Parochial Church Council minutes record the occasion of the re-opening in these words: 'The old church, so dear to Parishioners, is preserved not only as an historic relic of the past, but as a live Church, still the Parish church, where God is worshipped, and the sacraments are administered.'[28] (It is now no longer in sole enjoyment of the title 'The Parish Church,' the parish having become known as that of 'St. Andrew with St. Bartholomew'.) Unfortunately, despite the heroic efforts made to safeguard the ancient building for posterity, the structure is constantly under attack by the elements and by ground movement. Its maintenance is in consequence an ongoing concern for the parish but the Bishop would have been pleased if he could have foreseen how much dedicated care is given today by the Friends of St. Bartholomew's, and by the strength of the desire of so many associated with Churchdown to keep the old church open and in good order.

During an earlier visit the Bishop had become very aware that there was now a rapidly growing population at the main road end of the parish and that they had to come up to St. Andrew's or St. Bartholomew's if they wished to attend Holy Communion. He therefore advised that an 8 o'clock celebration of the Sacrament should be held at the Mission Room on one Sunday during every month. The parishioners in this area had appealed for such a concession at the end of 1922 when they stated their case by pointing out that there were now about sixty houses in this part of the parish which was 'daily becoming a unit more or less independent of Churchdown' as it had its own little shop and people were able to travel into town on the main road bus. These amenities now meant that the residents no longer had to go into the village centre for shopping. The seeds of a divided parish were slowly germinating - but the parting was not to come yet.

It was now generally accepted that there was the need to provide a more commodious place of worship, and one which would not be sited where the continuous noise of motor traffic was most disturbing during services. The Mission Room entrance, being on the main road was a source of anxiety to the Sunday School teachers concerned for the safety of their pupils, the room itself was far too small for their classes, the steep staircase was a deterrent to the old people, and the room was not a suitable place for gatherings during the week.'[29] In 1928, therefore, a fund was started towards fulfilling this aim.

While the congregation at the Parton Road end were making forward-looking plans, attendance at church services in the 'old' village were declining. The Methodist Church, in its 75th Anniversary booklet, records that one preacher remembers congregations of two or three at Sunday morning worship. There was, also, a considerable falling-off in attendance at the Anglican services and in 1924 the Vicar, the Rev. J. Cooke, in his report to the Bishop, stated that, to his belief, the causes were 'not due to agnosticism, but to carelessness and indifference,' and were a symptom of what he called 'the general unrest of the age and the craving for pleasure, amusements and recreation.' The devastating effects of war, as is so often the case, were persisting long after the actual fighting was over.

During the next year the saga of the church heating began and continued to dominate the Parochial Church Council meetings for some years to come. The basic problem was that the existing gas steam radiators were now old and needed to be replaced - and, of course, there was a shortage of money in the maintenance fund.[30] A scheme for the provision of an up-to-date hot water system of heating was approved for St. Andrew's but this could not be undertaken at the time because of the expense involved, the estimate of £350 being thought prohibitive. To make matters worse church finances were soon to be stretched to their limit by the additional outlay about to be incurred by the provision of extra burial space in St. Bartholomew's churchyard.[31] This was now a matter of some urgency owing to the increase in population (and, therefore, of future deaths). A local landowner, Joseph Champion, conveyed a quarter of an acre of his land on the hill for the extension of the graveyard but, even with this generous concession, the parish was faced with a bill for £150 for fencing and levelling. The total cost rose to £168.8.3 and this was mostly raised by voluntary subscription.

The 'constant complaints' at St. Andrew's about the heating were mollified by the acquisition in 1929 of two Tortoise stoves and a patent spring which was fixed to the main door 'to prevent as far as possible the inrush of cold air,' but, in 1927, St. Bartholomew's had to be closed for services during the winter months as the shortage of fuel made the cost of heating the old church too expensive.

In 1929 the Vicar was again speaking sternly about the neglect of giving which he described, in a memorable phrase, as showing a 'lean-ness of the soul.' This sounds a damning indictment but, in fact, many people were finding it genuinely difficult to make ends meet. This was the year of the great financial disaster known as the 'Wall Street Crash' when the collapse of the American Stock Market sent the whole world into deep recession; no place escaped the effects of this economic earthquake for the loss of trade and the industrial decline led, inevitably, to greater unemployment. The Parochial Council minutes two years later contain this entry: 'The year under review (1931), although so critical to the country, had no outstanding event to mark it as memorable in the parish. Of course, all have felt the effects of the 'hard times' and the P.C.C. have had difficulty in meeting the ordinary recurring charges.' In 1933 it was found necessary to use the Christmas Day offertory (which for the past thirty years had always been donated to the Waifs and Strays Society) as a supplement to church funds in order to meet current expenses. One can sympathise with the Vicar's 'cri de coeur' that 'the constant anxiety about money is disheartening.'

From about 1932 onwards membership of the Methodist Church showed steady increase but the financial position continued to cause concern. (One Sunday morning collection in 1933 amounted to just one shilling). The next year, however, it was seen that an extension to the schoolroom and improved kitchen and toilet facilities would be needed and, encouraged by an initial donation of £100 and by financially rewarding social events (there were twenty entrants in the Baby Competition but the name of the brave judge is not recorded) a Building Fund was started. Four years later the extensions, which cost £680, were opened with 120 present at the ceremony.

Another enterprising venture undertaken in these difficult years was the St. Bartholomew's Bell Appeal launched in 1933. At first the cost of repairing the bells (only one of which could then be safely rung) seemed beyond the means of the parish but, in the words of The Citizen': 'as a result of splendid co-operative effort enough money was given by parishioners to have the necessary repairs executed.'[32] A re-dedication of the old bells and the blessing of the new treble, given by the Misses Auden, relatives of the poet, in memory of their mother, took place in October, 1933, the Assistant Bishop of Gloucester officiating.[33]

Although not everyone in the parish enjoyed hearing long sessions of ringing practice, most local folk were fond of the bells which had been part of Churchdown life for centuries, summoning worshippers to service, proclaiming a celebration, or tolling for the passing of a parishioner; it was, also, the long-established village custom to muffle the bells for the ringing out of the Old Year and to remove the muffs for a joyful welcoming of the New Year. With the repairs carried out, and with the addition of the new treble, it now became possible to ring a full peal

146

on six bells, this being achieved in April two years later when 5,040 changes were successfully rung.

The bells of St. Bartholomew's, according to a spokesman for the restorers, Gillett and Johnston of Croydon, were, 'considered as a peal,' to be 'above the average,' and, on the afternoon of the Dedication, ringers from local churches, and from a church as far afield as Birmingham, gave demonstrations on Churchdown's bells of the different methods of ringing.

By 1933 the people of the community at the lower end of the village were bringing to fruition at last their plans for a new church; a freehold site had been procured at the lower end of Parton Lane (now Parton Road) and the first sod was cut on 3rd July, 1933.[34] The simple hall-type building was planned to accommodate about 200 people, and was so designed that the worship area could be screened off when social functions were held in the main section. The Bishop of Gloucester, when he dedicated the Mission Room as it was popularly called, on the 12th October, 1933, spoke of the growth of suburban development, which was such a feature of the decade, and of the need for there to be centres of religion in these areas; this, he said, the Mission Room would provide but he stressed that it was not to be looked upon as taking the place of the old Parish Church or of St. Andrew's which still remained the central places of worship.

Two years later the Mission Room was equipped and paid for, donations having come from far afield as well as from local and diocesan sources. The Vicar of Churchdown, the Rev. J. Cooke, called the generosity and enthusiasm of the residents who had equipped the building and undertaken, voluntarily, many of the tasks that had been needed to complete the project, 'an outstanding feature.'[35]

It soon became apparent, however, that the Cheltenham Road neighbourhood was going to expand very rapidly and that even greater facilities would be needed to meet the requirements, social and religious, of this part of the parish. The appointment of a curate was a partial solution but it was obvious by 1939 that a still bigger place of worship would be required in the foreseeable future. The outbreak of war meant such a scheme had to be shelved.

Business and Industry

The difficulty of obtaining employment in the 1920's and 1930's is described by the memoirs writer. In 1932 he was fourteen and ready (more than ready!) to leave school and go in search of work. 'There was no work anywhere,' he says, 'I trudged everywhere but couldn't get a job.' At last he found employment at Hitch's Poultry Farm in Brookfield Road for a remuneration of ten shillings a week (50p.) He began his duties at 8 o'clock in the morning and continued till 5 p.m., but he then stayed on for another hour to shut all the poultry houses. He worked on Saturdays and Sundays as well and was allowed one free half day a week. 'It was a bitter cold job in winter,' he remembers, 'for it was right open to the north wind which whistled through the wire fences.' He often suffered all day from wet feet and legs when the icy water in the buckets was accidentally spilled into his Wellington boots, 'but,' he adds, 'in summer it was grand.'

Hitch's was a flourishing business then, with an average stock of 1,500 laying hens and 6,000 to 8,000 young chicks, the surplus pullets being prepared for market and sent to Smithfield on the overnight train. The writer worked there for over five years, by which time his wages had risen to £1.10s., but he was by then the sole employee and when he had the offer of other work locally at a wage of £1.15s. he decided to leave. With this new income he was now earning fifteen pence more a week than his father who had given thirty years' service at Seeley's farm. The poultry farm closed in 1939-40 and the site, which at first was used as grazing ground, was sold later for building development.

Another enterprise which had been in Churchdown since 1928 was Hurran's Nurseries, the premises of which are on the south side of the main Gloucester to Cheltenham road. Alfred Hurran, the founder of the business, began working at a plant nursery in Lower Edmonton when he left school at the age of thirteen, and by twenty-five he had become foreman at another nursery in Essex. In 1909, with a capital of just ten pounds, he and his wife rented a corner site in Derby Road, Gloucester and, later, a stall in Gloucester market. After his war service, he and his sons developed their horticultural business on a more extensive scale and embarked on a new venture by buying over the property of what had been the Churchdown Fruit and Vegetable Company. Here they established the present flourishing and very well-known Garden Centre at Cheltenham Road East.[36]

In 1931 two local businessmen saw the possibilities of establishing an airfield in the locality and, so, they bought land on the north side of the main Gloucester to Cheltenham road and opened it up for use by the newly-formed Cotswold Aero Club. The advantages that a nearby airport would bring to Gloucester and Cheltenham were realised by both councils and they took the decision, despite some local opposition, to open a municipal aerodrome. Accordingly, in 1934, after receiving a favourable report from Sir Alan Cobham, the famous aviator, 160 acres were acquired on the south side of the same road and, in 1936, the aerodrome was granted its first operating licence - despite having then only a grass strip, a windsock and a small hangar.[37]

The Flying Club, an early member of which was the pioneer woman pilot Amy Johnson, now moved across the road to the new ground and here the training of pilots for the recently-formed Civil Air Guard Scheme also took place.

It was in 1937 that the Rotol Company, needing a testing ground, moved to Staverton and built a factory on the site of the old airfield (at a cost of £97,000) for the manufacture of airscrews and aircraft components. Churchdown now had a growing industrial giant on its boundary.

It had another also a little farther away when, in the late 1920's, the Gloster Aircraft Company moved to a site in Brockworth where it set up a light-aircraft manufacturing industry and, by 1937, was making the Gloster Gladiator for the R.A.F. Both these big industrial concerns brought employment to the locality, with quite a large percentage of the workforce coming from Gloucester, Cheltenham or farther afield, and many of these employees saw Churchdown as a desirable place in which to live. In consequence, new housing estates were built along the main road and at the lower ends of Pirton and Parton Lanes. It is recorded that, at the induction of the Rev. T. Jupp as Vicar of Churchdown in 1935, the Bishop was very critical of this development as being 'in the most inconvenient place from the point of view of social organization... without any regard to the parish's civic or corporate life...just dumped down on the roadside.'[38]

Local Shops

Despite the many changes that had taken place since the war shopkeeping in the village was much as it had been for many years; businesses were

Butcher's Shop in Chapel Hay Lane (premises now demolished).

Interior of the Forge, Church Road, about 1910, with F. J. Merrett the blacksmith.

privately owned and customers were greeted by name (unless they were 'strangers' when a certain polite wariness was in order.) William Colville and Son now kept the grocery store at the corner of Chapel Hay and bread was baked on the premises. Western's butchery business, established since 1925, still operated from the shop at the side of the old farmhouse called 'Chapel Hay', and slaughtering continued to be carried out in a small abattoir at the rear. Cove the blacksmith operated the forge at the corner of what is now 'Blacksmith Lane' and the premises of Merrett's, the builders and undertakers, were situated behind this smithy; nearby was Scotford's boot repair shop quaintly named 'Ye Chosen Boot Depot.' Garness's greengrocery shop was in Church Road, near the new Bat and Ball Inn, and Wood and Company's decorating business was on the corner of The Piece; Boakes' Garage, Green's, the coal merchant, and Potter's grocery store completed the services offered in the village.[39] A Churchdown resident, remembering the village in 1937, recalls milk being brought round in churns and a daily delivery of bread to customers' homes. These were the halcyon days of orders being collected by bicycle-riding errand boys who, having done the rounds of all the houses, would return later with the required goods or arrange for the delivery of the orders if they were too large to be accommodated in the bicycle basket.

The customer always received personal attention when making her purchases in the local shop, and while the leisurely process of weighing, cutting and packaging the goods was taking place there was opportunity for a pleasant exchange of news and views.

Careful budgeting and frugal habits were very necessary for most people as these were still times of low employment and small wage packets, but the people of Churchdown did not suffer the extreme economic distress of their near neighbours in the Forest of Dean or of those who lived in the Welsh mining communities, and neither did they experience the stark poverty of northern towns such as Jarrow where unemployment was so disastrous.

Royal Events

Whether or not these distressing topics were much discussed in the parish, the royal events of 1936 undoubtedly were. When, in January, King George V died and the Prince of Wales acceded to the throne as Edward VIII, the schoolchildren were able to listen to his proclamation as king, a wireless loud speaker having been installed at the school for the purpose.[40] By the end of the same year the new king had abdicated, his brother, the Duke of York, had succeeded him as King George VI and the Coronation had been arranged for the 12th May in the following year. The Coronation celebrations in Churchdown followed what, by now, was a time-honoured pattern. The day began at 9 a.m. with a short peal of bells rung before the 'United Coronation Service' which took place in St. Andrew's Church three-quarters of an hour later, and this was followed by a tree-planting ceremony in the Chapel Hay recreation ground. Sports began at 1 p.m. with a programme of the usual competitive races for which small monetary prizes could be won - small, that is, by today's standards, for the 7s.6d. awarded for winning the Cross Country Handicap was then quite a munificent sum, and a half-a- crown for coming first in the Girls' Needle-threading Event was largesse indeed. Ticket holders could partake of an Open Buffet in Western's Field and then they, with others, made their way to the United Services' Club to hear a relay of the King's speech. All sang 'Auld Lang Syne' and dispersed until it was time to make their way up the hill to gather round the bonfire and marvel at the illuminations. The day's celebrations were concluded by everyone singing 'God Save the King,' rendered, perhaps, on this occasion with special fervour.

The Building of the Reservoirs on Chosen Hill

The following year a major construction project took place when work began on the building of the first two reservoirs. The movement of heavy loads from the bottom of the hill to the top must have presented considerable difficulty, especially as at first the road was not surfaced beyond the entrance to the pine plantation and this section would soon have become deeply rutted with such excessive usage. It seems that a 'broad new road' which 'ran relentlessly up to the hilltop' was made especially to cater for the movement of all the construction traffic but, as no evidence of this now remains, it can have provided only temporary access.[41] The vast excavation work no doubt effectively destroyed any archaeological evidence which may have still survived after centuries of indiscriminate marl digging and stone quarrying.

When completed the reservoirs - vast, concrete-lined cisterns of still, dark water presenting a chilling sight - were covered with the symmetrical turf mounds we see today and on these the two small, Cotswold-type, stone huts were built to house the dials and gauges which register the consumption of water in the Gloucester/Cheltenham area. It is quite an alarming experience to watch these instruments whirling round at speed and thus demonstrating how enormous is the demand for water.

War Clouds Gather Again

There were local people who were upset to see 'their' hill so under attack and who deplored what they considered to be a marring of the landscape, but soon there was to be something far more disturbing to be concerned about - the threat posed by Hitler's aggressive intentions in Europe. By September it became apparent that the unthinkable, a second world war, was a very real possibility. Four years earlier the Rev. J. Cooke had written in the Parish Magazine,[42] 'We pledge ourselves again to work for peace. Today many people seem to be despondent about it - 'the next war' is spoken of - we are inclined to pin our faith on disarmament as the way to peace...or rely on the League of Nations...or we hope that a multiplicity of international conferences will bring the desired security of peace....men and women can have peace if they will.' The vicar was writing with foresight but most of his parishioners had probably then put such disquieting thoughts to the back of their minds; this they could now do no longer.

At the beginning of September steps for the protection of the civilian population in the event of war were put into action and local people were encouraged to take part in spare time civil defence training, classes being held in the village school and in the old tractor house in Parton Lane. Special emergency fire measures were advocated for rural areas as it was felt that, during air raids, the town fire services would be too fully engaged in their own locality to be able to respond to calls from outlying districts.[43] Sketches were published in the local newspaper showing how to construct garden trenches to serve as air raid shelters, and the supply and fitting of gas masks for the whole civilian population was begun. (For those who experienced this the sickening smell of the rubber masks will never be forgotten.) Arrangements were made in the parish for the reception of children who would be evacuated from Birmingham, and for the continuing of their education in the local school which they would share with the village children.

Despite reporting these grim preparations, *The Citizen* gave more than equal coverage to local events and continued to supply articles concerning the 'normal' interests and activities of its readers; no mere threat of total war could drive the sports news off the pages and there was still comforting dalliance with such reassuring topics as the planting of bowls with bulbs for Christmas.

When, however, reports came through of the Prime Minister's diplomatic missions to Germany as he tried to stave off the disaster of war, these always topped the headlines. *The Citizen* on 15th September, 1938, reported them in these words: 'Carrying with him the good wishes of his countrymen, the Prime Minister, Mr. Neville Chamberlain, set out by air from Heston on his dramatic mission to Herr Hitler, a mission arranged on the Premier's own initiative and cordially reciprocated by the Führer.'

Five days later the paper strikes a hopeful note: 'There are still storm clouds overhead and certain horizons are heavily banked with the menace of wrath. But upon the whole it may be said that the atmosphere is clearing, and there is a growing hope, not to say a conviction, that genial currents will prevail, this terrible depression pass away, and Europe and the World once again bask in the sunshine. If we can now witness the dispersal of the war clouds.....then we may say, indeed, that Mr.Chamberlain's peace mission to the German Chancellor has been as great and as dramatic a stroke as ever was accredited to a statesman.'

By the 21st September it was believed that the danger of war had been averted, and on the 30th the newspaper hailed the 'Premier's Triumph' in achieving at Munich 'A new No-war Pact with Germany', and, within another two days, it was seeing Hitler as the 'Partner of Britain.'

What was the reaction among the general populace to this 'Peace in Our Time' message? In Churchdown we can assume it was much as it was elsewhere. There were some who expressed disgust at what they saw as appeasement, others regarded it as a breathing space in which to make further preparations, but the vast majority felt an enormous sense of relief that the predicted horrors of total war had been averted; life could now go on - and the optimism of the bulb-planting would seem to have been justified!

People, in the village as elsewhere, now tried to resume ordinary life and to make plans for the future as if there was no menacing dark cloud hanging over it; to some extent they had come to terms with the sight of air raid trenches in the town parks and with the gas masks lurking in their cupboards. Then, on 23rd August 1939, the news was released that Britain would support Poland if that country were to be attacked by the German army. It was expected that this would deter Hitler from invasion but, on the 31st August, he ordered the advance, and at dawn next day his troops crossed the frontier of Poland.

At home, on this same day, the 1st September, a general blackout was imposed throughout Britain and the villagers, in company with all their compatriots, made frantic efforts to screen their windows with black paper or blankets or whatever came to hand. (As soon as they could be made proper blackout curtains usually replaced these temporary measures).

On the morning of 3rd September everyone who had access to a wireless set gathered around it, prepared with a kind of grim acceptance and determined stoicism which had been less evident the year before, to hear the Prime Minister address the nation.

At 11 a.m. he declared that Britain was at war with Germany.

Chapter 8

Churchdown during the Second World War

The Citizen on 4th September, 1939, quotes, with sad but resigned acceptance, the Prime Minister's words on the inevitability of war against Germany: 'His (Hitler's) action shows convincingly that there is now no chance to expect this man will ever give up his practice of using force to gain his will.' It then goes on to report the Anglo-French declaration issued by the Foreign Office to the effect that the governments of both countries 'solemnly and publicly affirm their intention...to conduct hostilities with a firm desire to spare the civilian population, and to preserve in every way possible, those monuments of human achievement which are treasured in all civilised countries.'

Printed on the same pages as these serious announcements are items of local news (concern over the cancellation of sports fixtures is featured on the front page of the issue on 4th September, 1939); this was a deliberate policy to sustain public morale by emphasising, as much as possible, that despite the tragedy of war, normal life continued...and to a surprising extent it did.

Of course as time went on most families had members called up for active service, and many civilians took part in local defence activities or contributed to the war effort in whatever way was possible, but the devastating air attacks which had been anticipated did not at first take place and when they did, in a semi-rural area like Churchdown (sandwiched though it was between two high-target industries, Rotol and Gloster Aircraft) bombing raids were sporadic and, fortunately, limited in effect.

In all about 100 bombs fell in the area but some failed to explode. The most serious incident within the parish was the bombing of Hurran's Nurseries; it is thought the raider mistook the glasshouses for buildings of the Rotol factory. Unfortunately, an employee was killed and extensive damage was done but the premises were rebuilt just as soon as the necessary permits could be obtained. A bomb which fell in a field below the station caused considerable local inconvenience because it damaged the water main, resulting in five water-less days for the village and a return to usefulness of the village pump. Bombs fell in King's Fields and Hucclecote Lane and sixty small explosives rained down in Brockworth Lane near Pressmead Farm. A stick of bombs fell in Parton Road and one of the residents remembers that 'when the lights went out and water and gas disappeared for a moment we thought ourselves in the thick of it!'[1] On the whole, though, despite structural damage and some loss of livestock, the village came through fairly lightly. In 1940 three airmen were killed at Staverton barrage balloon post and the airfield suffered disruption; there was serious loss of life at Brockworth when, on the 4th April, 1942, ten men, five women and three children were killed and two hundred injured. Some of the raids were made by single, low-flying aircraft and one local lady, renowned as something of a crack shot, fired off her gun at the German plane which was clearly visible in the moonlight; this, no doubt, relieved her feelings even if the enemy pilot was quite unaware that he was under determined attack from below!

The two big neighbouring towns were subjected to more devastating bombardment, Cheltenham suffering from two particularly severe attacks. On 11th December, 1940, over 100 high explosives and 2,000 incendiaries were dropped, 23 people being killed and 600 houses damaged. Two years later, on 27th July, Cheltenham's second worst raid resulted in the death of eleven people.[2]

One Churchdown resident has vivid memories of the big raid on Coventry and remembers 'the lurid colours in the sky as the city was being bombed.' She also recalls how the house in which she was living (Chosen Hill Farm) shook as the very powerful anti-aircraft guns which were sited near Birdlip were fired. (There was a nearer but smaller gun-site by the Cheltenham/Gloucester main road.) Nearly everyone soon learned to distinguish the sound of British bombers passing overhead from the ominous deep throb of the enemy planes.

The barrage balloons were very much part of the wartime scene in Churchdown. There were two balloon stations along Hucclecote Lane and another near Brockworth Court and, for those living at the nearby Chosen Hill Farm the clattering sound of the winches as the balloons were raised gave early warning of an imminent raid and that it was time to take shelter in the basement. In her *Village History*, Hermione Oram writes of the barrage balloons as 'one of the strange beauties of the war.'[3] 'Suddenly,' she says, 'the swinging silver monsters would appear, rising lazily and floating over the green hill. Just as suddenly all the children disappeared from the village streets as they were called in by anxious mothers.'

When the siren sounded people took shelter in their cellars, sought refuge in the cupboard under the stairs or even beneath the dining-room table. Some householders made a garden shelter by digging a trench and lining and roofing it; comforts in the way of blankets, camp beds, lamps and candles were installed and, when the warning was given, all trooped down carrying Thermos flasks and light refreshments and possibly wearing over their pyjamas, if it was night-time, those sartorial inventions of wartime, 'siren suits', all-in-one garments similar to modern track suits. *The Citizen* on 6th September, 1939, carried an advertisement for 'A.R.P. Shelters' which could be built in the purchaser's garden within three days at a cost of £12. These were of solid construction and had the advantage of two exits in case one became blocked, but probably few Churchdown people invested in them. In 1940 the Parish Council passed a resolution stating that public shelters were needed in the parish[4] and that some, at least ten, brick surface shelters *were* built, probably at the lower end of the village, is instanced by a note that, towards the end of the war, when these were demolished, it was estimated that 50,000 bricks had been used in their construction and that the erecting and taken down of such shelters had given employment to many.[5]

Many householders protected their window glass with netting, paper film or adhesive strips; the School Log Book has an entry that the windows were coated with 'Cerrux' as a protection from the danger of flying glass.[6] On receiving warning that a raid was imminent the staff and pupils were instructed to proceed to whichever neighbouring house possessing a cellar they had been directed. This arrangement caused some anxiety to mothers who had more than one child attending the school as brothers and sisters could thus be separated from one another while sheltering in different buildings.[7]

If any child arrived at school without his or her gas mask that pupil was promptly sent home to collect it. The carrying of one's gas mask was obligatory and, at first, everyone could be seen toting the ubiquitous brown cardboard box. Later these were concealed in cases of varying degrees of luxury and became almost a fashion accessory. 'Bride carries gas mask (encased in white satin perhaps?) reported *The Citizen* in 1939.

Gas attack was one of the threats most greatly feared in the early years of the war and householders were advised to make a gas-proof room in their homes by having materials ready to seal all openings and apertures. Citizens could undergo Anti-Gas training and become qualified to act as members of the public Air Raid Precautions (A.R.P.) service.

Much indignation was registered at the Parish Council meeting in October, 1939,[8] when 'it was learned with utmost astonishment that our Air Raid Wardens have been compelled to close down their post owing to the refusal of the A.R.P. authority to sanction any expenditure whatever on its maintenance... A fully-manned post ensures us prompt action in any grave emergency which may be suddenly sprung upon us.' The meeting begged the rescinding of this decision and, presumably, obtained their objective for there is no evidence that Churchdown suffered from lack of proper A.R.P. provision.

One branch of the service was the supervision of fire-fighting management and the training of local people in dealing with incendiary devices. Fire-watching rotas were established in every town and village; one of Churchdown's look-out posts was sited high on the roof of the Chosen Hotel from where a good view of the nearby railway line could be maintained. Businessmen and women who lived in the village but worked in one of the towns returned to their places of employment on those nights when they were on duty in order to take their turn at guarding the premises; such nightly rendezvous, solaced by such refreshments as food rationing would allow, became part of the wartime social scene. Many local people, especially those housewives who were unable by reason of family commitments to undertake full-scale civil defence work, became very handy at using the stirrup pump and sand bucket to extinguish incendiaries.

Most spectacular, and most detested, of all the parish air raid precaution schemes was the smoke screen. This was intended to protect the Rotol factory and its environs from air attack by enveloping the area in a cloud of dense black smog. The smoke pots were filled with a mixture of crude oil and paraffin and this fearsome compound was ignited when a bombing attack seemed imminent. A coded message from the War Office in Whitehall gave the factory authorities the signal to activate the screen but the success or otherwise of the operation was dependent largely on the prevailing wind direction. The dreaded fire pots were sited, not only around the factory, but also along the roads of the village and, when not in action, were stored in the little building (now a greengrocer's shop) in the forecourt of the Old House at Home in Brookfield Road. Soldiers from the Pioneer Corps stationed for a while at Woodfield Farm, operated the devices - and dowsed the fire when one, inadvertently, burst into flames. Then, as Hermione Oram so graphically describes; 'from all sides blackened Pioneers would gallop, with magnificent oaths, to put it out.' Once in action the smoke screen could last for several hours and then, again in her words, 'Larders stank, clothes reeked, babies' nostrils in the morning were two minute areas of jet; but homes and factories stood.'[9]

No bombs actually fell on the factory which was, of course, now fully engaged on the vital war work of making aircraft parts and equipment. A special team of aircraft spotters were always on duty on the roof so that they could give warning to the employees when it seemed absolutely necessary to stop work and proceed to the shelters. Lord Beaverbrook, the Minister of Aircraft Production, sent a special message to the company on 5th July, 1940, saying, 'Will you please tell your staff that I will welcome and rejoice in a decision by them to stay at their posts if the sirens sound and until the danger of bombing attacks is imminent. Such a demonstration of courage and devotion would in large measure defeat the enemy's purpose of damaging our production for defence.'

By now there were many local people in the Rotol workforce and, on the 14th September, 1939, *The Citizen* carried notice of a request from Rotol management for Churchdown home-owners to offer accommodation to the additional employees whom the factory needed. Later, emergency housing was erected on the site of what is now Parton Manor Infants' School to accommodate these incomers and their families - and so again the population of the village took on a rapid spurt of growth. In 1942 an overflow class for infants had to be accommodated in St. John's Hall in Parton Lane and, a year later, a new school was opened nearby with an intake of 208 children, with the Headmaster of the Village School, Mr. H. A. Lane, remaining in charge.

During the early years of the war the number of children attending the village school was increased by the intake of evacuees, 162 extra pupils being taken on roll. By 1942, many of these children had returned to their homes in Birmingham.[10] Most of these boys and girls were from St. Anne's Roman Catholic School which was in an inner-city part of Birmingham so Churchdown must have seemed strange territory indeed to them. They arrived carrying their gasmasks and clutching a few necessary belongings in carrier bags or little cases; they had left their families, homes and everything familiar to them and, at first at least, it was uncertain when they would see them again. All must have felt bewildered, many were frightened and tearful, others, no doubt, put a brave face on things, and a happy few were perhaps actually enjoying the excitement of such a new experience. They were accompanied by their teachers and their headmistress, Miss Hammond, and were made to feel as welcome as possible by a reception committee the members of which provided the children with a meal on their arrival, and then took them to meet their hosts and hostesses in the homes to which they had been allocated. The organization was carefully planned, it had in fact been established well before the actual outbreak of hostilities,[11] but no amount of well-intentioned kindness could really assuage the pangs of homesickness.

Most of the evacuees had known only a very urban environment and they now found themselves in a semi-rural village; local people remember how the town youngsters filed timidly along the very edges of the Churchdown roads, missing, no doubt, the reassurance of solid pavements, whereas the village children disported themselves in the middle of the road until they were obliged to give way to an oncoming vehicle.

Many of the hosts and hostesses must have felt distinctly apprehensive about taking young strangers from a very different background into their homes and, in fact, an 'Appeals Tribunal' was set up to hear complaints and smooth away difficulties as much as possible but, in many cases, things worked out better than might have been expected. At the outbreak of war, when a devastating deluge of bombs was fearfully anticipated, the continuance of normal life was hardly hoped for and so, perhaps, people were prepared to accept inconvenience and disruption philosophically. There was, too, some shifting in the evacuee population for during the first months of what became called the 'phoney war', when there were no air raids, many parents took their children back home. A number returned later when the Blitz began.

The lessons for both the local pupils and the newcomers were arranged on a shared basis. Classes for the Churchdown children began at 8a.m. and finished at noon while the boys and girls of the evacuated school were taught from 12.15p.m. to 4.15p.m.[12] It became necessary, however, for 'overflow' classes to be held in the Methodist schoolroom and at the Chosen Hotel.

A small group of mothers and babies from London were billeted in the village for a while, and there were also 'private' evacuees who left the heavily-bombed areas and came to stay with relatives or friends in the parish, or took rented accommodation in the village while the air raids were most severe.

Churchdown was regarded as a reception area but, as has already been seen, it was actually in a very vulnerable position between the two high-target industries of Gloster Aircraft at Hucclecote and Rotol at Staverton. Gloster Aircraft were makers of the Gloster Gladiators, Hawker Typhoons and Gloster Meteors (probably the first jet aircraft in the world to go into regular production). Spitfire and Hurricane propellers were built at Rotol plus other components and auxiliaries. The airfield at Staverton, which borders Churchdown parish, was used by the Royal Air Force as a Navigational School and the Empire Training Squadron for Commonwealth and Polish pilots was also based there. Mid-air refuelling was also one of the techniques developed at Staverton during the war and Rotol were still using the airfield as a test ground.

Just 'down the road' at Innsworth there was now an R.A.F. camp and airmen and airwomen, in their blue uniforms, were a familiar sight around the village as Churchdown offered, perhaps, a little more opportunity for social life and off-camp conviviality than did the hamlet of Innsworth. In the words of a local resident: 'We really saw the war through the thousands of men who passed through Innsworth. The platforms of the station were grey with hundreds at a time, leaving on special trains.'[13] This writer goes on to recall the arrival one evening of a trainload of Polish servicemen straight from Europe after Dunkirk. 'They were filthy and exhausted and hungry, and finding a bread van near the station, they ate its entire contents, dry.' The local baker remembers that while on his delivery rounds he saw the columns of men marching down Parton Lane to Innsworth.

In November, 1941, Churchdown was subjected to disruption by a major civil engineering project; the rail line through the parish was one of the main arteries of the country and two more tracks had to be added in order to cope with the increased traffic of wartime. The work necessitated

King George VI and Queen Elizabeth at Churchdown Station in 1940.

severing the access near the station to both Pirton and Parton Lanes and the only way to get from one side of the village to the other at these points was by traversing, in Oram's words, 'an airy plank' or by diving into the cutting and climbing out again.[14] Local tradesmen often had to take very roundabout routes in order to serve both parts of the parish which cost them time and petrol - but this was wartime so who could complain?

In the previous year, on 10th February, 1940, the station enjoyed the most auspicious occasion in its history when King George VI and Queen Elizabeth alighted on its platform from their train. The King and Queen were then driven up Station Road and out to the factories at Hucclecote which they were due to visit. The news that the royal visitors were expected was, of course, like all such events during the war kept secret, but it seems that quite a number of local people did somehow get to know and were present along the route to see the car with its royal occupants go by.

With so much industry and so many activities taking place in the neighbourhood, Churchdown was, certainly, now no longer a rural backwater - and probably its inhabitants did not wish it to be. In the parish, as throughout the country, there was a general desire to be contributing to the war effort and there were many projects in which it was possible to be involved.

Tradesmen's advertisements in Churchdown Parish Magazine, 1941

162

The farming community had, of course, a very important part to play and Winston Churchill emphasised this: 'Every endeavour must be made to produce the greatest volume of food of which this fertile island is capable.'[15] Accordingly, it was ruled that a proportion of all pasture land had to be ploughed for crop production - wheat and potatoes being the priorities. Churchdown farmers, though, while trying to comply with this, found that their land, particularly if it was on the hill slopes, was not necessarily suitable for arable use; it was, and is, chiefly grazing ground. At Hurran's Nurseries in the very first month of the war a big sell-off of stock at less than cost price was held so that growing space could be released for food production. The village had its own Food Production Club which a hundred members joined immediately on its initiation in 1940, a government subsidy being available to help with the purchase of seed potatoes and various horticultural necessities.[16] A number of people in the parish kept rabbits or poultry or even a pig or two (there were many houses and cottages in the village with gardens large enough to rank as smallholdings) and so a certain amount of off-ration food was produced; friends and neighbours benefited, for instance, when a pig was killed, and any locally-produced additions to other such off-ration 'treats' as dried egg, offal (very covetable) and 'Spam' were very welcome.

The introduction of Double Summer Time in 1941 helped gardeners and growers who wished to work on their plots after business hours, but problems were created for livestock owners; at Chosen Hill Farm, at midsummer, the hens were still being persuaded to roost at midnight!

In some places there was considerable use of volunteer farm labour but this does not seem to have happened to any great extent in Churchdown. This may have been because there was a camp of Italian Prisoners of War at Woodfield Farm and these men, not being regarded as high-risk internees, were employed on farmwork and, consequently, were allowed considerable freedom to go about the village. These Latin strangers proved a romantic lure for some of the local girls and, village gossip has it, fruitful relationships developed as a result.

Schoolchildren were encouraged to 'do their bit' by collecting wild rose hips, which being a valuable source of Vitamin C, were made into a syrup as a dietary supplement. Gloucestershire was, apparently the top county for achieving the highest total weight of hips gathered and, no doubt, the boys and girls of Churchdown were enthusiastic contributors to this success.[17]

Most things were in short supply and almost everything that could be collected *was* collected and anything that could be saved *was* saved. The Girl Guides collected waste paper for recycling, pushing old prams 'on their rounds.' At first a shed in the Vicarage garden served as their headquarters for sorting and storing but later they used another at the top of Cranham Lane. The Scouts performed a similar service by collecting scrap metal for melting down, but the tons of iron railings which were

THE STORY OF CHURCHDOWN

sacrificed nationwide to this scrap metal drive were not, it seems, always used.

The conservation of water was urged and it was unpatriotic to wallow in more than the specified two to three inches of bath water. Paper had to be used most economically but, as it has been said, great quantities of it went into 'telling everyone not to use it unnecessarily.'[18] Fuel, too, had to be saved as much as possible and one resident remembers the services at St. Andrew's Church being held in the old wooden vestry which could be heated by one electric fire - and it would seem from this that congregations had become rather sparse if all the worshippers could be accommodated in such a small space.

The Methodist Church also suffered from a falling-off in numbers and it was due to the efforts of two supernumerary ministers, the Rev. Warwick Armstrong and the Rev. A. F. Brown, that spiritual morale was saved from declining. The Vicar of the Parish, the Rev. T. H. Jupp, had joined the Navy in 1939 to serve in the office of chaplain and during his absence the help offered by retired clergy living in the neighbourhood was greatly appreciated. The Rev. Anthony Fuest came to the village as Curate-in-Charge and served until 1943 when Mr. Jupp, being then invalided out of the Navy, was able to resume the incumbency. The Rev. Frank Cherrington took up his duties as priest at the Church of St. John the Evangelist (previously the Mission Room) in 1940 and, two years later, St. John's Hall was built on land behind the church. It was no mean achievement to accomplish such a building project in the face of all the difficulties and restrictions of wartime and the hall was to have many and varied uses and to prove a valuable amenity for all the village.

The walls of any public place where people congregated provided space for the innumerable slogan-bearing posters which aimed encouraging directives, stern injunctions or guilt-provoking questions at the populace. Churchdown had its fair share of these: 'Make do and Mend,' 'Save for Victory', 'Dig for Victory', 'Careless Talk Costs Lives', 'Coughs and Sneezes Spread Diseases', and, sternest of all, 'Is Your Journey Really Necessary?'

It was unlikely that any but the most hardy and determined *would* have attempted to travel for mere pleasure; trains which were crammed to bursting point with service personnel encumbered with bulky kit, were at night eerily blacked-out. Petrol was in short supply and then, in September, 1939, rationed, and, as an imaginative but rather naïve scheme for bewildering any invading enemy, all the road signposts were removed. This certainly confused our own drivers especially if they were travelling in unfamiliar parts. Railway station names, including Churchdown's, were also taken down.

After Dunkirk, invasion of this country by the German forces seemed almost inevitable and in the forefront of home defence were the Local Defence Volunteers, soon to be called the Home Guard; when this force

PARISH NOTES.

Salvage.—More than three hundredweight of bones have been collected in the village and it is safe to say that very few bones find their way into the dustbins. But it has been brought to the notice of the Salvage Committee that a good deal of food is being thrown away. Food will sometimes go stale even in war-time, but stale food is good for hens and pigs. So if your neighbour keeps hens let him have the clearings from your larder and the leavings from your plates and pots. And please remember the pig-farmer, and be on the look out for bins bearing the legend—Pig Food.

During the month of April the Guides and Brownies alone collected 17 sacks of mixed waste paper, 6 cartons of cardboard, 10 bundles of mixed waste, 2 sacks of soiled newspaper, 7 bundles of clean newspaper, 11 bundles of magazines, 1 sack of rags. Next month I hope to publish the amounts collected by the Scouts and Cubs.

Torch batteries and worn out electric light bulbs may be deposited in receptacles at Messrs. Woolworth's in Gloucester, in a bin outside the G.P.O. at Cheltenham, or they may be given to the village collectors.

The next meeting of the Salvage Committee will be held on Monday, June 9th.

Since September, 1939, 18,330 dinners have been served in the United Services Club.

Notice of Salvage Drive in 1941.

was set up in 1940 there was an immediate response from those men aged between sixteen and sixty-five who were not scheduled for call-up in the armed forces. Enthusiasm was in no short supply but, at first, proper equipment most certainly was. One Churchdown resident who was a member of the local force recalls his early training which took place at Parton House where the Drill Sergeant, a veteran ex-Serviceman, had the recruits marching up and down the drive with anything that could be used as 'pretend' rifles. Eventually there was an issue of real weapons and proper uniforms.[19] This member of the platoon became attached to the Signals Section which had its headquarters at Parton Farm and, later, at William's poultry farm at Paynes Pitch where the poultry pens became offices.

St. Bartholomew's Church served as the signal station and from the tower messages were relayed to the Home Guard units at Rotol and Brockworth. At first the signalling equipment consisted of home-made lamps but these were later replaced by naval lamps, then field telephones and, eventually and splendidly, by modern army wireless sets; direct voice contact could then be established and the use of Morse Code abandoned.

When on duty at the church the men were housed in the room below the bells - and these always remained silent as they were only to be rung to give warning of invasion. Heating and lighting in the tower room was by paraffin lamps and burners as electricity had not been connected to the church at that time. High up as they were above the village, the men could look down upon the dense black fog of the smoke screen when it was in operation and see the anti-aircraft balloons floating serenely above it.

Training schemes took place with neighbouring units and, on one occasion, as this ex-member recalls, there were strict orders to detain any civilian coming on to the hill without an Identity Card. A local farmer went to collect his cows for milking while this rule was in force and he found himself held prisoner by some of the Gloucester Home platoon because, not surprisingly, he did not have this essential document with him. 'I never did discover what happened to his poor cows!' says our informant.

The occasional farcical incident during such manoeuvres did not lessen the fact that these practice exercises were undertaken in deadly earnest. It was envisaged as a possibility that the estuary of the River Severn could be the site of a seaborne invasion; back-up troops would be parachute-landed and they would then make their way overland to gain control, first of the major ports, next of strategic inland sites and then of airfields and factories. In such a contingency, the Vale of Gloucester with its two commanding hill positions, Robinswood and Chosen, its air-strips and industries, could well be targeted by the enemy.

The steps taken to impede the progress of an invading force seem, now, simplistic to say the least. Road blocks of various kinds were prepared,

166

the most usual in rural areas being 'tank traps' of concrete bollards or barricades of whole tree trunks, mounted on wheels, which could be swung across the roads when necessary. Once the advance of the enemy had been slowed, the local Home Guard, armed with such guns as they had, and home-made 'Molotov Cocktails' (bottles filled with petrol and tar), would then have their opportunity to tackle the foe.[20]

Another important part of their duties was to keep constant watch and report immediately any sightings of parachutist activity; St. Bartholomew's Church, high on the hill, was obviously a good vantage point for such surveillance.

It seemed to be the conviction of the Defence authorities that, having landed, the invaders would make an immediate and concerted assault on the nation's bicycles and so, on warning of invasion being given, all owners of bicycles and cycle shops were to immobilise immediately all their machines by removing essential parts and hiding them. Motor vehicles were to be put out of action either similarly, or by the emptying of their petrol tanks, but, it was stressed, the vehicles should first be driven off the roadway and then the parts removed and hidden in such a way that the enemy would be unlikely to find them![21]

While it was seen as desirable to block the highways in the route of the advancing enemy, the civilian population were urged not to throng the roads impeding the movement of British troops. A directive issued by the County Controller to the civilian population[22] 'In the Event of an Attempted Invasion', states that no citizen should 'spread rumour,' block the roads' or 'become a fugitive', but must 'keep his head clear and his mouth shut,' 'Stay Put' and 'Sit Tight.'

The county was divided into over one hundred separate zones in each of which a stock of essential foodstuffs was stored.[23] Invasion committees in each area were asked to survey all local water supplies, including springs, wells and ponds; citizens were to conserve water in every possible way, storing it in jugs, etc., and to refrain from flushing lavatories or taking baths.

The public were informed that in the event of a hostile landing it was their duty 'to stand firm' unless they received instructions to move and, on no account, to attempt to leave their homes 'for some supposedly safer area.' In areas where actual fighting was taking place they were to keep off the roads and ' carry out such duties in support of the Army as may have been allotted to them, or remain in their own homes or shelters.'[24]

These grim words reflect the state of tense readiness which prevailed in the dark days of 1940; it will be easily understood, therefore, why all older residents of the parish will never forget the incident which occurred in June of that year. It was a warm summer's evening and life was settled in its usual wartime pattern...and then, suddenly, the church bells rang. This was, of course, the agreed warning signal that invasion had taken place and, as one local resident puts it: 'it was a blood-chilling sound, and all we could think to do, remembering the instructions to civilians, was to immobilise our bicycles!'[25] The error is believed to have occurred because this was the time of the German invasion of the Channel Islands and it seems that *Jersey* was misinterpreted locally as being the nearby Gloucestershire town of *Dursley.*

At this time the Local Defence Volunteers/Home Guard was a fledgling organisation, ill-equipped, only very basically trained as yet - but great in spirit. As the war progressed it became a very efficient defence force but at the outset it is doubtful how much, other than harassment of the enemy, could have been done to repel full-scale invasion.

But this never happened, although it may well be said that the Luftwaffe (the German Airforce) invaded the airspace of this country. In late summer what has become known as the Battle of Britain began but it was a battle fought over London, the eastern approaches and major cities and ports. This bombardment was undoubtedly part of Hitler's invasion strategy but the Blitz did not destroy morale as he had thought it would and, in consequence, he had to halt his plans to attempt seaborne landings. We have seen that Churchdown was not directly affected by the major air attacks but the big provincial raids were close enough for the horror of what was happening to be realised in the village.[26] This was the time when the second wave of evacuees left the cities and came to places like Churchdown which had the great advantage of being less densely-built and congested.

The years of war dragged on; rationing tightened its grip, blackout now seemed a normal part of life. There was hardly a family not committed to the war effort in some way; women were recruited for service in the forces, factories or hospitals or worked on the farms or in the public transport service. Only the very young, very old or severely disabled, mothers with young children, or those already in essential ('reserved') occupations, were exempt from enlistment either in the fighting forces or in civil defence. Gradually people became more casual about the air raid sirens and postponed taking cover until attack in their locality seemed really imminent. Whenever possible all gathered around their wireless sets to hear the bulletins which gave them (suitably 'adjusted') accounts of what was happening on the wide and various war fronts. Almost without exception everyone who could tuned-in to hear the Prime Minister, Winston Churchill, address the nation for there was a power even in the gravelly timbre of his voice which spoke defiance against what might have seemed overwhelming odds.

In 1944, as the time for the Allied landings on the Continent drew near, it was obvious to anyone living in the vicinity of a main road that a tremendous build-up of military power was taking place. All the might of American and British heavy weaponry seemed to pour along the highways - not, of course, down Churchdown's narrow lanes but almost continuously along the major roads in the area. Along the rail tracks, too, rolled the locomotives of both nations, sometimes grouped five or six together and towed by one engine, all bound for transhipment across the Channel. Hermione Oram speaks of the sight of these noisy monsters passing through Churchdown Station and remembers their being 'a major spectacle' She adds that 'rumour, the ever-fertile rumour of wartime,' asserted that on one occasion General Eisenhower himself was held up at Churchdown, 'the line being tilted a little.'[27] Once the invasion was under way Red Cross trains came through, empty, and, in a short while, would return filled with wounded servicemen and women.

Now when planes passed overhead it could be fairly safely assumed that they were British or American for bombing raids on this country had ceased in the spring, but in the summer Hitler used his last two desperate trump cards by launching the flying bombs and rocket missiles. These were aimed at major conurbations and small places like Churchdown did not suffer from the horror of these.

The threat of invasion of this country was now believed to have passed and as early as October, 1944, letters were read at the Parish Council meeting which stated that the function of the Invasion Committee could now cease as the gravest danger was seen to be over.[28]

By the second week of May Germany had conceded defeat and 'Victory in Europe Day' was fixed for the 8th May; there was, of course, a great feeling of relief but celebration was tempered by the fact that the war in the Far East had not come to an end and many people were anxious about relatives and friends serving there or languishing in the notorious Japanese prisoner of war camps. The memory of those terrible images of the suffering in the German Concentration camps may, too, have influenced the public mood and perhaps it was for these reasons that the parish decided to mark the end of the war in Europe, not with great gala celebrations, but by holding a public Thanksgiving Service and this took place in Parton Court Field.[29]

Then, on 6th August, 1945, a stunned nation heard that an atomic bomb had been dropped on Hiroshima in Japan by an American bomber. Next day *The Citizen* printed the comment made in the *Daily Express*: 'The world has changed overnight. It is a different world from the world we woke up to twenty-four hours ago. The change has come with the knowledge that the first atom bomb has been dropped upon the Japanese.' The second was dropped on the city of Nagasaki on the 9th August and Japan capitulated on 15th August. The war was now finally over but it was to be a very uneasy peace and it was to be a very changed world.

One of the first things that Churchdown had to do was to make public acknowledgment that eighteen men and one woman had lost their lives in this second conflict and these additional names were inscribed on the Village War Memorial; plans were then put in hand for a Welcome

CHURCHDOWN VILLAGE WELCOME HOME FUND

PRESENTED TO

BY THE INHABITANTS OF CHURCHDOWN VILLAGE FOR SERVICES RENDERED TO KING AND COUNTRY DURING WORLD WAR 1939 - 1945

The 'Welcome Home' Certificate issued to returning service personnel at the end of the Second World War.

Home Fund to mark the return of men and women of the parish who had served in the war. The village Youth Club were the original promoters of the project and at the first public meeting, held in February, 1945, every local organisation was represented.[30] Money was raised in a multitude of different ways: the British Legion donated £100, Churchdown farmers each subscribed at least £5 'as a token of their gratitude to the local men and women of H.M. Forces for the splendid manner in which they have spared us all from the terrible ravages of war,' and a patron of the Chosen Hotel handed in money from his sale of eggs and 14s.3d. earned by his banjo playing. A 'Grand Variety Concert' was held at the Chosen in June and admission tickets sold at 1s.6d. each realised £15.10s. while £13.10s.6d. was raised from skittling for a pig at the United Services Club. By June, £810.0s.8d. had been banked for the Fund and the final balance, after expenses had been paid, amounted to £749.10s.

It was decided to give a cash payment and a certificate to every man and woman who qualified and a celebratory 'Welcome Home' supper was planned - but deciding who was eligible and who was not eligible to receive the monetary gift inevitably presented problems. The public were invited to send in suggested names and the list of these was to be exhibited publicly so that any objections could be voiced. In one case it was claimed that an applicant's name had not been put forward because the lists had been put up in public houses and such places were not frequented by this person or his family. It was stipulated that to qualify the man or woman must have served either abroad or in this country before V.J. Day and to have been resident in the parish before joining-up. This latter clause caused 'a lot of resentment and concern' because there were some who had just happened to be away from the village when they enlisted - it is obvious that the organisers needed the wisdom of Solomon.

Those who were eligible and who duly received their gift were most appreciative; R. M. H. Whitehouse, writing from *H.M.S. Collingwood*, expressed his thanks for 'a very charming certificate' and the 'magnificent sum of £7.50s.,' and V. Gregory, in a letter headed 'War Dogs Training School (R.A.V.C.)' writes of his gratitude to all who helped 'in the fostering of Goodwill' in 'the lovely village which means so much to us.'

The 'Welcome Home Supper' was held on the 5th September, 1946, at the United Services Club. The meal cost £31.5s.3d and in this total were included 'drinks' at £18.1s.7d. (which sounds generous), a 'boiling fowl' at £6, ox tongue at 5s.2d., cakes and bread. Bread and flour had been put on ration in July. 'Entertainers' (unspecified) were paid £4, but presumably not individually. This event, despite the initial problems and some feelings of disgruntlement, was enthusiastically attended and proved to be a great coming together, from their varied walks of life, of all the people of Churchdown.

Chapter 9

Post-War Churchdown

Political Change

A spirit of camaraderie and a sense of common purpose had been 'plus factors' of the war years and these had undoubtedly played a big part in the final achievement of victory; these same qualities of courage and determined unity were going to be needed almost as much in the years ahead. The wartime spirit of co-operation was needed to make new ideas work; the Labour Party, which swept to victory in the 1945 elections, had put before the electorate a challenging programme for change, and the people, particularly perhaps the voting men and women of the armed services, had picked up that challenge. There was a feeling that the depression that had followed the 1914-18 war must not, this time, be allowed to sink the country into stagnation. *The Citizen* seems to have reflected this when, in its comment column after the results of the election were realised, it describes the political landslide as evidence of the people 'yearning for wholesale change'.[1] In Churchdown the Labour candidate, B. J. Parkin, was returned with a majority of 949 votes.

There were to be many changes in the village and one, in no way connected with Government policies or political interests, had taken place before the war ended. Churchdown had grown enormously during the war years and so, in 1944, part of the village was divided off to form a separate ecclesiastical parish (though it was still to remain in the original civil parish), the 'main road' end of the village becoming from then on known as the 'Conventional District of St. John the Evangelist.'[2]

Education

Another development, this time in the field of education had taken place in 1944, the year when R. A. Butler introduced his Education Bill. The school-leaving age was raised to fifteen (this came into force in 1947) and free secondary education was offered to all children. The new secondary system was to be divided into three categories - grammar, technical, and secondary modern - with selection for each type of school being determined by the examination which came to be known as the

'Eleven Plus,' because it was at this age that pupils sat the test. This scheme was intended to place pupils in the type of school best suited to their abilities whether these were 'academic' or more 'practical' in nature, but, in fact, it was seen as divisive and those children who did not pass for the grammar school felt a sense of failure - which in very many cases was certainly not justified.

The first secondary school in the parish was built on a 22-acre site approached from Winstone Road and called 'Churchdown School.' It was opened in September, 1954, although the building work had not by then been completed and the headmaster, Mr. W. H. Morewood, took up his duties the following January; by March of that year construction and fitting-out was finally finished.

In another four years Chosen Hill School in Brookfield Road had been built and was officially opened by the famous naturalist Peter Scott on 13th May, 1960. The number of boys and girls then on roll was 270, three forms having been transferred 'en bloc' from Churchdown School and the additional pupils being admitted by 'eleven-plus' selection. The school, which occupied a site of over 15 acres, was designated 'co-educational grammar/technical' and it was envisaged that the number attending the school would increase annually by an intake of about 125, with a full capacity of the expected 700 being reached by 1964.

In 1970, however, a big change took place in secondary education when the comprehensive system was introduced. It had come to be realised increasingly that the selection process was creating a grammar school 'elite' and that the secondary modern schools, many of which were doing excellent work, were often seen by parents and employers as offering a 'second-class' education. The new scheme was intended to afford more flexibility for pupils to study subjects at the level best suited to them but, above all, the selection examination, which seemed, at the tender age of eleven, to label children as having 'failed' was done away with.

Strong feeling , however, now arose in the parish, not so much about the principle of comprehensive education as to the way it was to be organised in Churchdown. The Education Authority planned to keep both schools, Churchdown and Chosen Hill, as separate but equal and catering, in each case, for the full 11-18 range, but when a public meeting was held in January, 1967, only twenty-three of the six hundred people attending voted for this.[3] One of the objections voiced was that to have two separate, and possibly rival schools, would divide the village again; another concerned the limitation it was felt would be necessarily imposed on sixth-form studies by having these centred in two schools. The alternative scheme, widely favoured, was to have a 'two-tier' system with all pupils attending the one school for the earlier years of their secondary education and then moving on to the second school (probably Chosen Hill) to complete the later stages - which would include a very strong sixth form. A strong campaign, including doorstep canvassing, was mounted in support of this alternative but at the next meeting, held a fortnight later, the consensus of opinion had changed and, of the 500 parents attending, most were now in favour of having the two separate comprehensive schools both catering for the full 11-18 range. This decision inevitably led to some anger among those who still objected and there were allusions to the plans having been 'bulldozed through.'

The report of the special committee on the re-organisation of secondary education[4] stresses that the decision to keep both schools as separate entities had only been arrived at 'after the most careful examination of all the evidence' and that it was not to be thought that 'a decision had been reached easily nor that all had been of the same opinion.' Despite these 'teething' troubles the two schools have enjoyed friendly co-existence with both achieving good academic results and with a very satisfactory percentage of students proceeding to further education and university entrance.

Meanwhile there were important developments taking place in the primary schools of the parish. The growth in population meant that many more school places were now needed and by 1951 the Parton Manor Junior and Infants' departments in Parton Road became separated from the original village school under a newly-appointed headmaster.[5] The intake of children was largely drawn from the rapidly developing estates of the Cheltenham Road and lower Pirton/Parton area and, in consequence, space at the school never seemed sufficient. Sandycroft Hall and the church hall were used as extra classrooms to supplement the provision provided by the pre-fabricated huts of which the main school consisted. A new building programme was begun in 1964 but even before this was completed it was realised that there would still be insufficient accommodation and so the decision was taken to make the Infants' School a separate establishment. The new Junior School was then officially opened in May, 1967, by Charles Loughlin, the local member of parliament, and in 1988 new classrooms were provided for the Infants' School.

The Village School faced a similar problem of overcrowding and various classroom units were added, but in 1954 the building of the present premises was completed. The school, which stands on a six-acre site, is planned as two-form entry mixed primary for pupils aged 7-11 years, the infants' section being housed separately in the original old building and in auxiliary classrooms around the central play area. In October 1954 the official opening by Lt.Gen. Sir John Evetts took place, but the school had actually been in use since the beginning of the year.

Then in September, 1972, a third primary school was opened. This was built adjacent to the Church of Our Lady, and it catered mainly for the children of the Roman Catholic community, the Church being responsible for 20% of the funding and maintenance. There were eighty children on roll at the outset but this number has trebled since then.

Health Care

When the measures of the National Health Act came into effect in 1948 these affected everyone. Despite the seemingly great public benefits, *The Citizen* sounded a wary note when it said: 'Many months must pass before it will be safe, or indeed fair, to appraise the working of the National Health Service which came in to operation today.'[6] It seemed, too, to regret that there would now be no need for the laudable voluntary effort 'on countless flag days' which had helped to maintain hospitals like the Royal Infirmary in Gloucester.

At first, medical care in Churchdown was administered solely by the two resident doctors, Dr. H. G. Dowler and Dr. C. H. Drake, and by the District Nursing and Midwifery services. Surgeries were held in the doctors' private houses and these could become very crowded; Dr. Drake recalls almost having to push his way through to the door of his consulting room - especially as many patients took to turning up unduly early in order to be seen at the beginning of the list - and some surgeries lasted for as long as four hours. For many patients there was something rather cosily reassuring about consulting the doctor in his own home, while the long waiting sessions were alleviated by chats with fellow sufferers, most of whom were well-known to each other; but ever-increasing numbers began to make this system unworkable.

It soon became necessary for new doctors to join the practice, and for secretarial help to be provided in order to cope with the mountain of paperwork that accumulated. By the 1960's it became apparent that there would have to be a big change in the system and that new purpose-built premises were required; and so, to meet these needs, the Medical Centre in St.John's Avenue was built. A team of doctors, assisted by practice nurses and ancillary staff, are thus able to offer a very efficient medical service to local people living in what is now an extensive and quite densely populated area. Great changes have come about, indeed, since the days when Dr.Prance drove out from Cheltenham in a dogcart to visit his patients in the village! The network of health care is extended beyond the surgery through the work of community nursing sisters, health visitors, and social workers and by volunteers in agencies such as 'Age Concern' and the 'Meals on Wheels' service; help and advice can thus be given in their own homes to those who need it.

A dental practice has been set up in the village and this operates from a surgery almost adjoining the clinic; opticians and dispensing chemists, too, have premises in the new parade of shops in St. John's Avenue.

The Churches

The number of Roman Catholic worshippers in the parish increased

175

during the war years when the evacuees from St.Anne's School in Birmingham and the accompanying adults had come to Churchdown; Mass had then been celebrated at various, decidedly secular, venues - the skittle alley at the Chosen Hotel being one - and at one time as many as 120 worshippers were attending Mass at the Sandycroft Community Centre. It was seen that there was need for a church in the locality and in 1953 Canon Matthew Roche, the parish priest of St. Peter's Roman Catholic Church in Gloucester, instigated the conversion of the old brick barn at Sandycroft Farm into the Church of Our Lady of Perpetual Succour. The new church was dedicated in March, 1955, and the official opening, conducted by the Bishop of Clifton, the Rt. Rev. Joseph Ruddersham, took place in March two years later.

This building had served the congregation for well over thirty years when it was decided to take the bold step of demolishing it and embarking on the construction of an entirely new, more substantial and permanent church on the site. The foundation stone of this was laid in September, 1991, and the Dedication, by the Rt. Rev. Mervyn Alexander, Bishop of Clifton, took place in June, 1992. The church, which fronts the main road, is a very attractive building, modern but not austere, and that so ambitious a project should be undertaken and carried through in such short time was no mean achievement.

At much the same time as the first Our Lady's Church was built, an Anglican church, the first permanent one to be built in the diocese after

Church of Our Lady, Cheltenham Road East.

176

the Second World War, was under construction a few hundred yards farther along the road. This was the new St. John's which was to replace the Mission Hall in Parton Road. In April, 1957, the foundation stone was laid and the church was consecrated in March a year later by the Bishop, the Rt. Rev. Dr. W. Askwith. A vicarage was built adjoining the church in the same pleasantly simple and classic style; the church hall was added later and the whole complex, on its tree-shaded site with its attractive Garden of Remembrance, makes a pleasing feature at the Cheltenham Road end of the village.

How were the older churches faring while these new ones were developing?

The Methodist Church enjoyed some revival in membership in the immediate post-war years - 'a period of consolidation' as the anniversary booklet calls it. Although 1953 was the Golden Jubilee no special celebrations were held, but the Church was 'steadily going ahead, gathering strength as it were...' and progress was to come in all directions. As well as the Sunday School, a Junior Church was started and the Boys' Brigade and Girls' Life Brigade were formed. Afternoon meetings such as Ladies' Circle and Women's Pleasant Hour (the latter was non-denominational and held at St. Andrew's Church Hall) proved very popular. There was now a strong movement between the churches of the village to co-operate with each other as much as possible for joint services and activities. In 1967 plans were initiated for a new hall,

St. John's Church viewed from the north-east.

entrance lobby and toilet facilities to be added to the existing buildings, and improvements to the kitchen, provision of storage bays, a new committee room and repairs to the organ and roofs were all undertaken in the sixties and seventies. The Churchdown Methodist community today is very actively concerned in a number of social and charitable projects.

The Parish Church (which St. Andrew's had now become) celebrated its 50th and 75th anniversaries with great enthusiasm. The Golden Jubilee events in 1954 lasted from 22nd May until the 30th and began with a fête where rides could be taken on a 'sensational miniature railway,' portraits could be hand-painted, the usual rustic sport of 'bowling for the pig' entered, and a programme of music by the band of R.A.F Innsworth enjoyed. Special services were held throughout the week and an organ recital was given by the Cathedral Organist, Dr. Herbert Sumsion. The exhibition of local memorabilia which was staged at the Village School included some surprising items - a piece of glass from the chandelier in Hitler's retreat at Bertschesgarten, the tail fin of the bomb (now made into a table) which fell on Hurran's Nurseries, a collection of Wordsworth's poems signed by the poet, and, perhaps most surprising of all, 'a locket containing hair of Edward IV taken from his skeleton found entire in 1789.'

It was in connection with the Golden Jubilee that Hermione Oram wrote her popular *Village History* in which she looks back over Churchdown's past. In his letter in the Parish Magazine,[7] the Vicar, the Rev. C. Norton Tyzack, wrote of the fifty years that the parish was celebrating as being 'in one sense a long time,' but that when one looked up at the ancient church on Chosen one was reminded that, in another sense, fifty years is a very short period in the life of Churchdown.' Then he added that perhaps no other fifty years had seen such tremendous changes - a comment very relevant then and perhaps even more so today. The 75th Anniversary was also celebrated with the customary fête, a Flower Festival and a Parish Lunch.

Another event of some considerable local interest - and pride - was the broadcasting in 1969 of the B.B.C. programme 'Sunday Half Hour' from St. Andrew's Church. All the village churches were invited to take part and there was a combined choir of 70-100 voices. The Vicar said that he felt the broadcast had been a great success and many letters of appreciation had been received.

In 1964/5 the external appearance of the church was enhanced by the addition of a north porch with an entrance lobby and inner doors of engraved glass. This was given in memory of Canon James McGill by his widow, and it has proved of great benefit to all who come into the church - and, not least, to waiting bridesmaids or worshippers encumbered with wet umbrellas!

Three very beautiful memorial windows were installed in the nave in the sixties and seventies, each designed by the stained-glass artist

A herald of the Plastic Age in Churchdown! One of the first plastic wrappers to be used by the local butcher in about 1965.

E. R. Payne and representing episodes from Churchdown's history. The first new window was given by Charles Anderson in memory of his wife, and depicts the 7th-century king, Osric, who was founder of a monastery in Gloucester and ruler of the region which included Churchdown. The West Window in the North Wall of the nave, the gift of the family of Brian Cox, illustrates the story of the rescue of William of Gloucester from the collapsed trench on Chosen Hill by the intervention of St.Thomas Becket. Next to it and commemorating Norman Shelley, late Headmaster of the Village School, is the 'Hooper Window' showing the martyrdom of the Bishop in 1555 (see Chapter 4). The three windows form part of a planned, but so far incomplete, group of four, the colouring schemes of which were to represent spring, summer, autumn and winter respectively.

For most churches, particularly older ones, the cost of maintenance is an ongoing problem and the parish has had to meet some heavy expenditure during this second half of the century. In February, 1957, major repairs were carried out to St. Andrew's baptistry and to the south-west corner of the church owing to subsidence caused by standing water. An anonymous donation of £500 helped greatly to meet the cost of this work which amounted to £888.4s.11d.

In the next year an infestation of woodworm was discovered and, despite the efforts of a working party who tackled the chairs using paintbrushes and little pots of treatment fluid, specialists had to be called in to deal with the ceiling timbers. Interior church roofs can have few rivals in inaccessibility (and at St. Andrew's then even the changing of a light bulb entailed a horrifying feat of aerial acrobatics); consequently a warning was printed in the Parish Magazine at the request of the woodworm specialists 'that there should be no distracting interruptions when they were at work' as most of it had to be 'done at precariously high levels.'[8]

From the outset the heating of the church had given trouble, coke boilers had been superseded by gas heaters but there were complaints about fumes in both cases; when supplementary fan heaters were installed the problem then was noise which 'was not distracting at Evensong but could be at the 8 a.m. service.' In 1985 Halogen Quartz Ray electric appliances were fitted at a cost of several thousand pounds.

For many years the last of the obsolete coke boilers brooded by the south door but this iron monster came into its own at Harvest Festivals when it supplied splendid staging for a monumental display of foliage, fruit, flowers and vegetables. The decorating of the churches for major festivals was a parish activity enthusiastically undertaken; moss and primroses were collected for Easter, pumpkins and potatoes, burnished apples and well-scrubbed carrots were piled up among a riot of 'old man's beard' at Harvest, and local woods and gardens were raided for evergreens, holly and ivy at Christmas - never mistletoe for that was 'pagan'.

Beautiful floral displays, most professionally arranged, are now a regular feature throughout the year in the village churches.

The maintenance of an organ in good and tuneful order is a big commitment and the instrument at St. Andrew's has, over the years, proved demanding of both attention and expense; in 1979 it was found to need a complete overhaul. The cost, with the proposed changing of the action to an electro-pneumatic system, was, at the final estimate, expected to cost a staggering £25,000 and, so, nearly four years of unremitting fund-raising were entered into. A large thermometer was erected outside the church door and the gradual accumulation of donations was registered 'by degrees' on this. When £15,000 had been collected the Fund benefited from interest-free loans to cover the remaining deficit and, by 1983, the work on the organ was able to be undertaken.

St. Bartholomew's, perhaps fortunately in view of the cost of maintenance, no longer had a pipe organ but in 1967 an electric organ, replacing the American organ purchased in 1925, was given by an anonymous donor. Electricity had been installed in the old church in 1953, a memorial gift of £50 having been received to help towards the cost.[9] The new organ was donated as part of the Thanksgiving celebration held when St. Bartholomew's was reopened in 1967 after the closure which had been necessary while extensive repairs were again carried out - this time at an estimated cost of £9,700. The Vicar, speaking at the inevitable fund-raising fête, said that he regretted that there was need to add once more to the large number of appeals already taking place in the village - but the sign on the gate at Barn Hay where the event was being held put the case in stark words: 'Church on the Hill is Falling Down.'[10]

Three options had been put before the Church Council: one was to continue to use the building until this became no longer possible when it would have to be closed and left to become a ruin, the second was to restore it piecemeal over a long number of years, and the third was to make an all-out effort to do all that was necessary as quickly as possible. Of course, once again, the parish rose to the challenge, the last course of action being the one chosen, and, as a start, an Appeal brochure was delivered to every home. It was suggested that a list of donors, with the amount given in each case, should be published but there was criticism of this as approaching social blackmail.

In two years the cost of the work had been met through private gifts, fund-raising activities, with financial help from the church authorities and from the Historic Churches Preservation Trust. At the celebratory Evensong on Ascension Day, the Archdeacon of Gloucester, the Ven.W.T.Wardle, said that the parishioners had met a great challenge in restoring the 800-year-old church, which, thanks to them, would now be a shrine for centuries to come.

Unfortunately in this last decade St. Bartholomew's is again in serious trouble and at the present time the whole structure, and the unstable mound on which it stands, are being surveyed and monitored. A group of local people have formed the Society of Friends of St.Bartholomew's to help support the care of the old church.

In 1955 it was entered on the list of Buildings of Special Architectural or Historic Interest.[11] A letter from the Church Commissioners sets out the significance of this: 'By virtue of the provisions of this Act the effect of the inclusion of the Church in such a list is that if the building ceases to be used for ecclesiastical purposes, it will be an offence to demolish it or to alter or extend it in such a way as seriously to affect its character, without first giving two months' written notice to the Planning Authorities'

The church became a landmark by night as well as by day when, in 1953, Alfred Hurran, in order to mark the Coronation celebrations of Queen Elizabeth II, presented an illuminated cross which was erected on the tower. This spiritual beacon on Chosen Hill proved so popular that, in 1976, Leslie and Audrey Major gave, as a family gift, a permanent cross which could be lit at the principal festivals. When eventually this needed replacement an anonymous donor made the gift, in 1988, of the present cross 'in memory of loved ones.'[12] It was by now such a feature of the Churchdown skyline that financial provision was made for it to shine on every night throughout the year. How amazed St. Augustine's early missionaries would have been to see the Christian message so publicly proclaimed from the hill with such a long religious, but anciently heathen, past. The old pagan god Thor took his revenge, however, when, in 1971, he struck the tower with a lightning bolt! Fortunately, damage was not extensive but repairs to the structure and to the electric system amounted to nearly £400.

In 1954 another major parish project had been launched when the decision was taken to erect a church hall. This was to be sited on part of Chapel Hay and the building was to be so positioned that the length of ancient wall foundation to the south-east of the church (referred to in Chapter 3) should not be disturbed.

Good Friday Procession of Witness ascending Chosen Hill. The people of the local community have climbed Chosen for acts of worship from the beginning of the village's history.

A retired clergyman living in the parish, Archdeacon Tanner, offered a starting donation of £500 subject to further sums being raised from other sources, including voluntary contributions.[13] The contract for the work which was to cost £5,739.2s.3d. (some exact accounting here!) was signed in 1955 and the hall was ready for consecration by September, 1956. Speaking at this ceremony, which was very fully attended, the Bishop of Gloucester said: 'I am going to make a boast that there would have been nothing like such a gathering had this occasion been a political meeting...but it is a meeting of the Christian Church and here we all are. What is beyond our power? Absolutely nothing. Get on with it!'[14] From the foregoing it would seem that life in Churchdown in the twentieth century has been exceptionally marked by the need for fund-raising, but the records of many parishes give evidence of similar efforts, most communities having struggled throughout history to repair and improve their church buildings.

The last few decades, however, have been noteworthy in another respect - patterns of worship have changed considerably. Most churches have adopted a less formal approach and the laity have taken a much more active part in the services. Modern versions of the Bible have proliferated and the Church of England has seen the introduction of the Alternative Services Book - but not everyone has accepted these innovations gladly. In 1976 it is recorded in the Parish Minutes[15] that the Vicar, 'after three years of looking, watching and listening,' had reached the conclusion that, 'it was in the best interests of the parish to keep both traditions - the old and the new.'

One of the very positive advances in church life during this last half century has been the ecumenical movement which has seen the coming-together of Christian denominations for joint services and activities. This is being very positively achieved in Churchdown and is symbolised by the Good Friday Procession of Witness in which members of all congregations take part. The Cross is carried from Our Lady's Church to St. John's and then on to St. Andrew's and the Methodist Church and, finally, to the mound outside St. Bartholomew's. Here the Cross is set up and a short service is held around it; this gathering for worship around a simple cross on Chosen Hill may re-create the form of the earliest Christian services held when Christianity was first brought to Churchdown.

The Loss of the Railway Station.

There is one amenity which, regrettably, the parish has lost in the post-war period - its railway station. The station had catered in the past for a faithful, but to some extent limited, band of passengers. In the 1950's one could travel to Gloucester or Cheltenham for 9d. return but

Churchdown Railway Station in 1954

the station had no parking facilities and for those residents who lived on the new estates in Pirton and Parton it was more convenient to make the journey to town by car or bus. As motor vehicles took over as the favoured modes of travel and transport, many stations throughout the country were threatened with closure, Churchdown among them. Signatures were collected in the village on a petition asking that the

Rail tickets issued for travel on the last day of service from Churchdown Station on the 31st October, 1964.

184

The Station being demolished, 1967.

station might be kept open but, in October, 1964, the closure took place and 'Churchdown a Ghost Station from Sunday' was the heading in *The Gloucestershire Echo* on the 30th October, 1964.

Later the two outer lines were taken up, the tracks re-aligned, and the station buildings and platforms finally demolished. 'Weeds well-set where once there were flowers...demolition men at work....'is *The Echo's* epitaph for the demise of what was remembered as a friendly, and pleasantly rural, small station.[16]

An additional early morning bus service was introduced to help meet the requirements of those who had used the train for travelling to work or school. The main services through the village (currently nos. 97 and 98) are now half-hourly and there is a frequent service along the Gloucester to Cheltenham Road.

Major Construction Works in the Parish

In order to cope with the vast post-war increase in motor traffic, a great road building programme has been undertaken nationwide and Churchdown, too, has been affected by this as the M5 Motorway, opened in April, 1971, now skirts the parish on the eastern fringe. During the titanic earth-moving operations involved in the construction, evidence of a number of Romano-British settlements came to light, the most interesting locally being in the nearby parish of Upton St. Leonards. Here, among other remains dating from the second to third centuries, a corn-drying oven was discovered and examination was made of the vegetable residue it contained.[17] There was, as would be expected, wheat, but also a number of weed grasses such as brome and wild oat and, the now rather rare, rye grass darnel. The weed seeds also show that the same plants were growing then as are abundant in Gloucestershire today - chickweed, dock, bindweed, cranesbill, sorrel, field mint, mayweed, corn spurrey, orache, 'fat hen' (*chenopodium*) and self-heal, (this latter once a herb of high repute but now the bane of lawn-conscious gardeners). Dock, sorrel and mayweed are reported as being present in the largest quantities and all three are still found in profusion on waste ground locally.

The stripping of the top soil over much of the length of the motorway from Boddington to Upton, which includes the Churchdown stretch, brought to light pottery fragments, which indicated the spread of Roman occupation in this region.

In the 1960's, the Golden Valley by-pass from Elmbridge to Arle Court in Cheltenham was constructed and this bisected the parish again as the railway had done previously; it was, in fact, a comparable feat of civil engineering as it followed the same pattern, comprising a straight stretch, a cutting, and an embankment built up from the excavated material. The deep digging revealed the fossil-rich lias bedrock which underlies the whole area and this, in wet weather, became a morass of extremely sticky mud as the great machines lumbered back and forth - apparently haphazardly to the uninitiated onlooker. But, it seemed almost suddenly, apparent chaos was transformed, and a superbly straight and level road was laid, banked by carefully-graded slopes and spanned by graceful bridges; highly professional engineering, skilful operation, modern technology and high-powered machinery had effected this miracle and, in September, 1969, the by-pass was ready for the official opening. This ceremony began at the Cheltenham end where the Mayor, Miss May Dent, cut the tape and was then driven along the by-pass to its termination at Elmbridge where the City Mayor, Councillor Leslie Jones, was waiting to snip the ribbon at the Gloucester end. This new by-pass carries a heavy volume of traffic particularly as it is a 'feeder' road for the M5 motorway.[18]

Another major engineering project completed in Churchdown in the latter half of the present century, is the construction of the third reservoir on Chosen Hill. The late Hermione Oram lodged a protest with the North Gloucestershire Water Board about its siting which she affirmed cut through the Soldiers' Walk (allegedly used by the Royalist troops stationed on the hill during the Civil War) and the Iron Age Camp. The Board's reply was that, in 1936, the site had been surveyed by the Ministry of Works 'in view of the possible historical interest of certain features' but that the Ministry had concluded that these features did not warrant any special protection. The work accordingly went ahead but, as it happened, the excavation produced the first real evidence of Iron Age inhabitation of the hill (see Chapter 2).

Amenities, Events and Leisure Facilities

Very extensive house-building schemes have taken place since the war, particularly in the Parton and Pirton areas, and local amenities have developed to meet the requirements of a rapidly increasing population. For some years, starting in 1953, an hourly Gloucester city service (6A and later 1A) ran to Springwell Gardens, the residential development off Parton Road and, later, early in 1960, the 1B route went to Winston Road off Pirton Lane. There are new shops in St. John's Avenue, Chosen Drive, and in the village centre but one of the old buildings, the seventeenth-century farmhouse from which the Western family conducted their butchery business, has been pulled down and a large block of 'sheltered-accommodation' flats has replaced it.

Three other housing developments for the elderly have been built - Tynings Court, Priory Court (on the site of the now-demolished Chosen Hotel) and cottages and maisonettes in the Manor House grounds; there is a sizeable 'senior citizen' population in Churchdown and people who come to live in the village often do not wish to leave it when they retire.

Considerable outrage was expressed in the parish when it became known that plans were afoot to build on the Manor site which was regarded as being very much part of the traditional 'heart' of Churchdown, but protest was unavailing and the building went ahead. The facade and main external structure of the old house was, however, kept intact while the interior was redesigned.

A parcel of land in the Manor Orchard was donated in 1970 to the scouts and guides by Mrs. Brown, then the owner of the Manor House, for the building of their new headquarters. A condition of the gift was that work had to be started on the site during Mrs. Brown's lifetime and so, as the lady was by this time elderly and in frail health, a concerted effort was made by the scouts themselves, their parents, relations and friends to get the foundations duly dug. Two feet of excavation had just been achieved when Mrs. Brown's death occurred. The new building when finished was named 'Brown Lodge' and was dedicated to both Mr. and Mrs. Brown; their son, Sir Ralph Kilner-Brown, conducted the official opening. Strong feeling was aroused in 1981 when the branch library housed in the old Parish Hall at the corner of Sandfield Road and The Piece was closed down; The Citizen ran a headline: 'Tears as Library Shuts for Good' above a picture of the retiring librarian, Mrs. Cora Gough.[19] The accompanying write-up went on to recall the 'passionate campaign', supported by 1,900 users, which had been undertaken in an endeavour to keep this very popular amenity open. At the presentation of leaving presents to Mrs. Gough and her staff, the spokeswoman for the 'Friends of the Library' said that it was 'more than a library, it was a focal point of village life where people met their friends and enjoyed companionship.'

The present Churchdown branch of the County Library in Parton Road, which, following the closure of the Sandfield Branch all borrowers from the village now use, had been opened in 1966 by Lt. Col. A. B. Lloyd Baker, Chairman of the Gloucester Library Committee. It was the twelfth new county branch library to be built since the end of the war and is a very pleasing-looking building which has, apart from the main book section, a reference room and children's library. Despite the initial resentment at the closure of the village branch, most book-borrowers who are able to make, either by car, 'bus or on foot, the one-mile journey down Parton Road have come to appreciate the efficient and friendly service offered by the staff at the Parton library.

A few hundred yards farther up the same road another Churchdown enterprise, the Community Centre, has been established, and it was in 1965, at a meeting held at Churchdown Secondary School that the decision to build such an amenity was taken. The initial plans, in a scheme estimated to cost £50,00, were to have included an indoor swimming pool and a coffee lounge but such ideas proved over-ambitious because they were too expensive. By 1967 the Community Association, which by then had 1,500 members, had raised enough money to be able to purchase an 1¼-acre site from the Staverton Airport Committee. The Centre, which has a main hall, meeting room, lounge bar and skittle alley, was officially opened in February, 1975, by R. Kelly, Esq., of Chesford Construction, the contracting firm which had given much help to the project.

The very first booking was taken by the Pre-School Playgroup, and now classes catering for all ages and interests use the Centre on a regular basis, so that choice can be made from 'Keep Fit' and Karate, or arts and crafts of all kinds including wood-turning, lace-making, patchwork and quilting. Many societies hold their meetings there and these include the Probus Club (for retired business people), the Wine Circle, the Skittles League, the Bridge Club and groups specialising in fuschia-growing, the art of Bonsai or budgerigar-breeding. It seems that whenever a seed of interest is sown in Churchdown it soon grows into a flourishing society.

Among the annual events now held at the Centre is the Horticultural Show (which Swift saw inaugurated in 1902). There often seems to be an almost unquenchable optimism (or is it stoicism?) in the national spirit which refuses to be deterred by the uncertainties of the climate and still opts for holding outdoor events. The Horticultural Society has, however, decided in recent years to fight no longer with the problems of wind, rain and mud and also to avoid the considerable expense of hiring tents and marquees. It must be confessed, though, that there was an uniquely homely and 'village' atmosphere about the Show when it was held in a local field - despite the inconvenience of thistles, nettles and cow pats - and those who remember these occasions recall with slight nostalgia the special quality of pellucid light diffused through canvas, the sweet smell of damp, bruised grass and the rural accompaniment of the clucking, crowing and quacking of the poultry exhibits.

When, however, the organisers of the Coronation Celebrations in 1953 decided to stage an ambitious outdoor programme they took a brave gamble on the weather. King's Field, in Parton Lane, was hired for the occasion and the Chief Constable of Gloucestershire, Col. W. F. Henn, a local resident, performed the opening ceremony.[20] The first event was listed as 'Novelty Sports -for old and young to test your speed, skill and ingenuity,' and then followed displays by a number of local organis-ations. At 6.30 in the evening there was delightfully rustic-sounding 'Folk Dancing for All on the Green' and at intervals throughout the course of the day's proceedings the Gloucester Pipe Band provided musical interludes; then, at 7 p.m. came the big event - 'The Pageant of Churchdown Through the Ages.'[21] Photographs suggest that it was really rather splendid with some very authentic costumes and colourfully imagined enactments of scenes from the history of the parish.

The festivities concluded with a United Service of Thanksgiving and Dedication, during which the illuminated cross shone for the first time from St. Bartholomew's tower. Twenty-four years later, on the 7th June, 1977, the Silver Jubilee commemoration of the Queen's Accession was celebrated by another outdoor event this time taking the form of a 'Grand Carnival Procession' which wound its way along all the principal highways of the village. There are in Churchdown now well-supported dramatic and choral societies which attain a high standard of professionalism. In 1953 opportunity for participation in outdoor sports was greatly improved when John Daniels, the local builder, generously offered, rent free, thirteen acres of land to the parish for use as a playing field. A Playing Field Sub-Committee was formed to take charge of the development and maintenance of the ground and collections were made and donations invited towards the cost of preparing the field and providing the necessary facilities. In two or three years sufficient money had been raised to enable a pavilion to be built and this was opened in 1957 by the Duke of Beaufort. A good cricket pitch has been laid and on most weekends in the summer matches can be watched on this pleasant site. A recreation ground has also been opened in Parton Road and here the local junior football teams undergo coaching and practise the game.

In 1971 Churchdown Club celebrated its Golden Jubilee; by this time the membership had grown from the 320 at its inception to over 1,000. The Club has achieved quite a reputation for its sporting activities, the tennis, skittles and snooker sections all taking part in the County

The local bus from Gloucester to Cheltenham passing the Parish Council Offices in Parton Road.

Leagues. The bowling green is very well patronised by local and visiting teams - but perhaps few of the players realise, as they concentrate upon their game, that beneath the smooth green turf, human remains from Churchdown's ancient past still lie buried.

Local Government

With so many leisure activities available, Churchdown can, by no means, be considered a social, cultural or sports backwater and with the building of the parish's own Council Offices it can claim to have 'arrived' municipally too. These new premises were opened in September, 1991, by Councillor J. W. Threadingham, Mayor of the Borough of Tewkesbury, to which the village now belongs. Twenty-one councillors are elected to the Parish Council, seven for each of the three wards, Brookfield, Pirton and Parton; local matters have now been discussed and settled at Parish Council meetings in the village for over a hundred years.

It is the Parish Council's responsibility to maintain footpaths, public recreation areas and bus stops and to carry out minor environmental projects such as tree and flower planting. The Council are able to pass bye-laws on such matters as the fouling of pavements, and can impose penalties for infringement of these orders but, in actuality, fines for the committing of this particular nuisance are seldom, if ever, imposed; there are many dogs in Churchdown, most healthily exercised, and rarely is an offending animal caught *in flagrante delicto*.

The Parish Council also undertakes the overseeing of the street lighting and reports any non-functioning of lamps, but the actual erection or replacement of standards is carried out by the Highways Committee of the County Council. All the main residential areas of the parish are now adequately lit, but it was not until 1951 that the first street light appeared in the village and this only after a long and frustrating history of local opposition, delays over planning permission, and controversy about the locating of standards.

It was under the local government re-organisation in 1974 that a number of the Gloucester Rural Districts (of which Churchdown was one) became part of Tewkesbury Borough, to the Council of which six representatives from the parish are elected. Churchdown, which at the last Census had a population of twelve thousand and has been steadily increasing so that the number of residents is now in excess of fourteen thousand, is the biggest single contributor to the Borough Council Tax.

The Borough Council has a wide area of jurisdiction which includes refuse collection, street cleaning, the inspection of food premises in accordance with the Public Health Act, the care of listed buildings, the consideration of planning applications, the granting of licences, the care of Council property and, of course, the collection of the Council Tax. The newly-constructed burial area on Chosen Hill is maintained by the Borough, but the upkeep of St. Bartholomew's graveyard remains the responsibility of the Parochial Church Council.

One councillor represents Churchdown on the County Council which administers Education (the biggest item on the Budget) and Social Services; road maintenance and improvement (excluding that of motorways which are the responsibilty of the Ministry of Transport), libraries, major planning decisions, the checking of weights and measures and inspections to see that the Fair Trading standards are being adhered to, are all the responsibility of the County Council.

These three bodies maintain the many amenities and regulations which are part of modern day living in urban or semi-urban areas. Churchdown must now be seen to be in the latter category even though it fiercely defends its right to be considered a village.

In Conclusion - The Local Scene Today

From the vantage point of Chosen Hill many features of Churchdown's story can be seen around and below.

Despite modern building development much of the landscape is still farmland, mostly sheep or cattle pasture often showing the ancient ridge and furrow plough pattern. The neat hedges of the 19th-century enclosures predominate but where these have been rooted out, as they have on the Zoons land, an impression of the open-field system can be imagined. The traditional crops have, however, given way in places to stretches of brilliant yellow oil seed rape or the gentle blue of linseed; there are even some plantings now of a real alien - maize - an exotic to find in the Gloucestershire countryside It is not a heavily wooded landscape, as it has not been since, at least, Saxon times when so much forest was cleared and 'assart' encroachment made on the waste in order to provide more land for farming, but many splendid trees remain in fields and along the ancient hedgerows.

The level green expanse of the airfield with its long, straight runways is conspicuous across the landscape. It is now used mainly by operators of business aircraft and for training and general flying purposes. For many years a popular annual event was the Staverton Air Show with ultra-modern and vintage aircraft taking part and with displays of parachute jumping and aerial acrobatics being staged. The highlight always came at the end with the arrival, suddenly out of the blue, of the world-famous Red Arrows team and, during their breathtakingly daring manoeuvres, the sky above the village became streaked and criss-crossed with red, white and blue plumes of smoke. Many local people climbed the hill from where they could watch this amazing spectacle for free!

From Chosen some of the original lanes, a little straightened and 'improved', can still be seen marking time-honoured routes, but the railway, the by-pass and the motorway make few concessions to natural features as they cut across the countryside. Near Ermine Street and the remains of the Roman villa at the Noke, the huge labyrinth of the M5/A417 interchange has been carved out of the terrain where, centuries ago, there were vineyards. Seen from above this appears to be a confusing complex of approach roads, under-passes and roundabouts, the whole now landscaped with smoothly-graded grass banks replacing what, during construction, appeared to be acres of muddy devastation.

Ownership of a car is almost an essential for most of the working population of Churchdown for few people live, as once they did, within walking or cycling distance of their employment; there are now a number of major industries in the two towns and neighbourhood. To the south-west, towards Gloucester, the huge factory of the frozen foods makers Birds Eye/Walls can be seen and this is claimed to be the largest in Europe. A little nearer, and to the north-west, are the premises of Messier/Dowty (as the aerospace engineering company is now designated) and, nearer to the outskirts of Cheltenham the shining dish aerials of the Government Communications Headquarters (G.C.H.Q.) can be seen. Many local people are employed at these establishments or by the numerous building societies and insurance companies whose vast office blocks are conspicuous in and around the two towns.

R.A.F Innsworth now houses the recruiting, training, personnel, legal, medical and chaplaincy branches of the Service and over half the staff are civilian. Cordingley Close, off Pirton Lane, is a residential development of married quarters for the officers of the Camp and their families who, during their sojourn in the parish, soon integrate into the village community - as so many newcomers have in the past.

Many people use their cars for their shopping expeditions to one of the several supermarkets which are within easy motoring reach. Fortunately for those who have no transport, and for those who appreciate personal service, local shops still survive; long gone, of course, are the days when the exact quantity the customer required was weighed by the grocer into stout, blue paper bags, and biscuits were selected from rows of open-topped tins, but the 'core' of the village can be said to still retain some of its earlier character despite the enormous changes that have come about in the last fifty years.

On Chosen Hill itself comparatively little has changed; the metalled road which now runs right to the top is almost parallel in its last stretch with the ancient bridleway; the three new reservoirs, hidden like tumuli under their grassy mounds, and the tall aerial masts are the only prominent modern innovations. From the ramparts of the Iron Age camp along which one can still walk, the territory of what was once the Barony of Churchdown is stretched out below. The tower of the church at Norton, one of the original manors, can be seen to the north-west; the footpath to Elmbridge is still visible, crossing fields as it always did (but now, at the spot where it terminates, suburban Gloucester quickly takes over) and, on the south flank of the Hill, the way up which the people of Hucclecote climbed to church remains as an access path to the hilltop. The sub-manors of Pirton and Parton are now the most densely developed parts of Churchdown but, even so, pasture-land still surrounds the Court and the Manor.

Although partly hidden in places by encroaching undergrowth, the old stone steps up which worshippers, wedding parties and funeral mourners made their way to St. Bartholomew's can still be found; the fir trees, planted to commemorate Queen Victoria's Jubilee and now grown tall and rather spare, are showing the effects of a century's battering; the tump where the celebratory bonfires were built, and earlier, perhaps, the Armada warning beacons were sited, is almost covered with bramble and nettle except where a well-trodden path prevents these invaders from overtaking the site. The old quarries and marl-diggings, too, are almost buried beneath scrub but, when this is kept at bay, plants with a long history of culinary and herbal use flourish - 'good King Henry,' elder, dock, mercury, nettle and self-heal; hemlock, which is possessed of a strange, musty smell and a sinister reputation, abounds in places. The

Muzzle Well is still there in the woods below, the spring running as it probably always has done, but the trough into which it falls has suffered from the long-sustained attack of tree roots, and is sometimes nowadays subjected to the offerings of our modern 'throw-away society'.

The Sexton's Cottage, probably the oldest domestic building in the Parish, continues to be lived in (currently by the Verger); it has been altered considerably over the years and modernised to some extent, but is still, obviously, a very ancient structure.

Churchdown people can be interred in St. Bartholomew's Churchyard as has always been their right, and here, in the older part, are the graves of the yeomen of the past - the Danceys, the Holfords, the Bubbs and the Bridges - and, deep below them, the mediaeval villagers lie. The main Wyndowe family plot is at the east end of the south aisle, and, not far from the ancient yew tree, William Swift lies buried, his wife, Rose, beside him.

St. Bartholomew's presides over all - Norman built but added to, altered and repaired in every century since, and sited on the mysterious mound which may be many centuries older than even the Iron Age camp which surrounds it. As was said at the outset, we do not know when settlement on Chosen first took place but it must have been here, on this marly hilltop, that the story of Churchdown began.

View of Churchdown, Pirton and Parton areas, from Chosen Hill.

Notes and References

Chapter 1: The Hill and the Vale (pp 1-7)

1. William Dreghorn, *Geology Explained in the Seven Vale and Cotswolds*. 1967, reprinted 1973, p. 62. An alternative suggestion for the presence of sand in the locality is that it was washed down by the action of melt water following one of the Ice Ages.
2. Frederick Smythe, 'Geology of Churchdown Hill, Part I.' *Proceedings of the Cotteswold Naturalists' Club*, Vol. III (1865), p. 42.
3. D.E. Finlay, 'The Churchdown Reservoirs.' *Proceedings of the Cotteswold Naturalists' Club*, Vol. XXVIII (1943), p. 30.
4. J.J.D. Cooke, *Churchdown Through the Ages* (1939 printing) p. 11
5. Rev. Canon W. Bazeley, 'Churchdown and Mattesdune Before the Norman Conquest.' *Proceedings Cotteswold Club*, Vol. XXI(I) (1921), p. 22. Canon Bazeley points out that there is a spring of the same name at Sandhurst (Glos.) and that 'Muswell Hill', London, also seems to share a similar name.
   See also R. W. Murray, *The Church of St. Bartholomew on Chosen Hill, Churchdown and Some Parish Notes*, p. 33. PA 84/2.

Chapter 2:
The Early Years from Prehistory to the Norman Conquest

Early Settlement (pp 8-15)

1. Some variations of the name of Churchdown:
   1086 Circesdune (Domesday Book); 1221 Chyrchedone and Churchdon;
   1230 Chyrchesdon (e); 1300 Churchesdon(e); 1303 Schurchesdon;
   1483 Churchedon; 1543 Churchedown(e); 1584 Churston;
   1690 Churson (hence 'Chosen'?); 1719 Chorsdown (possibly sometimes 'Thorsdown.')
2. Bazeley, 'Churchdown and Mattesdune before the Norman Conquest.' *Proceedings Cotteswold Naturalists' Club*, (1921), p. 17.
3. Report No. 1407 by E.J. Wilson & Associates, Consulting Engineering Geologists, Gloucester, (1992).
4. Thos. Lloyd Baker, 'An Account of a Chain of Ancient Fortresses.' *Archaeologia*, Vol. XIX (1821), pp. 169-170.
5. A group of W.E.A. students worked under the leadership of Mr. Henry Hurst and in consultation with Mr. John Rhodes, Curator of Gloucester City Museum. Report published in *Transactions Bristol and Gloucestershire Archaeological Society (Trans. B.G.A.S.)*, Vol. XCV (1997) pp. 5-10.

6. E.M. Clifford, 'The Roman Villa, Hucclecote,' *Trans. B.G.A.S.*, Vol. LV. (1933), p. 323.
7. Barry Cunliffe in 'Gloucestershire and the Iron Age of Southern Britain,' *Trans. B.G.A.S.*, Vol. 102, (1984), pp. 5-15, gives a detailed account of life in hillfort communities.
8. Thalassa Cruco Hencklen, 'The Excavation of the Iron Age Camp on Bredon Hill, 1935-7,' *Archaeological Journal*, Vol. XCV (1938), pp. 21-26.
9. W.T. Swift, *Some Account of the History of Churchdown*, (1905), p. 7.
10. Wilson Report, No. 1407, p. 6.
11. In the garden of Mr. and Mrs. Sheppard, War Close, Pirton Lane, Churchdown.
12. Lloyd Laing, *Celtic Britain*, (1979. Paladin Books Reprint 1987), pp. 114-115.
13. Hurst Report, p. 10.
14. Information about the A 'La Tene' Strap Junction found at Churchdown, and now in the Gloucester City Museum, was kindly supplied by Mr. M.J. Watkins, Director of Archaeology.

The Roman Occupation (pp 15-19)

1. Bazeley, 'Churchdown and Mattesdune Before the Norman Conquest.' *Proceedings Cotteswold Club*, Vol. XXI(1), p. 20.
2. H.P.R. Finberg, *The Gloucestershire Landscape* (1975), p. 44.
3. Alan McWhirr, *Roman Gloucestershire*, (1981, Reprint 1986), pp. 92-93.
4. W.G. Hoskins, *The Making of the English Landscape*, (1955, Penguin Edition, 1985), p. 36, quoting from R.G. Collingwood and J.N.L. Myres, *Roman Britain and the English Settlement*,(1937), p. 209.
5. For plan see McWhirr, p. 100.
6. E.M. Clifford, 'The Roman Villa, Hucclecote.' *Trans. B.G.A.S.* Vol. 55 (1933), p. 323.
7. I am indebted to Mrs. Doreen Cratchley for the opportunity to see this lamp which was found in the garden of her father, Mr. Leonard Brown.
8. Bazeley, p. 18.
9. ibid. p. 21.
10. Peter Salway, *Roman Britain (Oxford History of Britain)* (1981, Reprint 1987). p. 738
11. A stone altar *'to an unidentified local Celtic god'* may be seen in the Corinium Museum, Cirencester.
12. A statue, believed to be of Mithras and found in Spoonley Wood, Glos., may be seen in the City Museum, Brunswick Road, Gloucester.
13. The edict of the Emperor Constantine in A.D. 312 made Christianity the official religion of the Empire. Other coins found in Churchdown include: (1) Claudius (Grove Rd.), (2) Constantine II, 330-335 A.D. (Cheltenham Rd. East,) and (3) a large gold coin showing Marcus Aurelius as Caesar, A.D.144.
14. Finberg, p. 47.
15. Angus Winchester, *Discovering Parish Boundaries* (1990), p. 31.
16. *The Anglo-Saxon Chronicle*, (Trans. G.M. Garmonsway, 1953). Everyman Library Edition (1986), pp. 18-19.
17. Recorded as such in *Domesday Book.*

The Saxon Period (pp 19-28)

1. H.P.R. Finberg, *The Formation of England, 550-1074* (1974, Paladin Reprint 1976), pp. 22-23.
2. ibid., p. 26.
3. Rev. J.D. Cooke, *Churchdown through the Ages*, (1939), p. 12.

4. Angus Winchester, *Discovering Parish Boundaries*, (Shire Publications, 1990), p. 30.
5. Grenville Astill and Annie Grant (Eds.) *The Countryside of Mediaeval England*, (1988, Paperback Edition 1992), pp. 136-8.
6. Carolyn Heighway, *Anglo-Saxon Gloucestershire*, (1987), p. 18.
7. W.G. Hoskins, *The Making of the English Landscape*, (1955, Penguin Edition 1985), p. 86.
8. Finberg, *Formation of England*, p. 80. 'The field is 'open' only in the sense that no obstacle separates one man's ploughland from his neighbour's. But there is no hint of communal ownership (in 7th-Century Wessex). The shares are clearly regarded as held by individuals, each of whom must be compensated for damage caused by his neighbour's default. We must think of these individuals as forming what has aptly been termed 'a community of shareholders.'
9. Finberg, *Formation of England*, p. 81.
10. R.W. Murray, 'Excavation at Chapel Hay, Churchdown,' *Trans. B.G.A.S.*, (1923), pp. 277-284. William Swift in his Diary, 12th September, 1893, (Glos. Record Office D3981/20) states: 'Richard Holford's grandfather could remember the stones (in ruins) of the building of a chapel...... that used to be in Chapel Hay Farm home field, next the Vicarage...... Henry states that he had dug up the bones of people in Chapel Hay.'
11. Heighway, p. 23, states that crouched burials found at Withington are 7th-Century.
12. Murray, p. 282.
13 This event is commemorated in one of the modern stained glass windows in St. Andrew's Church.
14. These early missionaries probably followed the advice given, over eighty years before, by Pope Gregory to St. Augustine which was that heathen sites should not be destroyed but asperged with holy water and Christian altars set up where the pagan rites had taken place. This, Bede tells us, was in the hope that the people, seeing that their temples were not destroyed, would 'abandon their error' and 'flocking more readily to their accustomed resorts' would come 'to know and adore the true God.' Bede, *A History of the English Church and People*, (Penguin Edition, 1982), pp. 86-87.
    See Sir Frank Stenton's *Anglo-Saxon England*, (Oxford History of England, 1988 Edition), p. 150, for reference to the history of the standing cross in England.
15. Bazeley, p. 29. 'The earliest mention I have found of Churchdown is the grant of the barony, including Churchdown, Hucclecote and Brickhampton by Aethelred Ealdorman and his spouse Aethelfleda, Lady of the Mercians, to St. Oswald's Priory, Gloucester.
    'I don't remember to have heard anything about a charter of Aethelflaed in consideration with Churchdown.' Letter dated 1.12.1924 by Rev. Wilkinson of Ozleworth.
    Rev. J.D. Cooke, p. 31: 'A charter dealing with the Barony, 'the 12 vills of Gloucestershire' is said to be preserved somewhere - but it is not known in the British Museum, P.R.O., the Bodleian, The Archbishops' Registry, York.'
    I am greatly indebted to Carolyn Heighway for advice about this and am also most grateful for the opportunity to read Michael Hare's paper, 'The Documentary Evidence for the Early History of St. Oswald's, Gloucester, 900-1086 A.D.'
16. A. Hamilton Thompson, 'The Jurisdiction of the Archbishops of York in Gloucestershire,' *Trans. B.G.A.S.* Vol. 43.
17. ibid., p. 86.
18. ibid., p. 87.
19. Hare, p. 37.
20. ibid., p. 38.
21. ibid., p. 39.

Chapter 3:
From the Conquest to the Eve of the Reformation   (pp 29-54)

1. David C. Douglas, *The Norman Achievement*, (Fontana Edition, 1972), p.165, citing R.A. Brown, 'The Norman Conquest,' *Royal Historical Society Trans.* Ser. 5, XVII (1966), pp. 109-30.
2. G.N. Garmonsway, Ed. *Anglo-Saxon Chronicle*, (Everyman's Library 1953/86), p. 219.
3. Carolyn Heighway, *Gloucester, A History and Guide*, (1985), p. 39.
4. Stigand probably acquired the estates during the reign of Edward the Confessor (1042-1066) when lands belonging to the Church were granted for political advantage. Stigand was deposed in 1070 (and died 1072) and so it is likely that the Barony and the estates of St.Oswald passed into the hands of King William who gave them to Thomas of Bayeux, Archbishop of York, as an endowment to offset the financial problems of the northern province. Thomas was the brother of Samson, Bishop of Worcester.
    See Moore, John S. (Ed.) *Domesday Book, Gloucestershire*, (1982), 2.1, 2.2, 2.3, 2.4, 2.5, and 2.9.
5. A. Hamilton-Thompson, 'The Jurisdiction of the Archbishops of York in Gloucestershire', *Trans. B.G.A.S.*, Vol. 43, p. 98. Charles Taylor, *An Analysis of the Domesday Survey of Gloucestershire*, (1889) p. 14.
6. R. Welldon-Finn, *An Introduction to Domesday Book*, (1963), p. 4. *V.C.H.*, Vol. II (1907), p.84, citing 'Gest. Pontif. Ang., 263n.'
7. A.H. Smith (ed.) *Place Names of Gloucestershire*, (English Place Names Society Edition, 1964-5) p. 120. Margaret Gelling, *Place Names in the Landscape*, (1984), pp. 138-9 and 142-3. Smith, p. 168.
    R.W. Murray, *The Church of St Bartholomew and Some Parish Notes*, (Private Paper) G.C.R.O. PA84/2:
    'I wrote to Professor Mawr of the English Place Name Society, asking if he could explain to me the meaning of the word Circesdune, and in his reply he said: 'The *s* which is so persistent in the early forms of Churchdown seems to me to be fatal to any suggestion that the first element in the word Circesdune is Old English *'circe'* Church, for that word is a feminine noun and would never have made its genitive in *s* before at least the 13th century. Beyond this negative statement I find it difficult to go at present. Personally I am inclined to think that the first element is Old English *cric* or *ciric*, a loan word from British meaning a barrow, and that the original name was *Cricesdun*, 'hill of the barrow,' that this by metathesis of the *r* became Circesdun, which would have been pronounced as Kirchesdun but was readily altered to Churchesdon through confusion with the common word *Church*. This is somewhat speculative but does fit the facts as I know them.'
8. A.H. Smith, p. 147.
9. Taylor, p. 177, estimates that Churchdown, Hucclecote, Bishop's Norton with Great Witcombe would equal 8,340 acres.
10 Welldon-Finn, p. 104.
11. ibid. p. 131. 'Rents varied appreciably; a shilling or eighteen pence (old currency) for fifteen acres frequently appear.'
12. ibid. p. 148. 'Radmen' or 'Riding-men' are to be found mostly in the West Midlands and Hampshire.
13. F.M. Stenton, *Anglo-Saxon England, Oxford History of England*, (1971) p. 473.
14. Finberg, *Formation of England*, p. 172-3. Letter from Bishop Oswald of Worcester to King Edgar: 'The men (milites, *cnihtas*, or fideles) must 'fulfil the

whole law of riding which belongs to riding-men.' 'They must pay church-scot, toll and pannage; lend their horses and ride on errands themselves; be ready to build bridges and to burn lime for church-building; erect a hedge for the bishop's hunt and lend their own hunting spears if required. In consideration of the fief ('beneficium') which they hold on loan, they must swear to obey with all humility and subjection the bishop as their lord and archiductor, their commander-in-chief'. p. 223: '...when the Bishop of Worcester complains of encroachment on his woodland, the defendant orders his *geneat* ...to ride round...and identify all the landmarks......We may safely identify the *geneat* with the countryman of superior status who will figure in the Domesday account of many manors, particularly in the west midlands, as a *radcniht* or mounted retainer'.

15. Court of John, Archbishop of York, 19th. Henry VI, 1441 (Abridged translation by Ethel Hartland. Gloucestershire Collection ref.10151).
16. *York Diocesan Records, Register W. Bothe, folio 142. Trans. B.G.A.S., Vol.43.* p.122.
17. ibid. *folio 130d.* ibid *Trans.* p. 122.
18. *Trans. B.G.A.S., 1946/7/8,* p.283. *Gloucester Corporation Records,* p. 316.
19. ibid. p. 316. (1320) also mentions the 'Millward' at Noke.
20. *Victoria County History, Vol. 4,* p. 435.
21. J.H. Bettey, *Church and Parish,* (1987), p. 23.
22. G.H. Cook, *The English Mediaeval Parish Church,* (1954), p. 20.
23. Rev. J.D. Cooke, *Churchdown Through the Ages,* p. 57.
24. Hamilton-Thompson, p. 112.
25. ibid., p. 115.
26. ibid., p. 109.
27. *Dictionary of National Biography* (D.N.B.) Vol. XLIX, (1897), p. 109. The state of enmity between the Archbishops of Canterbury and York is dealt with fully in *Thomas Becket* by David Knowles, (Stanford University Press, 1970), see pages 75 and 128 particularly.
28. William of Canterbury and Benedict of Peterborough, *Miracula S. Thomae Incipit Tertuis.* James Craigie Robertson, *Materials for the History of Thomas a Becket, Archbishop of Canterbury,* Vols. I and II.
    (I am indebted to the late Mr. A.Th. Arber-Cooke for translation from the Latin.)
29. Frederick Smythe, *Churchdown in Ye XII Century,* p. 167.
30. Paper by R.W. Murray, 'The Church of St.Bartholomew on Chosen Hill, Churchdown' p. 21, citing Vol. I, *Gesta Regis Henrici Secundi,* translated by F.B. Welch.
31. *Register of Archbishop Walter de Gray,* 1215-1245, (Surtees Society), Vol. LVI, (1870), pp. xxvi, 42, 121, 168, 270 give examples of transactions conducted in the barony. Hamilton-Thomson, p. 123, seems sure that the Archbishop was present in person.
32. ibid., p. xxiv.
33. ibid., p. 123: 'Thus Archbishop Gray was at Churchdown in September, 1224, November, 1225, and May and June, 1227; at Oddington in October, 1227; at Churchdown and Oddington in May and June, 1228; at Churchdown in January and February, 1230-1; at Oddington in May, 1232; at Oddington and Churchdown in October, 1235; at Churchdown in April, 1236, January, 1236-7; March, 1237-8 and April, 1241; at Oddington in January, 1250-1, and September and December, 1254, and at Churchdown in March, 1254-5. His visits were probably even more frequent as the number of documents in his rolls is small and his itinerary is very imperfect.'

34. 'Register of Archbishop Giffard,' (1266-1279) (ed.W. Brown, Surtees Society) (1904), Vol.CIX, pp. 114, 115, 124, xv, 123.

35. 'Register of Archbishop John Romeyn,' (1286-1296), (ed. W. Brown, Surtees Society) (1917), CXXVIII, pp. 200-201. *Trans. B.G.A.S.*, Vol. 43, p. 124.

36. 34 Henry II, Vol. 38 (1925), p.9. and 31 Henry II, Vol. 34 (1913), p.79. 'Pay R, our bailiff of Cherch' £32 7s 8d. for 12 doles of wine and 100 of the like with carriage.' In four years the name is variously given as 'Kyketon,' 'Kerketon,' 'Chyrked,' 'Chirchedon.' The king was holder of the barony at this time; it had reverted to him temporarily on the death of Archbishop Roger in 1181.

37. 'Register Walter Giffard' (Surtees, 1904) Vol. CIX, pp. xiii, xiv and 115. In the same year the bailiff was to pay Richard de Button 'our valet' £104 and to the 'poor matrons of Gloucester half a quartern of frumenty of our gift.' Pp. 121 and 124. He also gave 20s. to his relative, William of Greenfield, studying at Oxford.

38. *Trans. B.G.A.S.,* Vol. 43, p.124. 'Register William Greenfield,' (Part I 1306-1315, Vol. CXLV (1931); Part II (1311-1315, Vol. CXLIX (1934) 1 ff 92, 93.

39. *Calendar of Patent Rolls,* Henry III, Vol. XI (1913), p. 721.

40. *Trans. B.G.A.S.* vol. 43. p. 101, citing *Feudal Aids*, Vol. II, pp. 253, 258, 290, 296.

41. *Extracts of Court Rolls of Churchdown with Norton, Hucclecote, Witcombe and Shurdington, 1 Henry IV to 3 Ed. VI,* (abridged translation by Ethel Hartland) Gloucestershire Collection, ref. 10151. 'The Court of Lord John, Archbishop of York, 5th. Year of King Henry VI. (1426/27). Glos. Coll. Ref. 10151.

42. 'Court of John, Archbishop of York, Tuesday after the Feast of St. Andrew the Apostle,' *Extracts from the Court Rolls*, 17 Henry VI.

43. ibid. 19th. Henry VI. (1438/39). A 'tolcester' was a toll of a sester of ale due to the lord; it was about four gallons.

44. 'Pleas of the Crown for the Co. of Gloucester, Dudstone Hundred. No. 402.

45. ibid., p. 403.

46. ibid., p. 413.

47. ibid., p. 416.

48. ibid., p. 407.

49. *Register Archbishop Greenfield*, 1307, Surtees Society, Vol.145, (1931), p. 444.

50. Gwen Waters, *King Richard's Gloucester*, (1983), pp. 1 and 68.

51. *Calendar of Charter Rolls,* Vol.II (1906), p. 268.
    6th Oct.,1283: 'William of York (successor to Walter de Gray) for the profit of his successor and the good of the church of York, with the licence of the king and of the dean and chapter, ordained that 502 oxen, by the greater hundred, and 54 horses needed for agriculture in the demesne lands of the archbishopric, which oxen and horses with 1,000 sheep, to wit 500 withers and 500 ewes, the said archbishop has given and bequeathed to his successor in the see, should always be maintained whether the see be vacant or full, in addition to the 1,000 sheep above mentioned upon the manors of the archbishopric in the manner hereinafter determined: that is, in the bailiwick of Chirchedon.....'

52. Beyond the farmland of Churchdown itself were the fields of the sub-manors of Pirton, Parton, Hucclecote, Elmbridge and Brickhampton. The fields of 'Elbrugge' are mentioned in the *Gloucester Corporation Records* of 1347, p. 342.

53. *Inquisitions Post Mortem, Gloucestershire,* Vol.5, (1342), p.290. *P.R.O. Chanc. I.P.M., E.III*, file 66/10. 'John de Pyryton was seised in his demesne as of fee of one third of a messuage in Chirchesdon in the archbishopric of York........worth nothing beyond reprises........and 26s. rent of free and bond tenants. The reprises are held of the said archbishopric by the service of one sixth of a knight's fee.'

54. John Leland, *Itinerary in England and Wales*, (ed. Lucy Toulmin Smith, Centaur Press, 1964), Vol. 2, (1535-43), p. 57.

55. *De Comitatu Gloucestrie*, pp. 101, 433(B) (1221). I am indebted to the late Mr. A.Th. Arber-Cooke for translation and explanation.
56. Bennet, p.30. See also Cardinal Gasquet, *Parish Life in Mediaeval England*, (1906, 4th ed.), p. 12: 'The Council of Merton in 1305 set forth a schedule of things upon which tithes had to be paid by law; this included the cutting and felling of trees and woods, the pasturage of the forests, and the sale of the timber; the profits of vineyards, fisheries, rivers, dovecotes and fish stews; the fruits of trees, the offspring of animals, the grass harvest, and that of all things sown; of fruits, of warrens of wild animals, of hawking, of gardens and manses, of wool, flax and wine; of grain and of turf where it was dug and dried; of pea-fowl, swans and capons; of geese and ducks; of lambs, calves and colts, of hedge-cuttings, of eggs, of rabbits, of bees with their honey and wax, together with the profits from mills, hunting, handicrafts of all sorts, and every manner of business.' See also Gasquet, p. 10.
57. The names of Churchdown residents paying subsidy are: 'Rico. Pouke xiid., Cristin de Begworth viid. ob., Willmo Hoge, xiid., Willo atte Stret, viid. q., Alic. De Longforde, xvd.q., Rico Posth, xiid. ob., Johne Corndan, ixd., Johne Godseyn, lxd. ob.q. Walto le Longe, xid., Walto Takebat vid; Agnet la Longe vid., Walto le Rede, vid.ob.q.' (1327)
    At 'Oke' (Noke) the names of Johne Ines, Johne le Bonde and Galfro le Mulleward appear with Willo Laurence.
58. 'Court of the Manor of Thomas, Archbishop of York, (1300-1304). Glos. Coll. Ref.10151.
59. J.F.C. Harrison, *The Common People*, (1984) p.87, quoting the Sumptuary Statute of 1363, and the poet, John Gower (1375) *Mirour de l'Omme.'*
60. P.W. Hammond, *Food and Feast in Mediaeval England*, (1993), p. 12.
61. May McKisack, *The Fourteenth Century, Oxford History of England*, p. 203.
62. H.S. Bennett *Life on the English Manor*, (1987), p. 124.
63. Harrison, p.79. A death rate of about 45% is suggested.
64. Giovanni Boccaccio, *The Decameron* (trans. J.M.Rigg, Everyman edition, 1955) pp. 5-6.
65. *V.C.H.*, Vol. IV, p.434, citing Gloucestershire Record Office document D621/M7.
66. G.H. Cook, *Mediaeval Chantries and Chantry Chapels*, (1963), p. 21.
67. *Trans. B.G.A.S.* (1928), p. 198.
68. Public Record Office Chantry Certificate, no 13. (1546) names 'Our Lady Service in the Parish of Chursdon.'

Chapter 4: 'Times of Great Confusion' (pp 55-76)

1. The entries in the Parish Register read: '1640 - half leaf of register missing.' '1641-2 Whole leaf missing. Time of great confusion. Rebellion rages.'
2. Court Baron of Edward, Archbishop of York. 32 Henry VIII. 1540-41. Glos. Coll. Ref.10151
3. ibid. Held at Norton, 23 Henry VIII. 1531-32.
4. ibid. Held at Churchdown, 23 Henry VIII. 1531-32. Gloucestershire Collection, Gloucester Central Library.
5. Court of Manor of Thomas Archbishop of York in time of Reginald Bray, Chief Steward, at Churchdone. 2 Henry VII. 1486-87.
6. Court held Thursday after the Feast of St.Michael the Archangel at Churchden, 15 Henry VII. 1499-1500. G.R.O. D621.

7. *Victoria County History of Gloucestershire,* Vol. IV, p. 435, citing G.R.O. D184/M2.

8. 1584, 1616. Glos. Collection, C68.

9. Opening lines of the will of William Bishop, 1584 (G.D.R.5.59): 'I, William Bysshoppe within the Parishe of Churston...*Husbandman* beinge sicke in bodeye but whole of mynde of good and perfect Remembrance, laud and praise be given to Allmightye god, doe make and ordaine this my Last will and Testament in maner and forme following (that is to saye): First I comend my Soule to Allmightye god my Maker, Saviour and redeemer and my bodey to be buried in the Churche yarde of the Parishe Churche of Churston...' Will of Richard Blunte of Chursdowne (1614): 'I, Richard Blunte of Chursdowne...... *Yeoman....*' *Gloucestershire Wills 1607-31.* p. 199. Gloucestershire Collection, 39521C68

10. *Hockaday Abstracts,* (Glos. Coll.) G.D.R. 2.8 1545.

11. ibid. 168 Vol. 2, 1545.

12. ibid. Vol. 2 No. 244. 1545.

13. ibid. 1.77 1542.

14 ibid. Vol. 3.59. 1546.

15. ibid. Vol. 3.29. 1546.

16. G.C. Coulton, *The Mediaeval Village,* C.U.P, (1925), p. 320 - citing Stat. Henry VII, 1495.

17. I am indebted to Mr. Peter Ford, the present owner, for allowing me to read this study written by Mr. Ian Lord, grandson of the previous owner.

18. A dagger of a rather rare type, of the 13th-15th century, was found near a now blocked-up doorway at Ye Olde House. It may, of course, not indicate that the house is as old as this dagger which may have come into the possession of a past owner at some later time.

19. Rev. J.D. Cooke, *Churchdown Through the Ages,* (1939), p. 45.

20. ibid. p. 46. Thomas Thache was curate in the parish 1736-41.

21. *Calendar of the Records of the Corporation of Gloucester,* p. 443.

22. In 1535 the clear yearly value of the possessions amounted to £90.10s. 2d. *Victoria County History,* Vol. 2. p. 87.

23. *Letters and Papers, Foreign and Domestic, Henry VIII,* Vol. XIII Pt. 1., p. 575.

24. *Hockaday Abstracts.* (1536) P.R.O. Misc. Bk. 209/69d.

25. *Letters and Papers, Henry VIII,* Vol. 13, Pt. 1, No. 210.

26. Carolyn Heighway, *Gloucester, A History and Guide* (1985) p. 101. T.D. Fosbrooke, *An Original History of the City of Gloucester* (1819) 1976 reprint, p.105, gives *William Jennings* (King's Chaplain) 'last prior of St. Oswald's' as first Dean.

27. *Trans. B.G.A.S.* Vol. 43, p. 126.

28. *Suppression of the Monastries,* (Camden Society) p. 124

29. *Trans. B.G.A.S.* Vol. 43, p.127, citing *L.&P. Henry VIII,* Vol. 17, 640 (1154 no. 60).

30. *Victoria County History of Glos.* Vol.4, p.434, citing *L.& P. Henry VIII,* Vol. 17, p. 638.

31. Cooke, p. 39: 'In 1894 The Ecclesiastical Commissioners transferred these tithes to the Dean and Chapter of Gloucester Cathedral.' The rectory and advowson are now also with the Dean and Chapter.

32. Cooke, p. 39.

33. P.R.O. *Patent Roll 36 Henry VIII,* p.11, m.26. 'Grant by the King (March 14, 36 H.VIII) to Robert, Archbishop of York, in exchange for the barony of Churchdowne, the lordships and manors of Church-downe, Huckylcot, Norton, Shurdington, Wydcombe, (North) Cerney, Compton (Abdale) and Odyngton, Gloucs., and lands, etc., in other counties, by indenture of 6 Feb., 36 H.VIII - of certain rectories, churches, advowsons and lands in Yorks.

34. 35 Henry VIII. (1544/5). Glos. Coll. Ref.10151.
35. *Trans. B.G.A.S.* Vol. 56, p.204.
36. *Calendar Patent Rolls 37 Henry VIII* p.4 m.11.
37. *Hockaday Abstracts.* (1545) P.R.O. Parts for Grants, 474.
38. *Trans. B.G.A.S.* Vol. 56, p.204. Letter to William Paget, a privy counsellor and a Secretary of State upon whom Henry VIII relied.
39. *Hockaday Abstracts,* G.D.R. 177, 1542.
40. ibid. 1 IV. 172, 1543
41. ibid. 2 No. 8, 1545.
42.. ibid. Vol. 3. 59, 1546.
43. ibid. 352.
44. G.H. Cook, *Mediaeval Chantries,* (1963) p. 76.
45. Chantry Certificate VIII P.R.O. 22 No.33: 'The Pariche of Chursedon houselyng 283. (Survey in 37 Henry VIII). A Chauntrie or Service in the seid porche Churche of Chursedon wt certeyn land therunto app(er)teigne videlt (videlicet?) to yerelie value of ixs.vjd. and an Inventorie delyned of certeyn things to the same belonginge as in the seid fformer survey is mencioned and doth appear. The pcketoz (proctors?) and Substanciall men of the seid poche have at this p(re)sent upon their othes affirmed declared and p(re)sented unto us nowe Comyssions as well the seid land as goods and Cattell in the Inventorie mencyoned to appteigne and belonge unto their p(ar)ishe Churche and not to ony suche Service in man and fourme as att the other Survey was untruly certified.'
46. *Cal. Pat. Rolls, 12 Elizabeth I,* Vol. V., p. 42.
47. *Gloucestershire Wills 1588-96,* Glos.Coll. 39521 C68. William Blunt, Wood Hucclecote, 1589. p. 82.
   Richard Blunte, Churchdown, 1614. *Glos. Wills 1607-31.* p. 199.
   'Item: I doe give towards the Reparacon of the Parishe Church of Churchdon, iiis. iiijd.'
48. *G.D.R.* 20.6
49. ibid. 28. p 5.
50. A.H. Dodd, *Elizabethan England,* (1974) p. 102.
51. A. Tindall Hart, *The Man in the Pew, 1558-1660,* (1966) p.59. (Parish of Childswall.)
52. *G.D.R.* 20.6
53. J.H. Bettey, *Church and Parish,* (1987) p. 90.
54. *G.D.R.* 28 p. 5
55. ibid.
56. ibid. 29 p. 80
57. Tindall Hart, p. 25.
58. Lucy Toulmin Smith, ed. *John Leland's Itinerary,* Vol. II, (reprint, 1964) p. 57.
59. William Harrison, *Description of England* (1577) Bk. II, p. 280.
60. G.C.R.O. D621 M16.
61. A. Tindall-Hart, p. 27.
62. R.W. Murray, 'Church of St. Bartholomew', unpublished paper, pp. 30 and 31. P.A.84/2.
63. *Glos. Notes and Queries,* Vol.II, pp. 448 and 449. 'DCCCLVIII - A scarce pamphlet of 38 pages, written by "that worthy Divine, Mr. Henry Burton," 1641, and entitled "A Divine Tragedie lately acted, or a Collection of sundrie memorable examples of Gods judgements upon Sabbath-breakers, and other like Libertines, in their unlawful Sports, hapning within the Realme of England in the compasse only of two years last past, since the Book (of Sports) was published"...'

64. G.C.R.O. Parish Records, 1644. C.6/3.

65. *Hockaday Abstracts.* (1678).

66. ibid. *G.D.R.* p.207, 271.

67. Smythe, *Notes on the Church of St. Bartholomew, Churchdown*, p. 276.

68. W.T. Swift, *History of Churchdown*, p. 17.

69. J.H. Bettey, *Church and Parish* (1987) p. 105.

70. Articles of Visitation...in the Triennial Visitation of William, Lord Bishop of Gloucester, 1671 (Gloucestershire Collection J 4.5):

   3. VII. Is your Parson, Vicar, Curate, or Lecturer a man of a sober, honest and exemplary life? Is he vehemently suspected, or guilty of any Scandalous Vice? Is he contentious and ready to set neighbours at variance, and to encourage suits and contentions?

   5. III. Have you any in your Parish that Prophane and mis-spend the Lord's Day, by opening their shops, trading, buying or selling? Do any Vintners, Victuallers, Alehouse-keepers suffer any persons to tipple or game in their Houses on that Day? Declare the names of the offenders herein.

   5. IV. Do all the persons of your Parish, having no lawful impediment duly resort to your church or Chappel upon Sundays and Holy-days? Do they abide quietly with Reverence, Order and Decency, during all the time of Divine Service? Or is there any in your Parish that forbear to partake of the Common-Prayer? Present the names of the faulty.

   6. IX. Are there any in your Parish that being lawfully married, and not separated or divorced by due course of Law, do not dwell together as Man and Wife ought?

   6. XV. Do you know any persons that have presumed to brawl, fight, quarrel, or strike one the other in your Church, Chappel, or Church-yard? If such present their Names.

71. Dr. Frederick Smythe, vicar in the nineteenth century, disliked these panels for their, 'Elizabethan Style with skulls, bones and other repulsive, stiff and doleful decoration.' He also objected to the inscription from Horace which he considered pagan.

72. J. Smith, *Men and Armour for Gloucestershire in 1608,* (1902) p. 13 - 14.

73. Malcolm Atkin and Wayne Laughlin, *Gloucester and the Civil War,* (1992) p. 15.

74. J.R.S. Whiting, *Gloucester Besieged,* (1975) p. 9.

75. Swift, p. 14., considers that the local names 'War Close' (but also sometimes called 'Ward's Close' on old maps) and 'Bloody Man's Acre' reflect memories of skirmishes which took place in Churchdown.

76. J. Washbourn, *Bibliotheca Gloucestrensis,* (1825) p. lxxxvii (writing of Newnham) 'and there another church became the scene of bloody and savage confusion; a case too frequently to be deplored in these undistinguished struggles of civil fury....'

77. Atkin and Laughlin, p. 27, citing 'The Perfect Diurnal' a parliamentary newsheet, 20-27 February, 1643.

78. Notes by Mr. Ian Lord whose family owned Pirton Court.

79. Swift, p. 14. This local historian states that a room at Parton court 'is still known as 'the Prince's Room' but Mr. M. Dawson, to whom I am indebted for replying to my enquiries about this, knows nothing of such a room in Parton Court.

80. Rev. Beaver H. Blacker, ed. *Gloucestershire Notes and Queries,* (1887) Vol. III, p. 439: 'A Journal of the Siege of Gloucester' August, 1643: 'Friday night about twelve, Colonel Gerard's brigades of horse marched to Cheltenham Hill three or four miles from Gloucester, and feigned to skirmish with one another and made fires. This was done to draw out the besieged, upon intelligence that it was believed in Gloucester that Waller would come thither that night and give signs of it by fires; but they stirred not out of town; for Massey knew he had but gulled

his soldiers with the hopes of it, to hold out.' Atkins and Laughlin, pp. 112-3 definitely say 'Churchdown Hill.' There is no such place as 'Cheltenham Hill' and, if there were, it would be more like 8-9 miles distant from Gloucester and not 3 or 4 miles as the above passage states.

81. Carolyn Heighway, *Gloucester, A History and Guide,* (1985) p. 125. The words 'A city assaulted by man but saved by God' were inscribed over the South Gate when it was rebuilt after the siege.
82. F.A. Hyett, *Gloucester and her Governor During the Great Civil War,* (1891) p. 33.
83. H.P.R. Finberg, ed. *Gloucestershire Studies,* (1957) pp. 184-8.
84. G.C.R.O. D1421/6
85. From notes compiled by Mr. Middleton, in the Gloucestershire Collection, Central Library. R2 77.1.
86. *Gloucestershire Notes and Queries,* Vol. II, p. 500.
87. Samuel Rudder, *A New History of Gloucestershire,* (1779) pp. 306, 437, 516, 607, 814.
88. J. Smith, (1902) p. 13.
89. Will of Alice Huntleye, 1609. *Gloucestershire Wills, 1607-31,* p. 15. Gloucestershire Collection, Central Library 39525 C68.

Chapter 5: Times of Great Change   (pp 77-114)

1. The earliest was Horton in 1668 but this was by private act.
2. Jethro Tull's invention of the seed drill did not come into widespread use until the 19th century when open field farming had declined. Both 'Coke of Norfolk', a pioneer of more efficient land use, and Lord Townshend, known to history as 'Turnip Townshend' because he advocated the growing of root crops as winter feed for animals (many of which had, previously, been slaughtered at the onset of winter) both proposed the growing of new strains of cereals and vegetables and more flexibility in rotation patterns.
3. W.E. Tate, *The English Village Community and the Enclosure Movements,* (1967), p. 85.
4. The Tithe Map may be consulted at the Gloucestershire County Records Office G.D.R./T1/54.
5. J.F. Bayes and J. Roberts, *The Turnpike Roads from Gloucester to Cheltenham and* Tewkesbury, *Paper of the Glos. Society for Industrial Archaeology,* (1971), pp. 74, 75.
6. William Marshall, *Rural Economy of Glocestershire,* Vol. 1, (1796, Reprint 1979), p. 14.
7. ibid. p. 10.
8. J.F. Bayes and J. Roberts, pp. 74-84.
9. David Bick, *The Gloucester and Cheltenham Tramroad and the Leckhampton Quarry Lines,* (1969, 1987 edition), pp 9, 17, 22.
10. See Bick p. 69-69. for an amusing account of the early steam experiment.
11. See ibid., p. 51.
12. ibid. p. 52.
13. Railway Times, vol. III, p. 941, cited in *The Birmingham and Gloucester Railway,* P.J. Long and the Rev. W.V. Awdrey, Gloucester, (1987), p. 40.
14. Long and Awdrey state that there was a 'station' at Churchdown from 9th August, 1842 to 27th September, 1842.
15. 11th April, 1887, from a private collection of documents relating to Churchdown.

16. W.T. Swift, *History of Churchdown, (1905)* p. 65 and 'Statement by Fredk. Smithe, Chairman and Co-optative Governor of Wyndowe's School.'
17. *Victoria County History*, Vol. 4, p. 437.
18. From a paper cutting in a private collection, undated but probably about 1870.
19. J.J.D. Cooke, *Churchdown through the Ages*, (1939). p. 56.
20. Research pamphlet on Churchdown School from 1870 to 1970, p. 20. In a private collection.
21. 'A Statement' (1890), in a private collection. (also G.C.R.O. SC 1/7 p.184) This was, apparently, directed to the ratepayers of Churchdown with regard to the re-election of the existing governors.
22. In 1903 it became a council school under the Gloucestershire County Council. A body of managers was appointed and the Windowe endowment continued to be administered. This still exists today.
23. H.C. Middleton's private paper available in Gloucestershire Collection, Gloucester Central Library. R2 77.1.
24. J.H. Bettey, *Church and Parish*, (1987) p. 112: '...the inadequacy of the stipends paid to many of the ower clergy was recognised as early as 1704, when Queen Anne's Bounty was established to supplement the incomes of the very poorest of the clergy.'
25. Gloucester Diocesan Records (G.D.R.). B4/1/638.
26. G.D.R. 226a p. 290, 1713: 'Obadiah Dunn licensed to serve the cure of souls in the Parish Church of Churchdowne otherwise Chursdon.'
27. G.D.R. 282a p. 107
28. Gloucestershire County Records Office (G.C.R.O). Incumbent Acc. 2918 1/3. Swift, pp. 71,72.
29. G.C.R.O. *Gloucester and Bristol Diocesan Calendar*, p. 17.
30. Paper entitled 'The Church of St.Bartholomew and Some Parish Notes' by R.W. Murray, p. 32. G.C.R.O. PH84/2.
31. G.D.R. 284 p. 172.
32. G.D.R. 319a p. 100.
33. G.D.R. 334 b p.335; 334 b p.241; 344 fo. 19; 350 p.14; 350 p. 140.
34. G.D.R. 797.
35. Murray, p. 33.
36. Churchdown Methodist Church Guide, 1978.
37. ibid. Tenancy Agreement, 1890.
38. G.C.R.O. D3981/9 (1877).
39. G.C.R.O. D3981/13.
40. G.C.R.O. D3981/15.
41. Swift, p.75. and Oram, *A Village History*, p. 12. Swift records in his diary a wedding which took place in the schoolroom: 'Had scarcely swallowed my dinner when the Dr. (Smithe) with a man, John Austin, came to ask me to assist at the marriage of the latter with Susan Aitken - with a special license (sic) in Sch. Chapel without preparations of any kind in the matter of moving the furniture. Accordingly I did and I and Brown were witnesses to this singular wedding. The Dr. was very tedious - and read the words of betrothal over twice and muddled generally - and then was equally slow in the registration. Austin promised to send up the fees in a fortnight wh. is another singularity...Read Boswell's Life of Johnson one hour.' 21st June, 1897. G.C.R.O. D3981.
42. Martin Child, *Discovering Churchyards*, (1982), p. 52.
43. William Beale died aged 49 in 1773 and was buried in St. Bartholomew's churchyard as the parishioners of Hucclecote still shared the church on the hill and its graveyard.

44. 'That Robert Window be employed to trim and clear the Road to the Hill.' G.C.R.O. P84a PC/1, p. 81, 1898.
45. *History of Churchdown,* p. 30.
46. G.C.R.O. D3981/17; Oram p. 7.
47. G.C.R.O. D3981/19
48. Robert Atkyns, *Ancient and Present State of Glocestershire,* Part I., (1712, Reprint 1974), p. 336
49. Samuel Rudder, *A New History of Gloucestershire,* (1779, Reprint 1977), p. 341.
50. G.C.R.O., Singleton Will, SL 196.
51. ibid.
52. G.C.R.O. D3981/28 (1900) 'Major Selwyn-Payne had bought the lordship of the manor of Churchdown - Mr. Jones (J.H. Jones, Solicitor, of Barrow Hill, Churchdown) outbidden having offered £153. G.C.R.O. D3981/31 (1904) 'Lordship sold by Henry Ingles Chamberleyne to J. Lovegrove and by the trustees of the will of the latter to Major Selwyn-Payne.' Mrs. Hermione Oram, author of *A Village History, Churchdown, 1904-1954,* was Mr. Jones' grand-daughter.
53. G.C.R.O. D3981/8. During a time of severe drought in November, 1890, when Swift was anxious about the level of the water in his well, Mrs. Roberts was forbidden to wash the lower room floor, but on '20 January a smart shower of rain fell which filled the rainwater tub.' 'The Missus had not washed for over 5 weeks for want of water.'
54. Founded by Joseph Arch (1828-1919).
55. Nigel Scotland, *.Agricultural Trade Unionism in Gloucestershire, 1872-1958,* (1991) pp. 10, 16 , 33.
56. G.C.R.O. D3981/14.
57. By the third Parliamentary Reform Act of 1884 two million farm workers had the right to vote.
58. William Swift, *History of Churchdown ,*(1905), p. 70.
59. D.84 OV2/2.
60. Hargreave's Spinning Jenny, 1765. (Several shuttles on a wooden frame could be operated by one worker.) Arkwright's Water Frame, 1769, (used water power for spinning.) Crompton's 'Mule', 1779, combined the moving frame of the Jenny and the rollers of Arkwright's invention.
61. G.C.R.O. D.84 OV.2/2 (All money amounts quoted are old currency.)
62. G.C.R.O. D3981/22 (1895) and 'The Story of our Village' prepared by the Women's Institute, Churchdown, p. 53.
63. G.C.R.O. D.621 X 2i.
64. Available for reference at the Gloucestershire County Records Office.
65. Compton and other villages. G.C.R.O. Q/AP6
66. G.C.R.O. Q/AP8
67. G.C.R.O. D3981/13
68. ibid /11
69. The Abstract of Title of Draggett's Court (including nearby properties) names a house designated as a 'Police Station.' This was probably the house later called 'Melrose.' (Document in the possession of Mr. L.E. Copeland.)
70. p. 95.
71. G.C.R.O. D3981/14, 1886. Mr. Swift was a supporter of the Conservative party and went to their fete on Chapel Hay: 5.30 to 9.00 'listening to (Cheltenham Town) Band and the speeches of Mr. Stroud, Rickets, and Clifford, etc., A little nigger melody, etc. but the whole proceedings were very flat.'
72. G.C.R.O. D3981/13, 1885.

73. P.C. Minutes, G.C.R.O. P. 84a PC1/1, p. 32.
74. In 1882 Swift writes of the burial of an illegitimate child 'in a soap box and the name written in black lead pencil.' G.C.R.O. D3981/12
75. G.C.R.O. D3981/13.
76. G.C.R.O. P.84aPC. 1/1 p. 20. 'The Grotto' was so called because the builder obtained materials from the demolition of a summer house and buildings in a garden.
77. ibid. pp. 26 and 28.
78. ibid. p. 48.
79. ibid. p. 99 (1899).
80. G.C.R.O. P84a PC 1/1 p. 40.
81. Dr. Reginald Moore was Churchdown's first resident doctor and he was in practice in the village from 1900-1939.
82. G.C.R.O. D3981 1/11.
83. Churchdown Parish Council Minutes, p. 46. G.C.R.O. P84a PC. 1/1
84. P.84a PC. 1/1, p. 47.
85. G.C.R.O. D3981/24
86. The National Telephone Company's Directory for 1896-97 lists 'Gloucester Extension 80' as being at The Central Stores, Churchdown.
87. G.C.R.O. D3981/23.
88. These notes on the postal service of the village have been kindly supplied by Mr.L.E. Copeland, author of *Gloucester's Postal History,* (1988). The references to the first mail delivery are from a letter to the *Gloucester Journal,* 9th October, 1858, and from Post Office archive material.
89. Oram, *A Village History*, p. 10.
90. G.C.R.O. D3981/17 (1890).
91 ibid /20 (1893).
92. ibid /16
93. G.C.R.O. D3981/23.
94. 'Our Village' (W.I.) p. 50. This elm crashed across Chapel Hay on 11th February, 1928.
95. The 'Old House at Home; was sold by Agg Gardiner's Brewery Co. for £1,030 with G. Garness as landlord on 21 Sept, 1896. D3981/22.
96. Licence for the 'new hotel near station' was refused on 25th Sept., 1897. D3981/24.
97. G.C.R.O. D3981/15.
98. ibid. /18, 1891.
99. ibid. /25, 1898.
100. ibid. /29. and Parish Council Minutes, G.C.R.O. P84a PC, p. 82.
101. G.C.R.O. D3981/22
102. Oram, p. 7.
103. G.C.R.O. D3981/27. '17th Nov. Daily Mail Extract 3rd Nov. records wreck by Boers of an armoured train. Twenty men got back, fate of remainder, including Mr. Winston Churchill, unknown.'

Chapter 6: Time of Growth and Conflict (pp 115-130)

1. G.C.R.O. D.3981/26
2. G.C.R.O. D3981/28 School Inspector's Report, 20th June, 1900
3. G.C.R.O. D3981/28. P84 PC 1/1 Note 105, Feb. 1901 (Minutes Parish Council)
4. G.C.R.O. P84a PC 1/1, nos. 120, 124.

5. ibid., no. 125.
6. G.C.R.O. D3981/40
7. From brochure prepared by Churchdown Methodist Church to commemorate the 75th anniversary, 1903-1978.
8. G.C.R.O. D3981/31.
9. Oram, *Village History*, p. 16.
10 *The Citizen*, 1st December, 1904. The final account - £3,335.3.7d. - was submitted at the evening meeting held on the same day.
11. Oram, pp.16-27 has full details of the furnishings and additions to the church.
12. G.C.R.O. D3981/28
13. ibid /37, 12th December, 1908.
14. ibid /44
15. Churchdown Golf Club Rule Book, pp. 12 and 13. G.C.R.O. D6035/8/6
16. G.C.R.O. D3981/30
17. ibid. The first Show was held in 1902.
18. From an article by Owen Hyett in the *Churchdown Diary*, 1976, No.25, p. 22.
19. G.C.R.O. D3981/33. 23rd July, 1905.
20. ibid. 25th April, 1907.
21. ibid. /29.
22. School Log Book entries, February, 1900, and 21st November, 1902.
23. ibid. 17th November, 1904.
24. G.C.R.O. P84a 1/1, Parish Council Minutes, No. 188.
25. ibid. No. 197.
26. ibid. No. 201.
27. G.C.R.O. D3981/17/33.
28. ibid. /43.
29. ibid. /45
30. G.C.R.O. P84a 1/1 Parish Council Minutes, No. 216. D3981/45.
31. 1st January, 1914.
32. G.C.R.O. D3981/45.
33. G.C.R.O. P84a PC 1/2, p. 9.
34. J. Lenrup, p. 581.
35. G.C.R.O. D3981/46.
36. Parish Magazine, Sept., 1914 and Oct. 1914.
37. ibid. 27th November, 1915, p. 13. G.C.R.O. P84a PC 1/2. (see pamphlet reprinted from *Gloucestershire Chronicle*, 27th November, 1915).
38. ibid. February, 1916, p. 14.
39. ibid. 23rd January, 1917, no. 24.
40. Parish Council Minutes, March, 1917, No. 27. G.C.R.O. P84a PC 1/2.
41. ibid., 16th March, No. 16.
42. G.C.R.O. P84 VE 2/1.
43. Parish Council Minutes, No. 30 G.C.R.O. P84a PC .

Chapter 7: Between the Wars   (pp 131-154)

1. Parish Council Minutes, 17th October, 1919, No. 60. G.C.R.O. P84a PC 1/2.
2. ibid. 12th December, 1919, No. 70. The following was said of Dr. Moore: 'He does not need to have the fact emphasized that he is most highly esteemed and beloved by every parishioner and his resignation, if irrevocably decided on, will be for each and all of us nothing short of a Parochial calamity.'
3. Parish Council Minutes, 21st May , 1919, No. 49. G.C.R.O. P84a PC 1/2.

4. ibid. 6th and 17th March, 1919, Nos. 36 and 37
5. ibid. 17th March, No. 41.
6. Ref. Somerset House M95773, 28th October, 1919. 'This indenture made the twenty-eighth day of October one thousand nine hundred and nineteen between John Handcock Selwyn-Payne and John Henry Jones of Barrow Hill. All the Manor or Lordship of Churchdown the fee-farm quit and other rents... were duly granted and conveyed unto and to the use of the Vendor his heirs and assigns in fee simple and whereas the Vendor has agreed with the Purchaser for the absolute sale to him of the said Manor or Lordship fee farm quit and other rents for the price or sum of Two hundred and fifty pounds.'
   The late Hermione Oram who wrote *A Village History, Churchdown 1904-1954,* was his grand-daughter and she shared his great affection for, and interest in, the village.
7. This was donated by Miss Jessie Purnell and it was made from part of the old panelling thought to have come from the Tower Room at St. Bartholomew's.
8. Oram, p. 42
9. *The Citizen,* 4th April, 1921.
10. 'the miners worked once more on terms which now seem to us.....as remote and barbaric as serfdom' A.J.P. Taylor, *English History, 1914-1945,* Oxford 1965, reprint 1981, p.146.
11. Parish Council Minutes, 1922, Nos. 112, 115. G.C.R.O. P84a PC 1/2
12. ibid., March, 1933, No. 225.
13. ibid. nos. 129, 211 and P84 V.E. 2/3 (1922-9), No. 12.
14. This cottage has been converted into the modern residence called 'Chequers' in Pirton Lane.
15. Parish Council Minutes, Nos. 108 and 240 (1933). G.C.R.O. P84a PC 1/2.
16. Owen Hyett 'A History of the Churchdown 'Bus' in *'Country Tales',* p.21. The Bristol Tramways and Carriage Co. Ltd. had begun operating the No. 49 main road service in 1921.
17. Parochial Church Council. G.C.R.O. P84 VE 2/8.
18. Winifred M. Mills, 'Churchdown before the Change', p. 2. Unpublished paper in private possession.
   See also R.W. Murray, 'Excavations at Chapel Hay, Churchdown'. *Transactions Bristol & Gloucestershire Archaeological Society,* Vol. 45 (1923) p. 277.
19. School Log Book, 26th June, 1935.
20. Oram, p. 57.
21. School Log Book 17th June, 1930. 'Rec'd results of Scholarship Exam. There are two free places and four at reduced fees.' Secondary Education was not free until the Education Act of 1944.
22. Oram, p. 59. In 1933 the pond, which up to that time had, apparently, been used as a refuse dump, was filled with soil.
23. Parish Magazine, June, 1925, and 'Story of Our Village' (W.I. production), p. 32.
24. June 16, 1938, p. 8.
25. Parochial Church Council. G.C.R.O. P84 VE 2/8. It was purchased in 1933 on a mortgage of £260 which was paid off in 1953. Oram, p. 48.
26. G.C.R.O. P84 VE 2/8, 1925. The final cost of the work for which the parish was responsible was £713.16.2d.
27. Oram, p. 29.
28. G.C.R.O. P84 VE 2/8, 1926..
29. Oram, p.50.
30. G.C.R.O. P84a PC 1/2 1925. P.C.C. P84 VE 2/8, 1926.
31. G.C.R.O. P84 VE 2/9 for period ending 1934.

33. The Auden family were relatives of the poet, W.H. Auden, and they resided at 'Caer Glow' which was at the junction of Station Road and The Avenue.
34. The estimated price at contract was £461; the total cost of the hall and equipment was just over £737.
35. Oram, p. 51. Rev. J.D. Cooke *Churchdown Through the Ages, (1939)* p. 79. In 1936 there was considerable objection to the suggestion that the Mission Room should be called 'The Holy Redeemer Mission' (P84 VE 2/4 1936--1940) and it was then dedicated to St. John the Evangelist.
36. *The Horticultural Trade Journal,* 14th May, 1959, p. 17.
37. Parachuting took place at 2/6 per person per descent; car-parking was 1/6d a day and 10/- a week. *Gloucestershire Life,* 1971.
38. Oram, p. 53.
39. *Kelly's Directory,* 1939.
40. School Log Book, 22nd January, 1936.
41. Oram, p. 63.
42. 12th November, 1936.
43. *'The Citizen'* September, 1st, 3rd, 15th, 27th, 26th. Oram, p. 63.

Chapter 8
Churchdown during the Second World War   (pp 155-171)

1. Paper by W. Mills, *Churchdown Before the Change,* p. 5.
2. June R. Lewis, *The Cotswolds at War,* (1992, 1995 edition) pp. 96 and p. 102.
3. Hermione Oram, *A Village History,* p. 65.
4. G.C.R.O. PC 1/3, P84a., p. 93.
5. Lewis, p. 84.
6. School Log Book, July, 1940, p.18. The first meeting of the Parochial Church Council after the declaration of war was on 2nd September, 1939, and the minute states: 'the windows and doors being shielded in compliance with Government wartime regulations for safety. G.C.R.O. V 2/5 p. 84.
7. School Log Book, April, 1941: 'Alert sounded this morning. 9.30-10 a.m. spent in the shelters.'
8. G.C.R.O. PC 1/3 P84a, p. 83.
9. Oram, p. 65.
10. School Log Book, September 11th, 1942: 'The remnants of St. Anne's R.C. School, Birmingham, evacuees (three children only) returned to Birmingham to-day after a stay of three years.'
11. G.C.R.O. PC 1/3, P84a, p. 80. 19 May, 1939.
12. School Log Book, 11th September, 1939.
13. Mills, p. 5.
14. Oram, p. 65.
15. Lewis, p. 195.
16. Oram, p. 65. The Club came to an end as urgency diminished in about 1944. A Rabbit Club also existed.
17. Lewis, p. 216.
18. ibid. pp. 165 and 169.
19 From notes kindly lent by Mr. Henry Western.
20. Lewis, pp. 68 and 69.
21. AC/DA 5/2, p.11, Item 64 (Shire Hall Records)
22. Printed Notice to the Civilian Population in the Event of Invasion, F.W.B.

22. Printed Notice to the Civilian Population in the Event of Invasion, F.W.B. Cripps, CC Da 11/8. (Shire Hall Records)
23. AC/DA 8/51, p.10 Item 59.
24. AC/DA 5/2, p.5, Item 26.
25. Mills, p. 5.
26. Major raids were Coventry 14th and 15th November, Birmingham 20th November, Bristol 2nd December, 1940.
27. Oram. p. 66.
28. G.C.R.O. PC 1/3, P84a, p.130. October, 1944.
29. ibid. p. 132.
30. The Fund was officially set up in March with J.H. Western as Chairman, H.J. Western (to whom I am indebted for information about the Fund) as Hon. Secretary, and H.A. Lane as Hon. Treasurer.

Chapter 9: Post War Churchdown (pp 172-194)

1. July 27th, 1945. B.G. Parkin, Labour, was returned for Churchdown with a majority of 949.
2. The first split occurred in April, 1940, when, as Hermione Oram says in her *Village History*, (p. 52), the St. John's district was transferred to the Ecclesiastical Parish of Wotton St. Mary Without (or Longlevens).
3. *The Citizen,* 31st January, 1967.
4. Gloucestershire Collection, Central Library Gloucester, RR77.5, 13th November, 1967.
5. Mr. A.W. Cavill.
6. 5th. July, 1948.
7. May, 1954, p. 9.
8. Parish Church Magazine, April, 1958.
9. In memory of George Felix Smith of Chosen House. G.C.R.O. P84, VE2/6
10. *Gloucestershire Echo*, 28th June, 1965.
11. CW 3/12, p. 84, 16th March, 1955. Ref. 2106/11/A. File No. 166 (15th. April, 1955.) The restriction was not effective so long as the building was being used for ecclesiastical purposes.
12. It was erected and maintained by a group of parishioners under the leadership of Tony Johns.
13 G.C.R.O. P84, VE 2/6, p. 84, No. 52.
14. *The Citizen*, 25th. September, 1956. Now, after 42 years of use, it is planned to build a new hall.
15 G.C.R.O. P.C.C. Minutes, 1976, No. 15.
16. *Gloucestershire Echo*, 1st September, 1967.
17. The Motorway was opened in April 1971. P. Fowler and C.J. Walthew, Eds. 'Archaeology and the M5 Motorway.' *Trans .B.G.A.S.*, 1971, pp. 43-48.
18. *News and Journal*, 25th September, 1969.
19. 1st April, 1981.
20. 6th June, 1953.
21. Written and directed by Phyllis Temple Morris.

Select Bibliography

Abbreviations: Gloucester County Records Office - G.C.R.O.
Gloucestershire Collection, (Gloucester Central Library) - Glos. Coll.

General Local History

Finberg, Joscelyne, *Exploring Villages.* 1958. Re-print 1998.
Hoskins, W.G., *Local History in England.* 1959. Re-print 1985.
Iredale, David, *Discovering Local History.* 1973. Re-print 1977.
Riden, Philip, *Local History: A Handbook for Beginners.* 1983.
    Record Sources for Local History. 1987.
Tate, W.E., *The Parish Chest,* 1960. Re-print 1983.
West, J. *Village Records.* 1962. Re-print 1982.

Histories of Churchdown

Bazeley, Rev. Canon W., 'Churchdown and Mattesdune before the Norman
    Conquest', *Proceedings Cotteswold Club,* Vol. XXI (1). 1921.
Cooke, Rev. J.D.D. *Churchdown Through the Ages.* 1939.
Murray, R.W., The Church of St. Bartholomew's on Chosen Hill and Some Parish
    Notes, (unpublished paper, G.C.R.O. PA 84/2).
Oram, Hermione, *A Village History, 1904 -1954.* 1954.
Smythe, Frederick, 'Notes on the Church of St. Bartholomew', *Trans. Bristol and
    Glos. Archaeological Society,* Vol. XIII, 1888-9.
Swift, W.T., *Some Account of the History of Churchdown.* 1905.
Waters, Gwen, *The Churches of St. Bartholomew and St. Andrew, Churchdown -
    History and Guide.* 1989.
The Story of Our Village Within Living Memory. (Paper prepared by Churchdown
    Women's Institute, 1959. Glos. Coll. SP 642.)

Original Sources

Churchdown Parish Council Minutes of Meetings. G.C.R.O. P84a.PC
Churchdown Parochial Church Council Minutes of Meetings. G.C.R.O. P84 VE.
    (Permission to see these has first to be obtained from the Vicar and
    Churchwardens of the Parish).
County Council Records, Archive Department, Shire Hall, Gloucester. AC/DA, CC/A.

Gloucestershire Wills. Glos.Coll. 39521 C68.

Hartland, Ethel, Abridged Translations of the Manorial Rolls of Churchdown Barony. Glos.Coll. 10151. (The original rolls may be seen at the Gloucester County Records Office.)

Hockaday Abstracts. Glos.Coll. Vol.153.

Newspapers, Local. (*The Citizen, The Gloucestershire Echo*). Past editions may be viewed in the Gloucester Collection Library.

Poor Relief Accounts. G.C.R.O. DS4 OV.

School Logbooks, Churchdown Village Primary School (Application to see these should be made to the Headmaster.)

Smith. D.M., *A Guide to the Archive Collection in the Borthwick Institute of Historical Research,*York. 1973. This lists the Records of the Archbishops of York 1215-1576.

Swift, W.T., Diary. G.C.R.O. D3981.

Local Geology

Dreghorn, William, *Geology Explained in the Severn Vale and Cotswolds.* 1967. Re-print 1973.

Finberg, H.P.R., *The Gloucestershire Landscape.* 1975.

Finlay, D.E., 'The Churchdown Reservoirs'. *Proceedings of the Cotteswold Naturalists' Club,* Vol. XXVIII. 1943.

Smythe, Frederick, 'Geology of Churchdown Hill'. *Proceedings of the Cotteswold Naturalists' Club,* Vol.III. 1865.

General and Social History

Harrison, J.E.C., *The Common People.* 1984.

Pre-Conquest History

Chadwick, Nora, *The Celts.* 1971. Re-print 1986.

Cunliffe, Barry, 'Gloucestershire and the Iron Age of Southern Britain'. *Transactions Bristol and Glos. Archaeological Society,* Vol.102. 1984.

Cunliffe, Barry, *Iron Age Britain.* 1995.

Darvill, Timothy, *Prehistoric Gloucestershire.* 1987.

Hencklen, Thalessa Cruco, 'The Excavation of the Iron Age Camp on Bredon Hill, 1935-7'. *Archaeological Journal,* Vol.XCV. 1938.

Laing, Lloyd, *Celtic Britain,* 1979. Re-print 1987.

Lloyd Baker, Thomas, 'An Account of a Chain of Ancient Fortresses'. *Archaeologia,* Vol.XIX. 1821.

Roman

Clifford, E.M., 'The Roman Villa, Hucclecote'. *Transactions Bristol and Glos Archaeological Society,* Vol.LV. 1933.

McWhirr, Alan, *Roman Gloucestershire.* 1981.

Richmond, I.A., *Roman Britain.* 1955. Re-print 1986.

Saxon

Finberg, H.P.R., *The Formation of England, 550-1042.* 1976.
Garmonsway, G.N., *The Anglo-Saxon Chronicle.* (Trans.) 1953. Re-print 1986.
Heighway, Carolyn, *Anglo-Saxon Gloucestershire.* 1987.
Webster, Leslie, and Backhouse, Janet, (Eds.), *The Making of England.* 1991.
Whitelock, Dorothy, *The Beginnings of English Society, A.D.600-900.* 1952. Re-print 1986.

Norman

Douglas, David C., *The Norman Achievement.* 1972.
Galbraith, V.H., *The Making of Domesday Book.* 1961.
Hamilton-Thompson, A., 'The Jurisdiction of the Archbishops of York in Gloucestershire'. *Trans. Bristol and Glos. Archaeological Society,* Vol.XLIII, 1921.
Moore John S. *Domesday Book Gloucestershire,* 1982.
Taylor, Charles, *An Analysis of the Domesday Survey of Gloucestershire.* 1889.
Welldon Finn, R., *The Domesday Inquest.* 1961.
Welldon Finn, R., *An Introduction to Domesday Book.* 1963.
Wood, Michael, *Domesday, A Search for the Roots of England.* 1987.

Mediaeval

Bennet, H.S., *Life on the English Manor.* 1937. Re-print 1987.
Coulton, G.G. *The Medieval Village.* 1925.
Dyer, Christopher, *Standards of Living in the Later Middle Ages, c.1200-1525.* 1989.
Hammond, P.W., *Food and Feast in Mediaeval England.* 1993.
Hanawalt, Barbara A., *The Ties that Bound.* 1986.
Hilton, R.H., *A Medieval Society.* 1966.
Houlbrooke, Ralph, *The English Family, 1450-1700,* 1984. Re-print 1992.
Myers, A.R., *England in the Late Middle Ages.* 1952. Re-print 1972.
Platt, Colin, *Medieval England.* 1978. Re-print 1988.
Saul, Nigel, *The Oxford Illustrated History of Medieval England.* 1997.
Stenton, Doris Mary, *English Society in the Early Middle Ages.* 1951. Re-print 1985.
Wood, Margaret, *The English Mediaeval House.* 1965. Re-print 1983.

Tudor and Stuart

Ashley, Maurice, *England in the Seventeenth Century, 1603-1714.* 1952.
Atkyns, Robert, *The Ancient and Present State of Gloucestershire.* 1712. Re-print 1974.
Dodd, A.H., *Elizabethan England.* 1974.
Harrison, William, *The Description of England, 1577.* Ed. F.J.Furnivall. 1908.
Houlbrooke, Ralph, *The English Family, 1450-1700.* 1984. Re-print 1992.
Johnson, Joan, *Tudor Gloucestershire.* 1985.
Smith, J., *Men and Armour in Gloucestershire, 1608.* 1902.

The 18th-20th Centuries

Bovill, E.W., *English Country Life, 1780-1830.* 1962. Re-print 1963.
Copeland, L.E., *Gloucester's Postal History.* 1988.
Laver, James, *Manners and Morals in the Age of Optimism, 1849-1914.* 1966.
Lewis, June R., *The Cotswolds at War.* 1992. Re-print 1995.
Marshall, William, *Rural Economy of Gloucestershire.* 1796. Re-print 1979.

The Civil War

Atkin, Malcolm, and Laughlin, Wayne, *Gloucester and the Civil War.* 1992.
Beaver, Rev. H., and Blacker, H., (Eds.) *Gloucestershire Notes and Queries,* Vol. III.
    1887.
Finberg, H.P.R., *Gloucestershire Studies.* 1957.
Hyett, F.A., *Gloucester and her Governor During the Great Civil War.* 1891.
Washbourn, J., 'A Journal of the Siege of Gloucester', *Bibliotheca Gloucestrensis.*
    1825.
Whiting, J.R.S., *Gloucester Besieged.* 1975.

The Church

Bede, *A History of the English Church and People.* Trans. Sherley-Price, Leo.
    Revised Latham, R.E. 1955. Re-print 1982.
Bettey, J.H., *Church and Parish.* 1987.
Child, Mark, *Discovering Churchyards.* 1982.
Cook, G.H., *Mediaeval Chantries and Chantry Chapels.*1963.
Cook, G.H., *The English Mediaeval Parish Church.* 1954.
Cross, Claire, *Church and People,1450-1660.* 1976. Re-print 1987.
Dickens, A.G., *The English Reformation.* 1964. Re-print 1975.
Duffy, Eamon, *The Stripping of the Altars, Traditional Religion in England,
    1400-1580.* 1992.
Gasquet, F.A., *Parish Life in Mediaeval England.* 1906. Re-print 1909.
Harper-Bill, Christopher, *The Pre-Reformation Church in England, 1400-1530.* 1989.
Heal, Felicity and O'Day, Rosemary, Eds. *Church and Society in England, Henry
    VIII to James I.* 1977.
Platt, Colin, *The Parish Churches of Medieval England.* 1981.
Swanson, R.N., *Religion and Devotion in Europe, c.1215 - c.1515.* 1995.
Tindall-Hart, A., *The Man in the Pew, 1558-1660.* 1966.

The Countryside, Farming and Fields

Astill, Grenville and Grant, Annie, *The Countryside of Medieval England.* 1988.
    Re-print 1992.
Cantor, Leonard, (Ed.) *The English Medieval Landscape.* 1982.
Hoskins, W.G., *The Making of the English Landscape.* 1955. Re-print 1985.
Muir, Richard, *Reading the Landscape.* 1981. Re-print 1993.
Muir, Richard and Nina, *Fields.* 1989.
Rackham, Oliver, *History of the Countryside.* 1994.

Seebohm, M.E., *The Evolution of the English Farm.* 1927. Re-print 1976.
Slater, Gilbert, *The English Peasantry and the Enclosure of Common Fields.* 1907.
Tate, W.E., *The English Village Community and the Enclosure Movement.* 1967.
Winchester, Angus, *Discovering Parish Boundaries.* 1990.

Transport

Bayes, J.F., and Roberts, J., 'The Turnpike Roads from Gloucester to Cheltenham and Tewkesbury,' *Paper of the Gloucestershire Society for Industrial Archaeology.* 1971.
Bick, David, *The Gloucester and Cheltenham Tramroad and the Leckhampton Quarry Lines.* 1967.
Fowler, P. and Walthew, C.J., (Eds.) 'Archaeology and the M5 Motorway,' *Transactions of the Bristol and Glos. Archaeology Society,* Vol. XC, 1971.
Herbert, Nicholas, *Road Travel and Transport in Gloucestershire.* 1985.
Long, P.J.and Awdrey, Rev. W., *The Birmingham and Gloucester Railway.* 1987.

Index